'Rogues and Vagabonds'

Also by Lionel Rose

The Massacre of the Innocents:
infanticide in Great Britain 1800–1939
(Routledge & Kegan Paul)

'Rogues and Vagabonds'

Vagrant Underworld in Britain 1815–1985

Lionel Rose

Routledge
London and New York

First published in 1988 by
Routledge
11 New Fetter Lane, London EC4P 4EE

Published in the USA by Routledge
a division of Routledge, Chapman and Hall, Inc.
29 West 35th Street, New York, NY 10001

Set in Baskerville 10/11pt.
by Columns of Reading
and printed in Great Britain
by T.J. Press (Padstow) Ltd
Padstow, Cornwall,

Library of Congress Cataloging in Publication Data
Rose, Lionel, 1944–
Rogues and vagabonds: vagrant underworld in Britain, 1815–1985
Lionel Rose.
p.   cm.
Bibliography: p.
Includes index.
1. Rogues and vagabonds — Great Britain — History — 19th century.
2. Vagrancy — Great Britain — History — 19th century. 3. Great
Britain — Social conditions — 19th century. 4. Lodging-houses — Great
Britain — History — 19th century. I. Title.
HV4545.A3R67 1988
362.5'0941–dc19   87–33767

British Library CIP Data also available
ISBN 0–415–002575–3

Contents

Illustrations

Acknowledgments

I wish to express my thanks to the following for time and assistance accorded me in the preparation of this book: Chris Holmes and Nick Beacock of the Campaign for the Homeless and Rootless; Emlyn Jones of the National Association of Voluntary Hostels; Dr Michael Rose of the History Department, Manchester University; Dr Graham Davis of Bath College of Higher Education for an extract from his thesis, referred to in the Bibliography. My appreciation is also due for the yeoman service performed by my typist, Doreen Elwell and to Michele and Paul Connell for preparing the index.

For permission to reproduce the illustrations I would like to thank the Greater London Record Office, the Guildhall Library, the BBC Hulton Picture Library, the Public Record Office, and Chatto and Windus: The Hogarth Press.

I should like to take the opportunity here to draw attention to the ever-pressing need for donations by charities for the homeless in these difficult times. I am sure that CHAR and the NAVH, referred to above, would be only too willing to advise the enquirer.

1 Migrants, itinerants and the Vagrancy Law 1815–20

Imagine that some stratospheric time machine has whisked you back to hover over the British Isles in the period just after the Napoleonic Wars. From your vantage point the highways and byways resemble the tracery of blood vessels, and the human traffic is the life blood flowing to the vital organs. For the body economic of Britain those vital organs are the growing town of the early industrial revolution, and time-lapse photography (to stretch our technological metaphor a little further) reveals, in the decades after 1815, a strong current from the Northern and Midland counties towards those towns. In the coal-less South the movement is much more sluggish, but London exerts a powerful regional pull as the 'great Wen'. From the Scottish Highlands, where the crofter clearances are taking their toll, there is a flow towards the industrialising Lowlands and into England, as well as a transfusion to the overseas colonies. From overcowded and impoverished Ireland periodic potato blights, notably the disaster of 1821–2,[1] begin sending a continuous stream of emigrants (assisted by the development of cheap steam-packet services from 1818[2]), who concentrate in Lancashire and the South-west corner of Scotland, but progressively spread out to other urban centres, where they form distinct colonies in the dark and dangerous slum 'rookeries', like the notorious St Giles district of London.

The time-lapse sequence will also reveal blurry streaks, caused by more transitory passages: seasonal migrations of harvesters, including a high proportion of Irish who cross over in the late summer, travel extensively for work, and return home in the autumn;[3] navvies pursuing construction projects, such as housing, canal and, later, railway undertakings; unemployed 'tramping artisans', like shoemakers and ironfounders, searching about for work in an era long before employment exchanges and the telephone; and paupers and convicted vagrants being deported to their home parishes under the Settlement and Removal Laws. Pedlars, and migratory beggars and thieves add to this *mélange* of transients, and the whole flow-rhythm is affected by trade cycles and military and naval operations. The city of Bath, lying on the route of the Irish inflow from South Wales and Bristol towards London, witnessed the whole parade of itinerants. As S.S. Duncan, a Bath resident, observed in 1834:

> Failures of manufacturers, destruction of machinery, combin-
> ations &c, send many hundreds on the tramp. Soldiers' wives
> and children are scrambling in all directions after regiments
> ordered to new stations. Sailors ramble from port to port to find
> captains for certificates of service, or to find new or old ships, or
> to pass public examinations at public boards for pensions or
> prize money &c. Wives are hunting for runaway husbands
> (rarely the reverse); children for runaway parents. Agricultural
> labourers are occasional wanderers for employment.

And, he believes, a general mood of restlessness, generated by the economic and political ferment of that time, 'makes many leave the home of their youth with diminished anxiety . . . and easily led away to vice and shame.'[4]

The economic depression between 1815 and 1820 provoked widespread disorder, exacerbated by the new Corn Laws which protected the interests of the preponderantly land-owning Parlia-mentarians by barring foreign corn imports and keeping bread artificially expensive. Demonstrations, Luddism and calls for a widening of the franchise and the overthrow of the land-owning monopoly of power became the Radical response. Vagrancy increased as Napoleonic War veterans, some disabled, returned home demobilised and jobless; unemployment and astronomic bread prices sent many on the tramp to beg and steal to survive.[5] The ruling class blinkered themselves to the economic causes of vagrancy, preferring instead to see it as symptoms of the lower classes' own moral delinquency. In 1828 a Surrey magistrate, Randle Jackson, insisted dogmatically that there was no connection between unemployment and vagrancy, as vagrants were a sub-criminal class, a fixed element that persisted irrespectively of trade conditions.[6] He was, perhaps, faintly justified to the extent that workshy 'sturdy beggars' had been execrated since Tudor times – 'thieves and caterpillars in the commonwealth' Ralph Holinshed called them in 1586[7] – as intimidators of country folk in isolated hamlets, and a cheating menace in the towns. Henry Fielding, the famous novelist and London magistrate, wrote feelingly in 1753 of their ubiquity in ill-policed Westminster:

> . . . there is not a street in that liberty which doth not swarm all
> day with Beggars and all night with Thieves. Stop your coach at
> what shop you will, however expeditious is the Tradesman to
> attend you, a Beggar is commonly beforehand with him; and if

you should not directly face his Door, the Tradesman must often
turn his head while you are talking to him, or the same Beggar
or some other Thief at hand will pay a visit to his shop![8]

In 1806 the later eminent London magistrate Patrick Colquhoun,
surmised that among England's 10,000,000 people there were some
70,000 tramps, beggars, gypsies and the like, together with 10,000
wandering performers and dubious pedlars, and 10,000 lottery
ticket touts, whom he termed 'lottery vagrants'[9]. The landowners
conveniently blamed the existing Poor Law for sapping the
labouring classes' moral fibre and creating a nation of shiftless
scroungers. The Speenhamland system of outdoor relief and the
subsidy of low wages out of the rates (which the landowners had to
pay) was branded as the chief canker,[10] but the Tories who ruled till
1830 did not dare dismantle it, as they were loathed for their harsh
repression of radical unrest up to 1820, and it was their Corn Law
which made the continuation of Speenhamland a necessary buffer
against possible revolution. Between 1820 and 1825 trade conditions improved in the towns (though farm labourers remained
economically depressed) and, coincidentally, the Tory régime took
on a more liberal tone, typified in the replacement of the repressive
Lord Sidmouth by the reforming Robert Peel as Home Secretary in
1822. Though political agitation had died down, Peel was
confronted with a mounting crime wave, which had exercised
Parliament for at least a decade. Criminal commitments quad-
rupled between 1806 and 1826, though the population had grown
by less than half;[11] his answer was to improve the system of
policing, and to make the law more respected. In regard to the
latter he accelerated the reform of the archaic criminal code, whose
very savagery on paper – about 200 offences, including many non-
violent crimes against property, were technically liable to the death
penalty – had made it unenforceable in the courts. Updating the
penalties would improve their enforceability, and Peel effected
numerous reforms between 1823 and 1827, to be complemented by
his creation of the Metropolitan Police in 1829.[12]

The 1824 Vagrancy Act (preceded by the temporary 1822 Act)
belongs in this context of rationalisation of the criminal law, for it
was to make a clean sweep of the 27 pre-existing Vagrancy Acts,
extending as far back as Edward III's reign. It must also be viewed
in the context of Parliament's concern about the mounting costs of
public relief to the destitute, for ratepayers were groaning not only
under the burden of the Poor Law, but also the rapid increase in
the rate of 'passing' (that is, transporting) paupers and convicted
vagrants back to their places of origin. Here, I shall outline the
structure of anti-vagrancy law and the passing system just prior to
the 1822 Act.[13] The law defined three grades of offender, in
ascending order of seriousness, as the 'Idle and Disorderly',

'Rogues and Vagabonds' and 'Incorrigible Rogues'. The first included those who neglected to provide for their families, wilful idlers and those who begged within their parishes of settlement. The second included those who wandered outside their parishes to beg (professional itinerant beggars), men who deserted their families so that they had to fall back on parish poor relief, varieties of travelling entertainers and fortune tellers, and 'reputed thieves' and 'suspect persons' frequenting public places. The last refers to suspicious characters who loitered about and were deemed to be up to no good, though nothing specific could be proved against them. 'Incorrigible rogues' were recidivists previously convicted as 'rogues and vagabonds'.

Idle and disorderly offenders could be jailed by magistrates for up to a month; rogues and vagabonds were liable to be whipped, jailed for up to six months and then ordered to be passed to their home territory; likewise, incorrigible rogues were floggable and liable to up to two years' jail, with the possibility of impressment in the armed forces and even transportation. (The whipping of female vagrants had been abolished in 1792.[14]) To encourage the mopping up of this pestiferous breed, anyone who effected the arrest of a vagrant was entitled to a ten shilling reward from the rates.

As we shall see in a later chapter, lodging houses were notorious vagrant haunts, and the law empowered Justices to institute 'privy searches', or swoops against them, four times a year to haul in concealed offenders.

There were in fact two parallel but distinct systems of passing. The first came under the Poor Law régime, and originated from 1662; it empowered justices to order the removal of paupers – that is, those dependent on parish poor relief – back to their parishes of settlement. The complaining parish had to pay the cost of the entire journey back – which could be the length of England – and a deputed parish official had to escort the pauper all the way. An anomaly of the English removal laws was that they only applied to paupers who had a parish of settlement in England. Scots and Irish who had acquired no settlement in an English parish (for example, by length of residence, or renting of a substantial property) could not be removed, and might remain a charge on the 'foreign' parish's poor rate!

The other passing system came under the vagrancy law rubric, as noted above. Prior to 1814, the offender must have served at least seven days in jail or (if a male) received a whipping before a pass order was made. The Justice specified the most direct and convenient route back to the offender's home territory. Since 1744, convicted Irish and Scots vagrants could be returned home, too. Scotsmen were conveyed to the border and dropped there. Irish were conveyed to specified western ports – Bristol and Liverpool were the main ones – and the financial burden fell on those ports to ship the vagrants over to any point on the Irish coast. Unlike the 'Settlement Law' removals, each parish *en route* had to pay its share of the cost of conveying vagrants through its territory. Each parish constable escorting the vagrants would hand them over at the boundary to a neighbouring parish officer.[15] In practice, magistrates would arrange for one escort all the way to the county boundary before the transfer, and the cost would come out of the county rate. Hence was born the 'pass-master', a private contractor to whom the conveyance of vagrants was farmed out. It was therefore far more advantageous to any single parish to get a 'foreigner' convicted and passed as a beggar than as a pauper it had first relieved; not only would it have to pay only a fraction of the removal cost, but it could get rid of any Scots and Irish destitutes, too.

From the late eighteenth century it was evident that the vagrancy law passing system was being widely abused; scroungers were using it to get a free ride back home, or to any parish they claimed was their parish of settlement, and the costs of passing began to spiral.

An early inquiry into the scale and causes of London mendicancy had been mounted by the philanthropic Society for Bettering the Conditions of the Poor in 1803, but its findings and recommendations were only to be examined again in detail by a Select Committee on Mendicity in London appointed at the instigation of George Rose MP in 1815.[16] This Parliamentary interest in beggary was prompted by the only too visible signs of it during the post-Napoleonic Wars period, with the economic distress and high bread prices, and the costs to London parishes of giving some kind of 'casual' relief to the destitute arrivals who had no settlement there. It was doubtless also associated with the current concern about the scale of juvenile delinquency: the 1803 enquiry reckoned that two thirds of London beggars were children, and the 1815 Select Committee's Report alluded to the 'urgency of the evil' of begging by children, who were 'in the course of becoming the very worst of criminals'. Other evidence also highlighted the 'Irish dimension' in beggary and juvenile delinquency. (The 1803 investigation indicated that a third of all London beggars were Irish.) Observers were apt to contrast the shiftless Irish with the 'industrious' London Scots who, it seems, rarely appeared before the courts as beggars. Conspicuous Irish colonies had established themselves in various 'rookeries' around London, chiefly in St Giles, St Marylebone and St Andrew's parish Holborn. Poverty, improvidence, drunkenness, brawling, physical incapacities, neglect of their children, and a high level of unemployment were all ascribed to them by contemporary observers. But for all their ignorance and squalor they certainly seemed to have kissed the Blarney Stone when it came to telling tales of woe to philanthropic visitors. Montagu Burgoyne, who was associated with a charity for assisting destitute Irish in London, told the Committee:

> . . . you can never believe one word they say; they have so much ingenuity and so much imagination that they will make a story which on inquiry turns out to be without foundation; their tale of distress has touched the humanity of several persons, and they have sent for these people, and given sums of money to some of them, frequently to those who deserve it the least.

Another witness, Edward Wakefield, said of his visit to the St Giles Irish, 'I suppose I was amongst the greatest thieves in London'.

It would be desirable here to explain something of the background to the Irish, to explain their alleged predilection for charitable relief. Unlike England, Ireland had no parish poor law system until 1838. Traditionally, destitute Irish had obtained relief locally through church charity, or by outright begging; this was socially acceptable and a necessity in Ireland itself.[17] Overcrowding on the land and harvest failures drove legions into part-year or full-time begging and charity-seeking. Of Ireland's eight million people in 1838 it was alleged that two to three million begged or were totally destitute for part of the year at least.[18] Contemporary English observers were struck by the fecklessness and helplessness of the low-class Irish, and their influx into Britain was commonly viewed 'as an example of a less civilised population spreading themselves as a kind of substratum beneath a more civilized community'.[19]

The stereotype of the shiftless and scrounging Irishman was firmly fixed, but how true was it? English and Scottish textile manufacturers and mine-owners found Irish workers more adaptable and venturesome. They were readier to move around to seek work than the English, and much of the apparent 'vagrancy' was in fact the seasonal movement of Irish harvesters and the migration of Irish navvies to new construction projects. They filled an important gap in the contemporary need for a mobile, footloose labour force.[20] Many of the allegations that the Irish threw themselves disproportionately on local poor relief were based on prejudice, not fact, and some local analyses have shown that the numbers of Irish-born on poor relief only matched their proportion of the local population.[21]

Beggary was a side-effect of the arrival each year of thousands of Irish seasonal workers, viewed by the English as little better than animals: they poured in at rock-bottom fares packed as 'living ballast' in empty coal vessels returning from Ireland, 'huddled together like pigs and communicating disease and vermin on their passage'. The menfolk came first, followed separately by their wives and children, who begged their way to the districts they believed their menfolk had found work – even when reunited they customarily begged in the surrounding towns and villages while the men worked in the fields.[22]

References to a significant Irish presence among charity recipients and in the casual wards of the workhouses will crop up in the narrative; the Irish did have many vices, but we must take a balanced view and remember that as newcomers here they were bound to be bottom of the heap and among the neediest.

The 1815–16 Select Committee criticised the vagrancy laws because they technically imposed the same penalties on all kinds of offender, the genuinely distressed and the crafty scrounger alike.

In practice, however, the enforcement of the law varied widely; some magistrates were tough, others lenient. Many magistrates refused to order a whipping or imprisonment before passing what appeared to be genuine hardship cases. They had also concocted the 'walking pass' to give 'respectable' itinerants practical immunity from the law. These had originated by analogy with passes for discharged soldiers and sailors under an Act of 1803 which allowed them to return home, under what amounted to a licence to beg. 'Walking passes' for civilians were quite illegal, but were widely issued and recognised by magistrates, so 'deserving' cases could find their own way home by whatever assistance they could beg.

The Committee was highly critical of the policing, and the parochial structure of the unreformed police force goes to the heart of the whole failing of social policy towards the vagrant. Just like each parish's poor law provision, each parish constabulary was independent of its neighbour's. If a vagrant was hustled out of the parish, both the police and the overseer of the poor could wash their hands of him; he was the next parish's problem. This fragmentation encouraged a 'move 'em on' attitude, and there was no agency broad enough to take a wider view of the vagrants' problems. The reward inducement for the parish policemen was often self-defeating. If they tried to arrest a pitiful-looking beggar, the populace assumed they were after the 'blood money', and were liable to set on the arrester; magistrates did not care for over-zealous constables, as this forced them to pay out rewards excessively from the county rates.[23] Corrupt policemen engaged in collusive arrests of beggars for a share of the reward money,[24] or took bribes to leave beggars alone on lucrative pitches.

Ever since Tudor times vagrancy law had paid lip service to the 'House of Correction' as the appropriate receptacle for the convicted vagrant, a reformatory where they could be applied to productive work habits. The costs of equipping and staffing such places had led to their degeneration to common prisons by the eighteenth century,[25] and transportation remained as the only (theoretical) chance for the 'incorrigible rogue' to renew himself. The Select Committee, echoing the recommendations of the 1803 enquiry and those of Patrick Colquhoun,[26] called for wider agencies to deal with beggars and vagrants. Ideally, there should be county-based Houses of Industry, as a revival of the House of Correction in its original Tudor conception. And there should be a London-wide Mendicant Police Board; its constables would not be confined to a parish bailiwick, and it would double as a welfare agency, investigating the circumstances of each beggar and vagrant, with funds to give immediate relief to deserving cases, and only arresting the scroungers and cheats. (The Committee accused many parishes of delaying 'casual' relief to non-settled applicants, so forcing them into begging.) Discrimination of treatment and uniformity of enforcement was at the heart of these recommendations – but any ideas of supra-parochial agencies and a centrally organised police force were ahead of their time. British notions of individual liberty were firmly rooted in purely localised policing, however inefficient. High Tory repression of Radical discontent in the years to follow reinforced this hostility to creeping police-statism, and it was only later in 1829 that Robert Peel was able to create a metropolitan police agency – but without any specialised functions in relation to vagrants.

The only practical immediate reform was a clause in the Sturges Bourne Act of 1819 (a poor law administrative measure).[27] This allowed the removal of non-settled Irish and Scots back home once they applied for poor relief in an English parish. This now made them removable as paupers as well as beggars, and the provision was likely to have been influenced by the Select Committee's evidence of the burden such 'foreign' relief-seekers placed on the London parishes where they concentrated. The removal procedure for Scots and Irish was to follow the vagrancy law machinery – that is, a parish-by-parish cost burden for it would have been far too expensive for any single parish to bear the whole cost as under the procedure for English paupers. But by bringing more Scots and Irish within the passing system the Act's intention of relieving the pressure on London only served to intensify the already rapidly mounting financial pressures of passing nationwide; this crisis was to lead to another Select Committee in 1821.

2   Pass abuses and the Vagrancy Act of 1824

The mounting concern about the costs of 'Speenhamland' to support resident paupers, and the spiralling costs of passing vagrants, were not unconnected. A Bill introduced by James Scarlett MP in 1821 to 'peg' levels of poor law spending failed,[1] for the poor law was too sensitive an issue. Shortly before, Sir George Chetwynd, the MP for Stafford (who, as a magistrate, was familiar with the workings of the vagrancy laws[2]), successfully moved for a Select Committee on the Vagrancy Law with special reference to the costs of passing.[3] In 1806 it had cost an estimated £15,000 to pass vagrants in England, and in 1820 the official figure was £58,605. Chetwynd believed it was really nearer £100,000. The existing laws were a maze, and badly needed consolidating, he argued.

The Select Committee of 1821[4] revealed the increasing burden of vagrancy control to the community. For instance, Coldbath Fields House of Correction in Middlesex had in 1810 received 265 vagrants; in 1820 the figure was 1,287.[5] Middlesex had passed 540 vagrants in the year 1808/9, but 6,689 in the year 1818/19. Bristol had shipped across 265 Irish adults and 48 children in the year ending March 1814, but the figures were 885 and 268 respectively in the year ending March 1820. It cost Bristol £1,000 a year to ship the Irish, but it transported only a fraction of Liverpool's total, which averaged about 5,000 a year between 1814 and 1820.[6] Both ports were groaning under the financial burden. Bristol could not cope. Irish vagrants conveyed to the city were often left to slope off back to London or elsewhere.

The Committee learned about abuses connected with the reward system. The law entitled constables to the money at the time of *arrest*, not conviction, so they did not bother to turn up as vital witnesses at the hearing. And once the defendant was freed, his re-arrest earned the constable yet another reward! The City of London, which clamped down hard on vagrants, had scrapped rewards without any adverse effect on the rate of arrest.

Short spells in jail held no terrors for ne'er-do-wells, who looked on it as a convenient shelter: 'The vagrant himself, so far from shrinking, throws himself in the way of it, apparently solicitous for it, and in fact steps forward as a volunteer for prison.' The Committee recommended longer sentences.

But the pass system abuses were the most staggering. Constables and pass-masters ran tidy little rackets. One Midlands constable, who received 30 shillings expenses for each vagrant he passed to the county boundary, secretly arranged with a wagoner to convey them for five shillings, and he pocketed the difference. Pass-masters, who conveyed batches of vagrants in carts, turned a blind eye if they absconded en route, as this saved on the expenses they still claimed for; while the next county on the route was happier the fewer vagrants it had to take over, so nobody cared as the numbers thinned out.[7] Escorters held the pass orders of their charges, and retained them if they absconded; they could be sold to other pass-masters en route, who claimed full expenses on them when they were presented to the justices' clerks.

Even if constables and pass-masters tried to be honest, they were at risk from the rum and ruffianly people they had to escort single-handedly over the miles of countryside. Vagrants were supposed to be searched for valuables, as these were seizable to offset the travelling costs, but to try to do so invited violence. Middlesex in 1821 employed a 70-year-old pass-master, Thomas Davis, who admitted that many transportees 'bolted on him' – some up to a dozen times. He found it easier to give in to awkward customers. The overseer of the poor for Speenhamland in Berkshire told how his carrier nearly came to grief on asking his stroppy passengers to alight when his horse came to a hill it could not climb: 'they would ill-use and beat the driver, did he not carry fire-arms.'[8]

Habitual 'idle trampers' and Irish harvest workers knew how to exploit the pass system in all its aspects to get a free passage. There was a trade in forged passes – soldiers' and sailors' passes and the unofficial 'walking passes', and these could be used as a cover for a go-as-you-please ramble around the country. James Dawson Burn's step-father, an ex-soldier who begged and peddled in Scotland, obtained a soldier's pass in Carlisle in 1810 to travel to London to apply for a military pension. This enabled him to get relief in every parish they passed through: 'As this turned out a profitable speculation, we embraced nearly all the towns over half the kingdom.' Later, when his mother left his step-father because of his heavy drinking, she obtained a pass in London fraudulently as a soldier's widow, claiming Northumberland as her home parish. (This was a common dodge by vagrants – to name a parish in the border counties as your settlement, to get the most extensive conveyance.)

With the pass we visited nearly all the towns and villages on the east coast of England between London and Newcastle-on-Tyne. As my mother preferred taking the journey at her ease and her own time, she frequently had the benefit of the cash that the overseers [of parish paupers] would have had to pay for sending us forward in a conveyance, and at the same time she had the advantage of the intermediate relieving officers, who were often glad to get clear of us at the expense of a shilling or two.[9]

Irish harvest workers, flush with earnings, posed as destitutes to get a free passage home. They might get their dependants passed home first as 'paupers', while paying their own fare home, or arrange with friends that one of them carry all their pooled funds home as a fare-payer, while the others were shipped free as paupers. Otherwise they concealed their money in their clothes, or bribed a sailor to smuggle the money on board while the transportees were searched upon embarkation.[10]

The financial burden of passing vagrants was unevenly spread; counties not on the major pass routes got off lightly, while others suffered. Thus, in the years 1818–20, the East Riding of Yorkshire forked out £2,000, but the West Riding over £10.500. Middlesex had to pass its 'own' vagrants and expellees from the City to the tune of nearly £7,000 over the same period, while the City itself paid only £2,700.

The 1821 Committee's findings were followed by Chetwynd's consolidating (and temporary) Vagrancy Act of 1822.[11] It mitigated the penalties of earlier laws; whipping could not now be ordered by a single justice, only by a bench of magistrates at Quarter Sessions, and transportation for incorrigible rogues was abolished. Rewards were reduced to five shillings. The traditional classification of offenders was retained, and those caught 'openly and indecently exposing their persons' were now added to the list of undesirables.

Although the Act was intended as a 'liberalising' measure, it came in for bitter condemnation from civil libertarians, such as the Radical MP Joseph Hume. It got tangled up in a controversy about the arbitrary way the Middlesex justices were exercising their discretionary powers generally, but the Act itself received excessive blame as being oppressive.[12] In fact, there was a marked reduction in the numbers of vagrants committed and passed comparing 1820 with 1823, and striking examples included Norwich, where the prison intake of vagrants dropped from 330 in 1820 to 104 in 1823; and Hertford, where it fell from 283 to 26. In Bedfordshire passing costs in 1823 were a half of what they had been in 1820; in County Durham a quarter and in Cumberland a ninth.[13] The trade improvement in those years must take much credit though the farming areas were still depressed. But the figures certainly do *not* bear out Hume's claim that the Act was somehow a diabolical new instrument of oppression. The controversy came to a head over a curious case presided over by a Middlesex magistrate, David Williams. One William Lotcho was charged with indecent exposure, having been caught allegedly having intercourse with a prostitute in a side street one night in the East End of London. Lotcho maintained that he was just answering the woman's query about a street direction, and that the constable who caught them together had dropped an oblique hint that he would let them go for the equivalent of the reward money – in other words, the arrest was a frame-up. The street was very ill-lit, and the constable could not have had a clear view, said Lotcho, but the magistrate nonetheless accepted the constable's evidence. Hume unavailingly tried to clear his name in Parliament and attacked the magistrate and the Act, which in fact was to be modified in its final 1824 form. Indecent exposure has since then been qualified by the 'intent to insult any female', and, as we shall see, rewards were to be totally abolished.

As the 1822 Act's term expired, it was superseded by the permanent Act of 1824.[14] Hansard reveals no libertarian controversy in its passage, except for some doubt voiced whether the retention of flogging would have any reformative value.[15] Otherwise the only other reservation expressed was whether the revised wording would now protect innocent men from malicious charges of indecent exposure!

The new law went further than the 1822 Act towards 'liberalisation' by abolishing rewards completely (such 'blood money' was now disfavoured in policing generally and had been abolished in relation to property crime arrests in 1818). The passing of all convicted vagrants, English, Scottish and Irish alike, under vagrancy law procedure, was expressly abolished,[16] but, incongruously, non-settled Scottish and Irish poor relief applicants in England and Wales could still be removed under the Sturges Bourne procedure, which remained in force. An Irish beggar could not therefore be sent across the sea, but an Irish pauper could.

The classifications 'idle and disorderly', 'rogues and vagabonds' and 'incorrigible rogues' were perpetuated, and punishments were eased still further – a maximum of one month's jail for the first, three months for the second and a year for the last; only incorrigibles could now be whipped, but the Act did not specify the maximum number of strokes or the instrument of chastisement.

Soldiers' and sailors' 'licences to beg' were retained and now extended to prison dischargees, to assist their journey home. (Interestingly, a Gaols Act was passed later on the same day as the Vagrancy Act; this entitled ex-prisoners to a statutory mileage allowance from each parish they passed through on their way home.[17])

The 1824 Act, like its forerunners, was directed not just at vagrants but the whole class of shady undesirable and suspicious characters with whom society was then infested. It applied initially only to England and Wales. Scotland relied on some archaic laws, local borough statutes and other bitty enactments till it adopted the 1824 Act in 1871.[18] It embraced a whole gallimaufry of undesirables: beggars, fortune tellers and pedlars without licences; various street misdemeanants, notably 'riotous and indecent' prostitutes, and street sellers of obscene pictures; and those who offended against the Poor Laws, for example by throwing their dependants on poor relief by refusing to support them. Section 4 was aimed at the suspect characters the law could not pin specific crimes on but who were apparently up to no good, namely those carrying housebreaking implements; those found on enclosed premises 'with unlawful intent'; 'every suspected Person or reputed Thief' frequenting dock areas or public highways 'with intent to commit felony'; and those who 'wandered abroad' (that is, slept out) without visible means of subsistence and unable to give a good account of themselves. The Act continued the principle from earlier statutes of presuming the guilt of Section 4 defendants from their conduct, and the onus was on them to explain themselves; this runs counter to the general presumption of innocence in British criminal prosecution.

The Act became a convenient pigeon-hole in which to slot other undesirables as 'rogues and vagabonds' in later enactments; for instance, in 1838, shopkeepers who exposed obscene prints in their windows, and in 1898 those who lived on immoral earnings. Offenders against poor law discipline were to be brought within the 'idle and disorderly' rubric; for example from 1842 workhouse inmates who refused to perform prescribed work tasks or damaged their clothes or workhouse property; and from 1848, applicants for relief who gave false information about their means.

Although the 'privy searches' of lodging houses had been very laxly enforced by justices, it was retained in the 1824 Act. The Act made no reference to 'Houses of Correction'; any pretence that a reformatory system for vagrants existed was now abandoned.

Later commentators, in judging the Act from the viewpoint of their own era, were, I think, rather harsh. The 1906 Departmental Committee on Vagrancy called it 'simply a measure of repression' and in 1909 Swift Macneill MP branded it as a 'purely coercive' measure passed at a time of agricultural depression. But, as we have seen, the Act reduced earlier penalties, and while it offered no 'remedies' for vagrancy, how can one blame the Act itself when vagrancy is a phenomenon which we still have not cured in our own immeasurably more sophisticated age? The virtually pre-sumed guilt of 'Section 4' defendants has only been energetically attacked in more recent times (see Chapter 27) on civil libertarian (and racial) grounds and its retention in 1824 must be considered in the context of the limited policing capabilities of that period and the contemporary crime wave.

Whilst the increase in the number of vagrants committed to jail after the Act from 7,092 in 1825 to 15,624 in 1832[19] has been ascribed to the Act's sharper teeth, these in fact were years of deepening economic depression, and we have seen that the 1822 Act was marked, for its short life, by a *reduction* in vagrancy commitments at a time of (urban) prosperity. Moreover, by continuing to allow Scots and Irish *paupers* to be passed, the Act left a serious loophole. Scots and Irish scroungers, and persons pretending to be Scots and Irish, were getting free passages across country by the thousand each year, and the increasing burden to those counties that happened to be on the main pass routes from London to Bristol and Liverpool on the one hand, and Cumberland and Westmorland on the other, led to further Select Committees in 1828 and 1833.[20] The offenders were overwhelmingly Irish and pseudo-Irish; they outnumbered the 'Scots' by anything up to 15 to 1.[21] All the abuses associated with the pass system – the abscondences en route, often connived at by the pass-masters, and the racket in forged or floating pass certificates – persisted. To take just one example: on 10 August 1832 Warrington parish in Lancashire had assisted one John Smith and his two children (whose pass, issued at Portsmouth, declared them to be Scottish), and they were conveyed to Westmorland. On 27 August he reappeared with a pass under the name of John Watson. However, he had no Scottish accent, and was recognised from a fortnight before. His pass name, upon close inspection, was found to have been altered from 'Jane Watson', and he admitted to having obtained this pass from the woman in question in Warwickshire. He was tried and sentenced to six months' hard labour for defrauding the Warrington overseer of 2/6d.[22] The Scotch and Irish Removal Act of 1833, repeatedly renewed till the permanent Act of 1845, was intended to tackle these abuses and relieve the pressure on the intervening counties by throwing the entire cost of removing Scots and Irish paupers on the originating counties.[23] (These now had to decide whether it was more expensive to keep them on poor relief or to send them all the way home.) The law seems to have had a dramatic effect. In 1832, for instance, Berkshire had to receive for transit 4,559 persons at a cost of £1,139, but in 1834 only one was passed at a cost of £3.[24] However, Irish removals were to remain a nagging issue from the 1840s for opposite reasons from before, namely the unwillingness of destitute Irish to be forcibly returned home. Following the huge influx of refugees from the Great Famine of 1845-7, Lancashire, Glasgow and Clydeside, and parts of South Wales, were particularly swamped and keen to be rid of them.[25] The famine had a tremendous impact on the numbers of Irish settling in the mid-nineteenth century. England's Irish-born population rose from 293,000 in 1841 to 520,000 in 1851, and the figures for Scotland were 126,000 and 207,000 respectively.[26] Despite complaints of anti-Irish discrimination, in fact only a fraction of destitute Irish applying for poor relief were ever removed from Britain even at the height of the Famine,[27] and a high proportion of those who were removed subsequently slipped back into Britain.[28] The shift of removal costs entirely to the banishing counties from 1833 must have made it less worthwhile to remove Irish the further away they were from Ireland, and the high proportion of Irish on charitable relief, as frequenters of the poor law casual wards and as vagrants at mid-century, will be touched on in later chapters. Overall, destitute Irish were fairly safe to stay in Britain (though harder-pressed and poorer Scotland was less tolerant than England) as non-settled paupers.[29] The sheer numbers involved (about 250,000 starving Irish landed in Liverpool alone in 1847[30]) would have swamped the removal machinery, just as the sudden proliferation of Irish beggars in the streets made the Vagrancy Act almost unenforceable. The Liverpool Stipendiary magistrate instanced just one case at this time:

> The overseer brought up a woman for begging . . . I said, 'It is a clear case, a very bad case; send her to gaol.' The overseer then said, 'She has six children; if you send her to gaol I must take the children, and it will be a great loss to me.' I said, 'If this is to be the process, there is an end of the Vagrant Act in Liverpool' . . . I did not send her to gaol, and they were all sent into the workhouse.

The Vagrant Act, he said, was 'a dead letter in the whole place; we are choked out.'[31]

Once the famine crisis had eased, there was a long-term decline in permanent Irish immigration. Scotland took in an estimated 115,000 Irish in the period 1841–51, and 69,000 in 1871–81. In 1886 only 1,245 arrived.[32] Ireland's population was going down, reducing its own rural poverty and so shrinking the pool of destitutes who continuously fed the numbers of paupers and beggars in British cities. Whereas in 1845–53 47,000 Irish paupers were removed from Scotland, in the period 1879–90 2,942 were sent home.[33] The Irish dimension in beggary caused by flight from destitution at home decreased markedly after the 1850s, but the contribution to vagrancy and begging made by *seasonal* migrants would have persisted longer as their numbers in Britain held up at 24,000–30,000 a year from the 1850s to the turn of the century, and only started declining from 1908, a trend sustained over the next generation by the mechanisation of farming.[34]

To return to the 1824 Act's loopholes: Were there any abuses connected with the eligibility of discharged prisoners to passes? The 1834 Commission enquiring into the workings of the Poor Laws grumbled that as a misguided act of humanity magistrates were deliberately jailing vagrants in order to qualify them for a subsequent pass home.[35] However, despite this blanket assertion, the evidence it received showed in fact that English justices rarely issued ex-prisoners' passes as this would encourage vagrancy, since trampers would claim the most far-off parishes as their homes; in 36 of the 52 English and Welsh counties it was not used at all, and only 4 used it regularly. However, Middlesex was one of the offending counties, and seems to have been a prime source of mischief. Magistrates there seem to have been intent on using the Gaol Act passes to facilitate the passage of vagrants as far away as possible from the beggar-ridden metropolis. Cumberland and Westmorland were favourite claimed settlement destinations, much to their exasperation. In 1832, for example, Mr Hornby, a Cumberland magistrate, wrote protestingly to Mr Gregorie, a London JP, about being saddled with one Annie Duggan, a destitute passed from London. With motives mixing calculation and compassion Gregorie had convicted her of 'wandering abroad' so she could qualify for a prisoner's pass back to her (falsely) alleged parish of settlement in Cumberland once her fortnight's imprisonment was up. Gregorie gave a dismissive reply: London's need came first, and 'unless the visiting justices at the gaols in this county continue to enforce [the 1824 Gaol Act passes] it will be impossible to clear the streets of the metropolis of vagrants'.[36]

Assistant Poor Law Commissioner H.G. Codd had some interesting observations to make on the working of the Vagrancy Act in 1834.[37] It is striking that even at this date he could condemn the Act on the same grounds as its critics a century later; that this motley catch-all law made no distinction between the unfortunate and the ne'er-do-well:

> For instance, a person sleeping in the open air may do so
> without evil intent but if he has no visible means of subsistence
> and cannot give a good account of himself, which, if a stranger in
> the place in which he is apprehended, it is not likely that he will
> be able to do, he is liable to be committed to the same yard or
> ward with reputed thieves, wretches having obscenely exposed
> their persons, gatherers of alms, or if a female, with common
> prostitutes.

Was there then no attempt in practice to distinguish between the blameless down-and-out and the parasite; to help the former and penalise the latter? This leads us into the next chapter.

3 Mendicity Societies, and poor law casual relief to the 1840s

We have seen that proposals for an official vagrant police were pie-in-the-sky in the early nineteenth century, but more limited local initiatives, both parish-run and voluntary, were being started at that time. It was widely accepted that 'indiscriminate alms-giving' – charity with more heart than head in it – was the real root of the begging evil. If the public were confident that some organised aid was readily available to the genuinely unfortunate, impulsive hand-outs would cease and professional beggary would wither away. In 1819 Manchester began a public Vagrant Office. Police could issue relief tickets at their discretion to itinerants; these entitled them to overnight shelter and next morning the beadles would escort them to the parish boundary. In theory, therefore, there was no excuse for begging; but the police themselves were insufficiently discriminating and it was alleged that by 1832 increasing numbers of Irish were arriving to take advantage of the public shelter.[1]

Voluntary Mendicity Societies ran on similar lines. Subscribers received pads of relief tickets, which they would issue to beggars instead of money. The vagrants would take this to the Societies' offices where they would be interviewed, and particulars recorded. If apparently 'deserving' they would receive food, overnight shelter and perhaps an emergency dole. Societies also employed corps of private constables who patrolled the streets, issuing tickets and arresting known fakes.

Bath appears to have established the first Mendicity Society, the 'Office for Investigation and Relief', in 1805.[2] The city was a traditional Mecca for bogus cripples who played on the sympathy of wealthy invalids who came for the waters, as well as being on the Irish migration route between Bristol and London. The Society was claimed to have reduced street beggars by 90 per cent between 1805 and 1834.[3] A 'Society for the Suppression of Public Begging' was founded in Edinburgh in 1812, and Kendal's Vagrant Office, established in 1818, was said to have reduced beggars by 80 per

17

cent within a year.[4] By the 1820s similar societies were springing up all over the country.

London's Society for the Suppression of Mendicity was founded in 1818 by William Henry Bodkin, an overseer of the poor and secretary to the Houseless Poor Association.[5] The capital was then infested with beggars posing as French war veterans. The Duke of Wellington became a patron, as did Queen Victoria later; and her son, the Prince of Wales, gave donations among numerous other high-born notables and public figures, who were a constant target for the begging-letter writers.[6] At its height in the nineteenth century it employed eight constables and in 1860 had an income of nearly £4,000.

The constables (who worked closely with the new Metropolitan Police after 1829) patrolled the West End, where beggars were most prevalent. They were far more vigorous than the pre-1829 parish constables: in 1820 in the parish of St George, Hanover Square alone, Mendicity Society police were said to have made 273 arrests, compared with only 23 by the parish's own specialist force of 18 vagrancy constables.[7] The Society's constables, who were non-uniformed, were less conspicuous than the post-1829 'Peelers', but more prone to assault, not only by beggars resisting arrest but also by passers-by who sympathised with the beggars. On one occasion a Society constable was thrown onto a kerbstone with such force that a spinal injury kept him in hospital for four months.[8] Two generations later, the risks were similar. In 1900 a beggar 'H.B.' successfully prosecuted at Bow Street on the evidence of a Society constable, shouted to the latter from the dock that he would 'put a knife into the officer and kick his brains out', adding, 'I hope to live long enough to go to the gallows for you.'[9]

The Society built up an invaluable register of beggars, which the Metropolitan Police were able to draw on in detecting previous offences; by 1900 it had accumulated records of 72,800 'beggars and imposters', and this was why London achieved more convictions of recidivists as 'incorrigible rogues' than any other part of the country.[10] As well as issuing tickets (recipients had to go to its office in Red Lion Square in Holborn), it ran a labour yard at Lincoln's Inn where applicants might be sent for stone-breaking or oakum-picking as a 'test' of their genuineness before getting relief. It also distributed free meals by the tens of thousands a year; its peak period was 1838-47 when the number of meals issued ranged between 110,000 and 239,000 a year. This was the period of the 'Hungry Forties', aggravated by the Irish famine influx.[11] Whereas in January 1828 it gave 379 meals to Irish down-and-outs, in January 1848 Irish recipients numbered 21,578.[12] The peak period for successful convictions was 1835-52 when it was achieving 600-1,500 a year;[13] its later history and decline will be traced in Chapter 11. The Society's most enduring success was to lie in following up begging letters on behalf of subscribing clients.

From its inception the 'Dicity' rapidly acquired a folk celebrity, and its supposed gullibility was lampooned in W.T. Moncrieff's play, *Tom and Jerry*, a semi-burlesque romp through London's *demi-monde* high and low, staged in 1828.[14] In a beggars' hang-out in St Giles Mr Jenkins tells the assembled rag tag and bobtail that the Mendicity Society 'have kindly purwided a fund for us gemmen', They picked him up recently and put him to some work task, but 'says I, gemmen, I can't vork, cause vy, I'm too veak – so they guv'd me two bob, and I bolted.'[15] However, a very different picture was presented by 'Castigator', the anonymous author of a pamphlet entitled 'The Mendicity Society Unmasked' in 1825. The Society was accused of a mean-minded 'unholy inquisition' of the poor, and that through incomplete and amateurish checks on supplicants' backgrounds it was unwarrantedly blacklisting deserving cases. Its investigators included some wholly unsuitable characters, said 'Castigator', including a 23-year-old habitué of low taverns, who happened to be the brother-in-law of the Society's manager. Nonetheless, whatever the London Society's failings, it was still highly active when, by 1848, many provincial societies had foundered after the high hopes of the 1820s as they crumbled under the numbers of scroungers that gullible ticket-issuers were sending them.[16] But its aspiration to eliminate 'indiscriminate charity' was disappointed; even in 1861 it had only 2,400 subscribers,[17] a drop in the ocean of London's population.

From Tudor times, the poor law had a vaguely defined responsibility to assist the 'impotent poor' of the parish, such as the crippled, regardless of settlement, but not the 'sturdy vagabond'. The pre-1834 poor law did give discretionary relief to 'casuals' (that is, the non-settled) and overseers of the poor found it simpler to offer them a few shillings on condition that they left forthwith, rather than go through the expensive rigmarole of formal removal.[18] Indeed, parishes were suspected of winking at begging among resident workhouse inmates as an economy. Paupers were often allowed out on a Sunday – and private workhouse owners who ran miserly establishments on contract with the parishes regularly allowed the inmates out to find food by their own efforts – and this provided the occasion for some opportunistic begging. William Hale, a Spitalfields silk manufacturer, recalled in 1815 how, on coming out of chapel one Sunday, he saw one of his parish paupers crying '. . . have mercy, have pity on a poor blind child.' It transpired that she hired a blind child for begging on her Sunday leave from the workhouse.[19] (Sabbath-day churchgoers were prime quarry for beggars.)

Professional beggars, perhaps trailing broods of pitiable-looking children, sometimes made a comfortable living as peripatetic 'overseer-hunters' accepting parish doles to move on. Edwin

Chadwick revealed the depths of the cadgers' cunning in his report to the Poor Law inquiry in 1833.[20] If refused relief by an overseer they had the right of appeal to magistrates, who were far more gullible and susceptible to supplicants' well-rehearsed tales of woe. One Whitechapel parish officer told Chadwick how he carefully interrogated itinerants, say, as to the topography of the route by which they claimed to have arrived in London. But even if they were caught out, they changed their story before the magistrate – it was then their word against the parish officer's, and so it was the latter who felt as if he was on trial as a bureaucratic skinflint. One woman, Mary Shave, who had been refused relief, immediately joined the queue of like persons outside the justice's office where she gossiped about her grievance. An eavesdropper ahead of her in the queue posed as Mary Shave before the magistrate and received relief in her name. She had disappeared by the time the real Mary Shave's turn came!

A Spitalfields overseer told Chadwick of a pauper called Ansler whose ragged family lived in a filthy hovel. One morning he fortuitously caught them by surprise in bed when he walked in on a visit. In their confusion they had no time to secrete the items on the table, to wit 'a large piece of beef, a piece of mutton, and parcels of tea, sugar, bread, butter &c'. Ansler never applied for relief again.

The same overseer had developed his own tricks for catching out such scroungers. Before entering their rooms, he always knocked softly near the bottom of the door, as if a child, to take them by surprise.

The new Poor Law Act of 1834, which set the framework for poor relief till the post-1945 'Welfare State' legislation, aimed at standardising the regimen of local relief around the country under regulation from a new Poor Law Commission (later the Local Government Board) in London. Parishes were to be combined into much larger 'Unions' for operating common, larger-scale work-houses, and the ultimate ideal was to confine aid to 'indoor relief' – that is, degrading upkeep into the workhouse as opposed to assistance at home.

Under Section 54, parishes were empowered to give temporary relief, in kind only, in cases of 'sudden and urgent necessity' regardless of the applicant's place of settlement; this was the 'casual relief' for which itinerants were eligible upon receipt of an order from the parish relieving officer, who screened applicants.

It was evident that the parishes were evading their responsibilities and widely refusing help to some really desperate cases. This was brought to the Poor Law Commission's attention by the new Metropolitan Police. As a city-wide force their responsibilities transcended the narrow bounds of the old parish constables, whose only concern was to push down-and-outs out of their patch. The Poor

Law Commission likewise took a wider view, and they were both confronted with the obstinate parochialism of the local poor law authorities.[21] The ordinary Peeler was in daily contact with the flotsam on the streets of London, and often displayed common humanity to the obvious hardship cases, ignoring the Vagrancy Act and trying to get workhouse relief instead. Contemporary police registers of pick-ups contain phrases like:

'Found . . . deserted by parents . . .'
'Found destitute and ill in the streets . . .'
'Found in the streets in a state of insanity . . .'

The procedure became almost standard: the policemen would conduct the vagrant to the workhouse, which shut its door on them. The vagrant got temporary shelter in the police station while application was made to a magistrate, who had to order the workhouse to take him in under Section 54. A case from December 1837 was typical. A constable brought an obviously very sick vagrant John Morgan into Thames Street police station in Greenwich. The master of the Greenwich workhouse refused to take Morgan over, 'as he had committed an act of vagrancy by sleeping in a barn on the previous night, and . . . he must be taken before a magistrate [i.e., that he should be prosecuted under the Vagrancy Act and not saddled on the workhouse]. The master said it was fortunate he had not gone to rest, or he should have been much displeased at being disturbed.' The police constable then went to Mr Stranger, relieving officer of Greenwich, but could not make anyone hear after having knocked at his door for a considerable time. It appears that the police were reluctantly forced to book Morgan under the Vagrancy Act after all.

But the parishes had their side of the story, too. They had been trying to tighten up against scroungers since 1834, and, they claimed, once it got around that a transient had been relieved in a Union, that Union became a target for clamorous and belligerent scroungers who could make the relieving officer's life unbearable. As the Lambeth relieving officer complained in 1842:

It has been the constant practice lately for all travellers and mendicants to come to my house at all hours of the evening, requesting admission into the house for the night and knocking at doors and laying about [*sic*], refusing to go away without their request being complied with. . . .

But as soon as one relieving order is given, this opens a flood-gate to more applications, and the workhouse ward where they are sheltered becomes 'a scene of riot and noise throughout the night'.[22]

The police, complained the parishes, habitually sent vagrants to the relieving officers' homes, where they made a nuisance of themselves. As a group within the workhouse they were disruptive and insolent, and they upset the resident inmates. Indiscipline was not their only threat. As Colchester Union complained, by next morning 'every article in their rooms swarms with vermin. . . . The most horrible and loathsome diseases pervade most of them, and it is by such persons as these that fevers, cutaneous disorders &c are communicated to the regular inmates.'[23]

Following police complaints, the Poor Law Commission had, from 1837 to 1839, issued increasingly strict orders to the Unions to admit destitute casuals under section 54.[24] It commended the Hatfield Union (Hertfordshire) arrangement for warding off scroungers from the parish: this was a workhouse-run 'mendicity society'-type system of relief tickets issued to parishioners, to discourage monetary charity.[25] In 1841, recognising the disturbing influence vagrants could have in the workhouse, the Commission authorised Unions to build separate quarters for them, away from the main body of the workhouse, and empowered them to exact a work task in return for food and overnight shelter.[26]

However, a new snag immediately arose. Whilst workhouses had legal disciplinary powers over disobedient paupers 'maintained' in them, many magistrates mistakenly believed that overnight casuals were not strictly 'maintained' paupers, leaving the workhouses without any sanction against casuals who refused to perform work tasks, or tore up their own (ragged and verminous) clothes to force the authorities to issue replacements before they were discharged.[27] This problem was met by an Act of 1842[28] which expressly made casuals who committed the aforementioned offences punishable as 'idle and disorderly' under the Vagrancy Act, and empowered the workhouses to detain the casuals for up to four hours after breakfast for a work task. The foundations of the English casual ward system had been laid. It did not apply to poorer Scotland, whose traditional poor law excluded relief to able-bodied, male, *settled* indigents, let alone vagrants from outside. In Scotland licences to beg were being issued well into the nineteenth century.

4 A gallery of beggars (I) sick lurkers, praters and screevers

It is perhaps difficult for us to visualise what an integral – if unwelcome – part of the colour of street life the beggar was at the period of the 1824 Vagrancy Act. So varied and raggedly picturesque were they, that a picaresque literary sub-culture grew up around them, a product of myth and folklore in which the 'Jovial Beggar' was somewhat enviously depicted as the carefree antithesis of the work-bound 'flats' (mugs) they preyed upon.

St Giles, with its dark and dangerous warren of alleyways and tottering houses, was the most notorious nest of beggars and thieves in London, a sinister but fascinating netherworld.[1] Pierce Egan's celebrated rakish literary romp, *Life in London*, published in 1821, includes a conducted visit into the 'Holy Land' (the ironical nickname for St Giles), where this rum romanticism is embodied in a description of the 'Noah's Ark', a beggars' dive, where all the fakes strip off their disguises, count their daily gains, tuck in and revel. The poor blind wretch who begs with a dog 'can here *see* and enjoy all the good things of this life, without even winking'. The crippled beggar on crutches is 'the first to propose a dance after he has carefully deposited his stilts, and to join in a reel'. The starveling beggar is telling off the cook 'for sending in rumpsteaks without the garnish of pickles and horseradish'. The pregnant beggar relieves herself of the cushion under her dress, proposes a toast to begging and sings:

> There's a difference between a beggar and a queen
> And the reason I'll tell you why:
> A queen cannot swagger, nor get drunk like a beggar
> Nor be half so happy as I, as I.

W.T. Moncrieff's dramatisation of Egan's book, staged as *Tom and Jerry* at the Adelphi in 1828, included a bit part for a real-life beggar, the well-known peg-leg negro fiddler, Billy Waters, who

had a pitch outside the theatre.[2] In the 'Holy Land' scene[3] where
the beggars are living it up, 'Soldier Suke' orders a sumptuous
repast of 'shoulder of veal and garnish – Turkey and append-
ages, – Parmesan – Filberds – Port and Madery', at which Billy
chips in: 'Dat dam goot, me like a de Madery. Landlord, have you
give this bag of broken wittals, vot I had give me to-day, to some
genteel dog vot pass your door . . ?' (This is a reference to the
'broken victuals' or scraps received in a day's begging, which were
then sold to the decent poor or as a dog food, while the beggar fed
on luxuries.)

Broadsheet ballads with long antecedents contain many a merry
song extolling the supposed careless joys of a beggar's life. The
'Cadger's Ball', of around 1849, celebrates a fictional last fling
among the St Giles beggar fraternity, just before it was due to be
pulled down for the New Oxford Street development. The whole
cast of tricksters – the starving, the dumb, and the crippled –
minus their disguises, cavort so furiously that they bring Mother
Swanky's dilapidated den crashing down about them:

> Some pitched in the road bent double
> Some was smashed with bricks down brown.
> So the Cadgers saved the Crown the trouble
> Of sending Coves to pull it down.[4]

An artist, John Thomas Smith, was inspired in 1817 to go about
London making a pictorial record of the ragged pageant of beggars,
under the title *Vagabondiana*.[5] (Some are reproduced on pages
26–7.) This was the heyday of street begging 'characters' when
French war veterans, real or bogus, played on the public's
sympathy with ghastly wounds (real or fabricated), and a later
generation looked back on it nostalgically undoubtedly exaggerating and rose-tinting the reality. One veteran beggar told Henry
Mayhew, the great journalist, in 1861, of the 'good old days' of the
French wars when he lived in a beggars' dive in Pye Street, ruled
by 'Copenhagen Jack', the captain of the Pye Street beggars who
allocated the pitches and beats each day, and shared the profits:
'Those were fine times for beggars. I've known many of 'em bring
in as much as thirty shillings a day. . . . Yes, we lived well. I've
known fifty sit down to a splendid supper, geese and turkeys, and
all that, and keep it up until daylight with songs and toasts.'[6] To
Charles Lamb, the poet and essayist, beggars were a legitimate
part of the London scene, 'so many of her sights, her lions. . . . No
corner of a street is complete without them . . .' Even if you suspect
they are bogus, he said, 'Shut not thy purse strings against painted
distress', for even if imposters, they were worth paying for the
entertainment value. And he regretted their 'passing', as he saw it,
driven out of existence by reforming busybodies.[7] However, this

notion of the colourful street beggars of one's youth now fading away contains a strong element of nostalgic fantasy, for Charles Dickens, a generation later, was saying just the same thing. Curiously, for a man who loathed the begging letter writers who pestered him, (as we shall see later), he had a soft spot for the street beggars, whom he lamented in 1852 as 'Gone all gone; as defunct as the box-seat of the York mail.'[8] He blamed the Peelers for chasing them off the streets; the tattered ex-soldiers and sailors, and the runaway negro slaves of yore, the quick-witted, ready-tongued, impudent rascals were now replaced by a dull, unimaginative crew of sham pedlars: 'The spirit of street mendicity and mendacity is broken; the genius of beggars' invention has shrunk into the envelope of the ill-worded begging letter.' Dickens' impressions were belied by his contemporary, Henry Mayhew, whose long interviews with the mendicant underworld showed that if some of the more crudely flamboyant street paraders had disappeared by mid-century, there was still plenty of inventiveness, and the skilled begging letter writer was now the aristocrat of his profession.

Estimates of varying sobriety about beggars' earnings also took off into legend and folklore. Mayhew judiciously reckoned that a mid-century run-of-the-mill earned less than eight shillings a week,[9] putting him on a level with a farm labourer. In 1869 Howard Tallack, Secretary to the Howard Association for penal reform, reckoned a 'low average' weekly income for a begging family at £1, and claimed that many had higher incomes than curates, clerks and schoolteachers.[10] The Howard Association in 1882 put beggars' earnings typically at two shillings to half a crown a day, the earnings of an unskilled labourer.[11] But averages are misleading, for as James Dawson Burn observed: 'The difference between a common beggar, who earns his living by cadging for scran and the genteel high flyer, is as marked as the distinction between a peasant and a peer.' Burn likens the high flyers to actors in skill and merit, 'artistes', who were 'no mean ornaments to their profession'. And within the begging fraternity there was a noticeable snobbery – the sophisticated practitioner disdaining the 'common cadger'.

However, fancies of beggars' pots of gold teased the public imagination, and even figured in one of the Sherlock Holmes adventures. In *The Man with the Twisted Lip*, set in 1889, one Neville St Clair who had earned £2 a week as a journalist found he could better himself earning £700 a year as a witty street beggar on his City pitch. Conan Doyle was grossly exaggerating, but he was obviously inspired by the stories, apocryphal or otherwise, of beggars who had reputedly left fortunes. The Regency period seems to have been the most extravagant example: the lame crossing sweeper on the Kent Road who left £1,500 in his will

Figure 1 *A sample of the variety of beggars to be seen on the streets of London just after the Napoleonic Wars. They include a married Scottish pedlar, blind beggars, a 'Billy-in-the-Bowl' and a crossing sweeper. The negro 'chaunter' with the ship on his head was Black Joe Johnson. (Source: J.T. Smith,* Mendicant Wanderers Through the Streets of London, *1883 edition, earlier published as* Vagabondiana, *1817. Courtesy, Guildhall Library of London.)*

to a considerate City gent; the Scots beggar arrested in Durham with £900 in securities concealed in his clothes;[12] and the negro beggar who was said to have earned enough to retire to the West Indies,[13] to cite just a sample. More credible are references to beggars with tidy but far lesser sums of 30 shillings or £2 found stitched up in their clothing by arresting constables.[14] A pedlar companion of the mid-Victorian self-styled 'King of the Beggars', George Atkins Brine, died with £54 in sovereigns sewn into his clothes; it paid for his funeral, and Brine pocketed the £39 balance.[15]

Accounts of beggars' 'fortunes' must be taken with a pinch of salt; as a type, beggars were mostly spendthrift, and readily frittered their takes on blow-outs and booze.[16] Sir Nathaniel Conant, the Bow Street magistrate, told the 1815–16 Select Committee on Mendicity that stories of beggars' hoards were exaggerated for they seldom had more than a few shillings on them. This was endorsed nearly a century later by W.H. Davies, the 'super-tramp', who maintained that most tramps treated their earnings as easy-come easy-go.[17]

The 'lays' and 'lurks' (masquerades and performances) of the beggar fraternity boasted ancestral lineage, and Victorian and Edwardian beggar-sharps would have understood and used some of the same cant as their Tudor forebears – words like 'prig' (a thief), 'skipper' (a barn), to 'pad' (to walk the highways), 'ken' (a

lodging house), 'standing shallow' (begging near-naked), and
'toby' (the highway) – to mention but a few.[18] Changes of social
environment in the industrial revolution opened up new varieties of
dodge, and the spread of literacy spawned the begging letter
industry.

The varieties of street beggar were legion,[19] and I cannot hope to
be exhaustive within the confines of this book. There were
physically disabled beggars. Some could contort their limbs,
strapping them up for hours to fake the loss of an arm or leg.
(Following the Crimean War, like the French wars forty years
earlier, there was a crop of disabled war veterans, genuine and
fake.) The 'Billy in the Bowl' or 'sledge beggar' sat 'paralysed' in a
cart. James Dawson Burn tells of 'handbarrow beggars' found in
rural Scotland in the early nineteenth century. They were carried
from farmhouse door to farmhouse door, and it was up to the last
farmer to arrange the dumping of these pesky incubi onto his
neighbour's premises. Closely related were the 'sick lurkers', like
the 'wheezers' (bronchitics), shivering ague beggars, and consumptives suitably made up to simulate hollow-eyed pallor; and there
were 'accident lurk' beggars, the apparently crippled victims of
mine explosions, shipwrecks and the like. They displayed horrific
wounds, craftily prepared (known as the 'scaldrum dodge'); a
mustard plaster would take the skin off, and an application of
potash to the raw flesh produced an excruciating but convincing
simulation. Another trick was to smear dirty fat on the fingers, tie
bandages round them tightly, and the melting fat gave the
appearance of dripping pus. A horrifically septic leg could be faked
by tying bandages very tightly round the calf, leaving a gap which
rapidly swells with blood; a slice of beefsteak placed over the
exposed part gave an even more shocking effect. Some beggars
burned their skin, or pricked it all over to simulate ulceration. But a
painless dodge described by Mayhew entailed smearing the skin
with soft soap, then applying vinegar to make it blister, so creating a
festered effect. And of course there were deaf and dumb, and blind
beggars – though the latter might have their genuineness tested by
boys who stalked them to see if they could nab money from their
collecting boxes.

The disability might be real, but the actual cause of it invented
to win sympathy. A police inspector, reporting in 1869 on beggars
in Oxford Street and Regent Street,[20] instanced Messrs Alfred
Middleton and Samuel Johnson; the former had no legs and the
latter a withered arm. They dressed as sailors, purporting to have
been the victims of a shipwreck, 'but the truth is that many years
ago Middleton, while employed as a docker at the London Docks,
met with an accident, and had both his legs taken off in the
London Hospital, and it is a great question whether his companion
has ever been to sea.' Middleton was very aggressive when drunk,

'the wooden stumps worn by him being somewhat dreaded in the neighbourhood from the use he makes of them in his encounters'.

Fake epileptics – 'counterfeit cranks', the Tudors called them – survived into the twentieth century. Bloody froth from soap in the mouth and pricked lips, accompanied by convulsions on the ground would quickly draw a crowd and a cascade of pennies for the poor fellow. The Mendicity Society in 1900 reported the arrest of the 75-year-old self-styled 'Soap Fits King' for a performance at East Dulwich.[21] In 1906 George Sims, the Edwardian near-equivalent of Henry Mayhew as a recorder of low life, stated that 'soap fits' were still used, though less commonly.[22]

Topical beggars, exploiting the rapid dissemination of news in the era of mass circulation newspapers, would follow the gravy train of recent railway collisions, fires, mining disasters, storm damage, severe frosts, shipwrecks, and redundancies due to technological change or trade recession. They could be highly organised. 'Accident lurkers' might even have leaflets printed, describing the disaster and appealing for assistance, left at people's houses for a touch when they came calling later. Others stood in groups singing in the street. One group of 'unemployed' textile workers even had decorous begging verses printed on leaflets:

> For now our labour it is stopped
> And we've no work to do
> Oh! let thy loving kindness, Lord
> Compassion on us shew. . . .
>
> May God who did Elija feed
> Your generous hearts incline
> To give to us a little aid,
> Or we must surely pine . . .

The 'servant lurkers' pretended to have lost a job through illness and came knocking at the doors of wealthy homes, and played upon the sympathies of servants who answered the knock. Good research helped: a knowledge of the local gentryfolk, and the ability to reel off accurately the names of notabilities in the district where one claimed to have worked previously, gave the story the ring of truth; and a respectable appearance and correct servant-like demeanour added conviction.'Respectable beggars', as contrasted with the blatant ragamuffins, made a virtue of tidiness in their threadbare but decent clothing, and put on a show of shame in being reduced to beggary. Their line was about some personal misfortune which had reduced them from prosperity to sudden penury and shrewdly struck a psychological chord among passers-by, for a sense of insecurity was easily touched in the era before the Welfare State. The 'ashamed beggar', Mayhew tells us,[23] 'exercises a singular fascination over old ladies who slide coppers into his hand quickly, as if afraid that they shall hurt his feelings. He pockets the money, heaves a sigh and darts an abashed and grateful look at them that makes them feel how keenly he appreciates their delicacy.' Such oblique begging was well known to Charles Dickens who instances the trickster accosting a traveller with some story about a desperate need to reach Dover that night: he is seeking help from a relative for his homeless family in London, but lacks the funds to speed his journey. The supplicant cannot bring himself to beg, he says, but he happens to have a comb to sell: 'Sir, I implore you in the name of charity to purchase a tortoise shell comb . . . at any price that your humanity may put upon it and may the blessings of a ouseless family awaiting with beating arts the return of a husband and a father from Dover upon the cold stone seats of London Bridge ever attend you Sir . . .'[24]

Patters in this vein, however, had a practised fluency about them that would betray their artifice to acute observers like Mayhew and Dickens.

Any householder with a reputation as a soft touch – clergymen were favourite targets – would find his doorstep not infrequently occupied by unexpected callers, total strangers seeking charity. One mid-Victorian victim, the Reverend J. Hornsby Wright,[25] had a fund of experiences that left him wiser. One apparently respectable woman called, stating that she was a dressmaker on the brink of ruin through someone else's financial default. He gave her a shilling and said he would visit her at home; but he arrived sooner than expected, and found her tucking into rumpsteak and well stocked with gin. Another woman, with five children and an incapacitated husband, so she said, called on him after he had given some shoes to her crossing-sweeper son. She duped him for a time with this charade and made a convincing display of religious piety, till he later found she was a notorious drunkard and 'strumpet'. Her fancy man actually hid in a cupboard when he visited the woman for a prayer session!

Beggars stood mutely appealing in the street with placards stating their distress round their necks. 'Screevers' chalked their appeal on the pavement. 'Screeving' also referred to pavement artistry (and begging letter writing). Pavement artists needed no talent; they could work from a stereotyped design,[26] or else they sat with paintings on a card, bought from seedy artists who toured the common lodging houses.

Pious beggars or 'praters' specialised in street hymn singing, or as 'tramp parsons' went in for street evangelising, followed by a collection coaxed by appropriate verses from the Bible, like Psalm 37, verse 25: 'I have been young but now am old, yet I have not seen the righteous forsaken, nor his seed begging bread.'

Praters needed to learn passages of the Bible off by heart, and to lace their talk with biblical references; as a type they survived into the inter-war years of this century. A Moody and Sankey hymn book was a tool of the trade; some beggars stole hymn books while at Salvation Army services;[27] and child praters turned the hymns learned at Ragged Schools to profitable use in front of theatre queues.[28]

Negro beggars deserve a special mention. There was a conspicuous sprinkling of them in the period after the French wars, some having seen service in the Navy. They were considered quite a sight, and I have already mentioned the celebrity of Billy Waters. A contemporary was Black Joe Johnson who sang sea shanties, whilst on his head a model ship pitched and rolled with head movements.[29] Within the beggars' brotherhood they were accepted on equal terms. (George Orwell wrote in 1933, from his *Down and Out* experiences, that all races mixed equally at the bottom of the social heap.) In fact the public seemed to have had a soft spot for them, and in 1838 it was noted that they often occupied the most lucrative pitches in London.[30] One sure-fire money-prompter was to pretend to be a runaway slave from America, suitably made-up, though as Dickens sardonically observed in 1852 the beggar's bowed back 'marked as with scars from the leathern and wiry claws of the slave-driver's cat' was belied by its 'dull, sable obesity'.[31]

The publication of Harriet Beecher Stowe's *Uncle Tom's Cabin* aroused sympathy for the American negro in Britain and beggars with flattish noses found it profitable for a time to black-up.[32] George Atkins Brine, the footloose cadger, took up for a time with Linda, an American coloured girl from New Orleans, who had arrived in Britain searching for her English sea captain husband. Brine passed her off as a runaway slave, printing pamphlets of her 'life' as *The Adventures and Sufferings of Jessie Brown in her Flight from Slavery*, and for a period they made a good living in village lecture tours and public recitals of slave songs.

A proportion of street beggars were deserving cases, as the aforementioned police inspector's report acknowledged in 1869; the only alternative for cripples and the like was the parish workhouse, 'an institution which I have always found very much dreaded by the poor'.[33] It is evident from his report that there were numerous veterans in regular pitches who were left alone by the police. He contrasts the 'orderly' and well conducted ones, with the public nuisances like 60-year-old Mary Crawley who was 'troublesome, importunate and not unfrequently abusive' and spent her earnings on drinking bouts. Between the beginning of 1863 and the end of 1864 she had been brought before the courts 14 times for begging and twice for being drunk and disorderly, serving on average a month's jail each time. Her record indeed illustrates what was commonly recognised, namely the utter futility of short jail terms under the Vagrancy Act.

The begging fraternity, he found, was 'very intelligent' with a professional pride of its own. Beggars' wits were sharpened by their mingling in the common lodging houses with men of higher education by which they 'acquire a tolerable address and a fair amount of information necessary in many instances to assume a character or occupation when applying to the unwary for . . . aid'. They were shrewd judges of character. The Howard Association in 1882 noted, for example, how they made a particular set at women, who, 'tender-hearted and simple-minded' creatures, 'cannot resist the whine and humbug of the tramp'.[34] They also knew how to work systems to their own advantage. The 'charity hounds', as we shall see later, exploited the lack of liaison among charities. And migratory beggars sometimes deliberately got themselves arrested to help them on their itinerary, looking on a few days in jail as a rest: 'Thus, a man leaving London to go through Essex to Ipswich might commit some small offence, in order to be sent to Chelmsford gaol, some twenty miles on his journey, and on reaching the borders of Suffolk another offence would ensure his conveyance to Ipswich.'[35]

This unsavoury (but sneakingly enviable) quality of unscrupulous guile in the professional sponger is well illustrated in the life of George Atkins Brine, the 'King of the Beggars'.[36] He was born in 1812 in Sherborne, Dorset, a postman's son, and died in Sherborne workhouse in 1883, having spent life as a rover, beggar, petty con-man and thief; his roof (when not in jail) being the workhouse tramp wards and the common lodging houses. There is no space to detail his career; I can only pick out a few dodges and experiences – his time on the 'runaway slave' lurk has already been mentioned. As a 'sick' beggar he simulated rheumatism and dropsy – the latter effect being achieved by blowing out the skin with a blow pipe 'such as butchers use for blowing out a calf'. One of the several female companions of his career teamed up with him, posing as rheumatic beggars at Holywell Spring in Flintshire, but they betrayed themselves when one night in their lodgings their drunken hijinks brought the plaster down on their landlord below. At other times he was a colliery disaster victim, a begging letter writer (posing as a clerk with failing eyesight and an unemployed clergyman tutor), a quack medicine seller, a fake epileptic, a poetry reciter on Brighton Esplanade (conveying the impression to the gentryfolk of pitiful social come-down) and a former Church of England cleric. In the last dodge he called on dissenting ministers, claiming to have resigned his living on a matter of conscience, and to be now without employment. (A similar trick was, incidentally, played by Jewish pseudo-converts to Christianity, who leeched on the Society for Promoting Christianity among Jews by claiming to have been made outcasts by their community.) From Brine we learn how tramps preyed on each other: in one casual ward he had his clothes stolen, but at a lodging house he stole a doctor's certificate from another beggar to help him in one of his 'sick lurks'. Brine also tried the 'respectable' dodge of coaxing money by insisting that he was *not* begging: the method was to apply as a sick man to local gentryfolk's homes for a letter of introduction to some neighbouring charity hospital; his pathos and pride in *not* wanting money would usually ensure that some was pressed into his hand.

His relationships with women were fairly transitory. Women beggars were usually low-class prostitutes, and unemployed servants with no references who had drifted into the vagrant life. Brine asserts with unusual frankness in a Victorian publication that sexual freedom was 'one of the many charms that induces men to continue to tramp'. Women would take up with tramps as their 'doners' ('wives') for a time but eventually they would go their separate ways.

Tramps were said to use a secret sign language, chalked on fences and trees, to indicate to followers likely prospects at a particular house, and warnings where the reception is likely to be hostile to beggars (see the Cadger's Map, Chapter 7, for examples). W.H. Davies, however, claimed that this was a myth as beggars were not likely to spoil good pickings by revealing them to others. However, there is evidence of such signs being used at least into the 1940s.[37]

Documentation was an indispensable tool of the 'high flyer', the 'genteel beggar' who was the cream of his profession. Screevers and 'gag-makers' (concocters of fake testimonials, known as 'slums' or 'fakements') made a living composing for themselves or servicing a clientele in the common lodging houses. Mayhew cites a tariff at mid-century of a shilling for a 'petition', 2/6d for a letter countersigned with forged signatures ('gammy monekurs') and 10 shillings for a manuscript for a broken down author.[38] The testimonial might be the account of some personal disaster, like the bearer's shop burning down, attested by the signature of some local worthy, like a JP or clergyman; and there might be appended the 'delicates', that is counterfeit signed donations lists, useful as an additional prompter. The presenter, of course, had to look and act the part, too, before his victim.

There is no doubt that of all forms of beggars the begging letter writer was detested as the most pernicious and parasitical by the class of people to whom beggars commonly applied. 'Screeving' was already a highly developed industry in 1815, when thousands of 'twopenny post' petitions were arriving at the doors of the wealthy and famous – and such non-highway solicitation was outside the vagrancy law.[39] Lord Shaftesbury in 1853 denounced begging letter writers as 'lucrative, profligate and comfortable' parasites who dined 'on the fat of the land and on all the luxuries of the season'.[40] It was their word-craft, intelligence and mendacious imaginativeness that really got under the skin of their victims, and in 1850 Charles Dickens fulminated against them in *Household Words* as 'pestilent knaves' and the 'scum of the earth . . . dirtying the stream of true benevolence, and muddling the brains of foolish justices with inability to distinguish between the base coin of distress and the true currency we have always among us'.[41] They came in an infinite range of shabby-genteel guises, and Dickens, as a celebrity and known sympathiser with the poor, was only too familiar with the begging mail. The begging letter writer

> has been in the army, in the navy, in the church, in the law; connected with the press, the fine arts, public institutions, every description and grade of business. He has been brought up a gentleman; he has been at every college in Oxford and Cambridge; he can quote Latin in his letters (but generally misspells some minor English word); he can tell you what Shakespeare says about begging, better than you know it.

Dickens was smarting from an experience with a character who had written to him posing as a struggling playwright with an ailing wife. Dickens aided him, but subsequently found he was an impostor and took him to court for fraud. Much to Dickens' shock and chagrin the magistrate showed more sympathy for the trickster than Dickens. He praised the former's literacy and obvious intelligence, regretting that he had been reduced to deception as a means of livelihood, and acquitting him – leaving Dickens, as he ironically put it, 'with a comfortable sense of being universally regarded as a sort of monster'.

Henry Mayhew had much to say about the begging letter writer;[42] he too was vitriolic, describing him as a 'hypocritical scoundrel', with his warped talent and penetrating cunning. The screever must have a knack for the insinuatingly coaxing turn of phrase; he (or she) must have a good hand, and do the homework well, for he must be able to drop names and make allusions about past events and places that are accurate. If the appeal works and is followed up by personal contact, the screever must have acting flair, with (in a woman's case) 'an artistic eye for costume, an unfaltering courage, and . . tears and hysterics at immediate command'.

One example will give some flavour of the technique. One of Mayhew's informants received a letter from a supposed military man, claiming to have been formerly stationed in Malta and have made the acquaintance of a member of the addressee's family who was out there at the same time (this timing was obviously researched). The writer was now in difficult circumstances:

My father was a large landed proprietor at Peddlethorpe,
—shire. . . . From an informality in the wording of my father's
will, the dishonesty of an attorney, and the rapacity of some of
my poor late father's distant relatives, the property was, at his
death, thrown into Chancery, and for the past four years I have
been reduced to – comparatively speaking – starvation.

He then relates his plight, and rounds off the appeal with an
explanatory piece of local intelligence (again carefully researched):

My object in coming to this part of the country was to see an old
friend, whom I had hoped would have assisted me. We were in
the same form together at Rugby – Mr. Joseph Thurwood of
Copesthorpe. Alas! I find that he died three months ago.

Many begging letters were, however, more amateurish and
simple, and could be amusing rather than insidious. Sir Richard
Tangye, a well-known Birmingham industrialist and philanthropist
of the later nineteenth century, was a frequent recipient. His mail
included requests for money to start a Gaelic centre in Birmingham,
to develop an invention for 'Discovering Lost Vessells [sic] at Sea',
and to buy a new wig, as the correspondent's job depended on his
having a full head of hair![43]

How did screevers do their research? As we shall see when we
look at life in the common lodging houses, in the thieves' kitchens
there were often local resident intelligencers, who, for a fee, would
supply newcomers to the area with choice bits of information. But
professional screevers relied largely on their own resources,
consulting Church Year Books, Debrett, *Who's Who* and other
directories as essential tools of the trade, and scanning the posh
papers for news of the fashionable world generally. They also kept
registers of victims with notes on their susceptibilities, how much
they were good for and whether they were worth milking again.
Mayhew quotes from a captured register book. For example:

'Lincoln, June 19th.
Andrew Taggart [address]. Gentleman. Great abolitionist of
the slave trade. [Posed as] tradesman from U.S. who had lost his
custom by aiding the slope of fugitive female slave. By name
Naomi Brown – £5. N.B. To work him again, for he is good. . . .
Grantham July 1st.
Charles James Campion – Westly House – Gentleman –
Literary – Writes plays and novels. [Posed as] distant relative of
George Frederick Cooke[44] and burnt-out bookseller – £2–2. N.B.
Gave me some of his own books to read – Such trash. . . . Went
to him again on the 5th – Told him thought it was wonderful,

and the best thing out since the *Vicar of Wakefield*. Gave me £1
more – Very good man – To be seen in the future.'

The London Mendicity Society, early in its history, undertook
the following-up of begging letters on behalf of subscribers, and
this remained a key activity into this century. Even the royal family
passed on begging letters to it.[45] By 1900 the Society had
accumulated 229,000 letters, and fifty years' experience indicated
that a quarter of all writers were 'downright imposters', another
half 'undeserving' and the remainder 'deserving' in different
degrees.[46] The Charity Organization Society, a charity-liaison
operation, performed a similar service after its formation in 1869,
but despite such policing efforts, the professional begging letter
industry flourished into this century. In 1874 it was claimed that
successful screevers could earn at least £5 a week, nearly a
professional salary.[47] George Sims[48] in 1906 described how
organised syndicates, operating from common lodging houses,
pooled their takings. One 'firm' even had its ledgers and employed
a corps of collectors. Rowton Houses, the working men's hotels (see
Chapter 8), were said at this time to afford 'capital shelter' to such
operators, as the proprietors would not allow police onto the
premises to make enquiries.[49]

Between the wars, 'screevers' were still working from lodging
houses,[50] and the last reference I have found to such a traditional-
type practitioner is in Mrs Cecil Chesterton's *Women of the London
Underworld* (1938). The female trickster she described posed
variously for example as the mother of a large family, a deserted
wife and a seducer's victim.

5   A gallery of beggars (II) children

A phenomenon of early industrial Britain, with its rapidly growing and therefore youthful population, was the spawning of juvenile crime and beggary on an alarming scale. Orphaned, exploited and unwanted children took to the streets, where they lived by their wits. In 1816, of the 3,000 inmates under 20 in London's jails, nearly a half were under 17.[1] And of the estimated 60,000 vagrants in England after the Napoleonic Wars, 15,000 to 16,000 were reckoned to be under 15.[2] An enquiry inspired by the Quaker philanthropist Peter Bedford in 1816 into the 'Causes of the Alarming Increase of Juvenile Delinquency in the Metropolis' highlighted among its findings the connection between vagrancy and crime. The case of 8-year-old 'E.F.' was typical. His mother was immoral, and he had already been stealing for two years:

> In Covent Garden Market there is a party of between thirty and forty boys who sleep every night under the sheds and baskets. These pitiable objects, when they rise in the morning, have no other means of procuring subsistence but by the commission of crime. This child was one of the number; and it appears he has been brought up to the several police offices upon eighteen separate charges. He has been twice confined in the House of Correction and three times in the Bridewell.

A generation later Mayhew was describing how these urchins slept among the animal pens at Smithfield,[3] and Ashley Cooper in 1848 listed arches, porticoes, sheds and carts, sawpits, outhouses, and in one case, the iron roller in Regent's Park, as shelters for the estimated 30,000 'street Arabs' in London.[4]

In 1803 it was stated that three-fifths of all beggars in London were children, and that Irish children formed a third of all child beggars.[5] The Select Committee on Mendicity of 1815–16 expressed alarm about the prevalence of juvenile begging, and called for the withdrawal of young offenders into special schools. Young children were useful begging earners for under the age of seven they were not criminally liable under the vagrancy laws. A train of pathetic infants – the punier and sicklier-looking the better – was a highly lucrative aid to an adult beggar; child beggars could reputedly bring in four shillings a day each in the mid-Victorian period.[6] Youngsters were hired from parents in the slums: Mayhew cites a tariff at mid-century of 9d for one child 'without grub' to 2/6d for a 'school of children, with a surcharge of 2d for a child kept out after midnight'. But individual charges must have varied according to the suitability of the child; there would have been a premium on lame or blind children, for example. Ribton-Turner mentions the case of a woman who begged for years with 'her' baby, which never got any older! Applicants for parish relief would claim for concocted broods of offspring, and their landlords, who had an interest in seeing their tenants in funds, would swear that the children were genuinely theirs.[7]

They were instructed to sob at the approach of a victim (babies were pinched to make them cry), and in St Giles rookery around 1815 there was at least one training school where some old woman taught young girls the arts of attracting attention to themselves in the street.[8] So bold and tenacious were such youngsters that they would pursue their quarry 30 or 40 doors along a street, begging lustily all the way. Street Arabs learned instinctive acting ploys. One boy told Lord Shaftesbury 'that he never received so much money as by putting on rags, assuming a melancholy face, and then standing before the door of a cookshop and gazing into it with wistful looks'.[9] Nearly 50 years later, young Arthur Harding, a denizen of the Nichol slum in Bethnal Green, went with other youngsters to Liverpool Street station, pestering travellers to carry their bags, and astutely appealing to them with patter such as 'You wouldn't say that, Madam, to a starving child, would you?' or 'I haven't got anywhere to sleep tonight; would you like to see me sleep on a cold winter's night out on the street?' And along theatre queues they would go cap in hand pleading 'Mummy and Dad's in prison or the workhouse and we're all on our own, and my little sister's over there, she's crying'.[10]

Another dodge was for a child to stand sobbing in the street, and tell some sympathetic passer-by that an item they had been carrying in an errand had been jogged out of their hands in the crowded street and there was no money at home to buy more.[11] Yet another was to beg, and exploit the well-known maltreatment of children by parents when they did not bring enough money home, by *pretending* that they would be beaten if they did not raise the cash.

Such exploitation by parents avid for drink money was certainly common. The *North British Daily Mail*, which ran a series of articles on the 'Dark Side of Glasgow' in early 1871, featured items on youthful begging, relating how slum children, raised amid drunkenness and vice, were deliberately put out in freezing weather to beg, sing, or sell newspapers, ill-clad and shoeless (perhaps deliberately to maximise the pathos), with threats from their parents if they did not bring enough money home.[12] The investigator, after giving a ragged six-year-old girl some money she was begging to buy a scone, secretly watched her as she then entered a close, and overheard the conversation:

'What did he gie ye?'
The child mentioned the sum which was correct.
'It is a lie', said the woman, 'he gied ye mair.'
'No he didna,' said the little one with child-like earnestness – 'as sure as dathe.'

The mother shook the child violently, warning her with strong language to 'see and get mair next time', then went across to the whisky shop opposite, to spend the child's earnings.

Before the State became directly involved through legislation with children in moral and physical danger, among the private philanthropic efforts to assist Street Arabs was the Ragged School movement; Ashley Cooper became involved from 1843 and the Ragged School Union was formed in 1844. Improvised schools, using sheds or even railway arches, were set up for the young urchins; a meal and the possibility of night shelter were inducements to attend, but, as we shall see, there is evidence that these malnourished but razor-witted waifs were using the schools, not for moral upliftment, but their own convenience as a place to go between begging stints. Cooper virtually admitted as much in Parliament in July 1849, when calling for government aid to emigrate such youngsters to the colonies.[13] Attendances at the schools, he said, were interrupted by the boys' spells in jail, and from lessons they went straight to their begging pitches. He cited one episode:

Fourteen or fifteen of these boys presented themselves one Sunday evening and sat down to the lessons, but as the clock struck they all rose and left with the exception of one who lagged behind. The master took him by the arm and said, 'You must remain; the lesson is not over.' The reply was, 'We must go to business.'
 The master inquired, 'What business?'
 'Why don't you see, it's eight o'clock; we must go catch them as they come out of the chapels.'

Whilst for boys begging was a stepping stone to more serious crime (and as beggars and crossing-sweepers they might already be reconnoitring for more experienced thieves), for girls it led into prostitution.

Seasoned girl beggars could become difficult to handle by their elders when they got to a certain age. Dr Thomas Barnardo, who began his mission to rescue street waifs in 1866, told in the 1880s of the traffic in girl beggars by parents, who might sell them outright for five shillings. One informant, who lived in a Stepney lodging house, told him how the landlady bought girls from tenants for begging purposes, and worse: 'Sometimes they buy 'em for a year, or two years or three years, and sometimes they sell them right out. But they ain't much good to anybody when they gets grown up; for then they are *known* and generally *goes to the bad*'. (Barnardo began mounting 'philanthropic abductions' to rescue by illicit seizure children at risk.)[14] George Atkins Brine hired a brood of children to beg with as 'Motherless' and raked in over 30 shillings in five hours, but this lucrative 'lurk' was cut short by one of his assistants, a rebellious girl who seems to have been fed up with the way her mother exploited her and her sister to blue the hire charges (2/6d in Brine's case) on drink. She began blabbing the truth to passers-by, and Brine had to make off quickly.

Street waifs might launch themselves as precarious street entrepreneurs, such as tumblers outside theatre queues, pedlars, crossing-sweepers and shoe-blacks. As crossing-sweepers they came up against older and more established sweepers on the more profitable thoroughfares.[15] Young sweepers totally autonomously formed themselves into companies, with rotas and strict rules about the allocation of custom. Henry Mayhew found these companies controlling the crossings in the Trafalgar Square area. Girls might be admitted to the companies: one twelve-year-old girl he interviewed earned 6d to 8d a day between 9 am and 4 pm; brooms cost 2½d and could be expected to last a week.

It was the other traditional waifs' enterprise of shoe-shining that gave John Macgregor, a barrister and Ragged School teacher, the idea of organizing shoe-black brigades to give employment to London's Street Arabs during the Great Exhibition of 1851, when hundreds of thousands of visitors would be in London.[16] The Shoe-Black Society was born, and by 1852 employed 120 boys. It provided approved lodging accommodation, free from the baneful influence of the common lodging houses;[17] it arranged pitches, with a promotion system as an incentive. Some of their earnings was banked to build up savings, and through close links with the Ragged School Union, there were possibilities of assisted emigration for likely lads. The Society grew over the next 20 years. By 1877 it was employing 385 boys, and earnings had risen to over £12,000 that year compared with £650 in 1851. The Home Office gave its blessing to authorised pitches, and the police protected the uniformed members of the Shoe-Black Brigades from free lance competitors who were harassed quite nastily – police would kick non-Brigade boys' boxes into the road to get broken among the traffic, and generally hustle the lads on. The Brigade was not popular among the poor; it was seen as organised regimented philanthropy, treated preferentially over individual initiatives to scrape a living.

In 1867 a similar system of 'Industrial Brigades' was started in Edinburgh. The raw material was the urchin mob who hung about Waverley station, begging and odd-jobbing.[18] A hostel with strict rules on church and school attendance and general behaviour was established, and shoe-blacks and crossing-sweepers were allotted protected pitches. A contemporary poem, 'The Shoeblack Brigade', published in Edinburgh newspapers, radiated optimistic prospects for youngsters in the scheme. A young lad meets a friend and 'stunnin' news that the Shoe-Black Brigade was recruiting more youngsters:

> Awa' to the office we skirted wi' speed
> To see an they any mair laddies micht need
> And the manager, seemin' to fancy our looks
> Spak kindly; and writin' our names in his books
> Speered wha we belongt tae? had we e'er dune ocht?
> Wi' wha, an' at what sort o' bizness we'd wrocht?
> A' whulk bein' answered, he'd trust us he said;
> Syne fitted us out for the Shoeblack Brigade.

And the poem ends brightly, affirming the good earnings to be made from willing work for the Brigade.

After the 1870s the London Society went into decline. Only the sort of youths who could take the discipline would stick it out; the more independence-loving or wayward ignored it, and the numbers it employed were a mere drop in the ocean of London's waif population. By 1904 it was down to two hostels (from nine in the 1870s), and one of those had ceased recruiting boys in favour of cripples and deformed adults. By this time compulsory education was helping to keep youngsters off the streets, and for the myriad of youthful moonlighters there was now a wider range of casual jobs – as errand boys, van drivers' mates, newsvendors, and so on – as industrial society matured.[19]

In early and mid-Victorian Britain, Irish and second generation 'Irish Cockneys' figure prominently in the ranks of Street Arabs, but there was also a small minority of Italian beggar children and street performers who have a very interesting story.

Italian immigrants and vagrants were present in Britain in noticeable pockets by the 1830s.[20] They were noted for their practice of putting their children out to entertain in the streets, where their exotic looks attracted attention. In 1831 one such beggar boy, Carlo Ferrari, who used to display white mice in a cage outside the Bank, was murdered by the body snatchers Bishop, May and Williams in Bethnal Green.[21] (To digress here: the Ferrari case led to the Anatomy Act of 1834 which expanded the legitimate provision of corpses for dissection and put the 'sack 'em up men' out of business. Ferrari was not the first youthful beggar to fall victim to body snatchers. 'Daft Jamie', a young simple-minded beggar of West Port in Edinburgh, was one of the victims of Burke and Hare, as transpired at their trial in 1828.[22])

The Italian immigrants concentrated in particular districts. Saffron Hill in Clerkenwell, London, became 'Little Italy', and in the early 1840s there was at least one lodging house in Birmingham inhabited exclusively by Italians, where they kept their musical instruments, monkeys and other small animals.[23] Italian organ-grinders were familiar by the mid nineteenth century, but there was a sinister side to this street entertainment. Traffickers known as *padroni* imported children from the impoverished south of Italy, Naples and Calabria particularly, by persuading parents to enter into a contract for an enticing lump sum to bind the children over for say two years to be taught a *virtu* (accomplishment) in England so that one day they could become as prosperous as the *padroni*. The *padroni* sent agents to go round the shops in the villages, asking which customers had bad debts. They were approached with an offer sufficient to pay off the debt in return for their children – an 'offer they couldn't refuse'! The unfortunate children were then walked all the way from Italy through France and entered England exhausted, having been forced to beg or perform all the way. Not speaking English, they were helpless tools of the *padroni*, forced to perform in the streets as organ-grinders, jugglers and so forth, living as semi-slaves in lodging houses.[24] The girls were obviously in moral danger, especially as they developed physically earlier than their English counterparts. One large-scale operator, Giuseppe Delicato, had houses in Birmingham, Plymouth and Hanley; he was a notorious seducer of young girls, and in fact brought over whole families to beg, taking nearly all their earnings, and ditching them when they ceased to be of use.

There was a similar traffic on a smaller scale from Germany, for there was a small cluster of German lodging houses in Whitechapel in the early 1850s. In 1851 one Conrad Stumpf was stopped at Cologne by police with a party of 19 children, contracted from parents in Hesse and Nassau, and stopped from getting any further.

In the 1870s it was said that the Italian children were expected to earn at least four shillings a day; one observer in 1892 put their earning potential at 10 shillings a day.[25] Sometimes they ran away, taking the instruments with them. (The *padroni*, assuming quasi-property rights over them, even advertised publicly for their return.) But it was not only the *padroni* who abused these children, for often Italian immigrant parents exploited their own offspring in just the same way.

The British government took no action before 1877 (there were no immigration controls then). However, the Italian government had been alerted by its own ambassador in London who was shocked when one night, emerging from a diplomatic function, he was surrounded by a crowd of child beggars speaking his language; it was customary for them to hang about the fashionable areas when there were balls. His report led to a swingeing Italian law of 1873 banning the recruitment by *padroni* of children under 18, but in the absence of any control at the British end, the flow continued.

In England the Italian Benevolent Society was formed under the auspices of the Italian Embassy to assist the return of stranded Italians back home. In 1876 the Education Act made compulsory the education of children up to 10 years old. The Italian Benevolent Society approached the London School Board and asked that the act be applied to Italian children, too. This was done, but the *padroni* simply dispersed to outer London and the provinces where the school boards did not bother.[26] In 1877 the Charity Organisation Society, having conducted its own inquiry into the problem, presented its findings to the Home Secretary, who instructed the Metropolitan Police to enforce the Vagrancy Act, and the Industrial Schools Act (see Chapter 16) more strictly. The crackdown led to an increase in the number of children sent home but they only returned with their parents, and by 1892 it was said that all this policy had achieved was to 'reduce slightly the number of *padroni* and increase the number of parents'.[27] Apart from dispersal, the *padroni* also evaded the Vagrancy Act by instructing their young tools not to solicit money but only to pick up coins voluntarily tossed to them, for busking was not a Vagrancy Act offence (see next chapter).

The 1889 Prevention of Cruelty to Children Act enabled the newly-formed NSPCC to move in, and its reports indeed bear out the claim that parents rather than *padroni* were figuring as the villains by the early 1890s. In October 1891 the *Child's Guardian* adverted to heartless Italian parents, and cited a recent Society prosecution of a father who forced his daughter to drag a two-hundredweight organ in the rain, soaked through, while he 'walked leisurely by her side'. The continuing weakness in the law was the lack of immigration control and the lightness of penalties under the 1889 Act, which only made a small dent in the *padroni*'s profits.[28]

The pathos of child-begging inspired a genre of maudlin parlour songs, sentimentalising the child's pleadings, or comforting the audience's conscience by spiriting the expiring waif into the bosom of the angels.

Isabella Vivien's *The Beggar Boy* of 1883 pleads:

> I have a mother good and kind
> To comfort her's my only care,
> For I've as true a heart you'll find
> As thou who live a choicest fare.
> Then give your mite and heed my lay
> And Heav'n will bless you on your way.

W. Paxton's *Underneath the Gas Light's Glitter* (1885)[29] carries the same soulful appeal:

> Underneath the Gas Light's glitter
> Stands a little fragile girl
> Heedless of the night winds bitter
> As they round about her whirl
> While the hundreds pass unheading
> In the evening's waning hours,
> Still she cries with tearful pleading,
> Won't you buy my pretty flowers?

An Angel's Message to a Dying Street Arab (1886) conveys to him the dubious consolation of a blissful after-life, as does *The Beggar Child's Dream* (1884). It tells of a freezing waif forlornly looking in through the window of a house where children are revelling in Christmas merriment.

As he sinks into oblivion:

> He slept and in his dreaming lo!
> He saw a figure stand
> Within a bright and happy glow
> And hold him to its hand.
> He clasp'd it tight and pass'd away
> Beyond the realms of night
> And with the dawning of the day
> Awoke to perfect light.

6 Crypto-beggars: pedlars, crossing-sweepers and buskers

Up to 1870 pedlars were supposed to take out an annual excise licence of £4[1] but the expense led to widespread evasion. Pedlars, authorised or not, were essential retail distributors in rural areas before the railway era, and were welcome guests at remote farmhouses for the news of the outside world they brought.[2] Traditionally, they sometimes operated as criminal couriers, for example secretly ferrying contraband whisky across from Scotland to England to avoid the excise duty; and peddling might be a cover for migratory thieves dealing in stolen goods.[3]

The Pedlars Acts of 1870, 1871 and 1881 radically changed the law in a 'free trade' direction[4] by replacing the licence with a cheap annual police permit (set at five shillings in 1871). The police were supposed to issue permits when satisfied with the applicant's bona fides and good character. In practice, many police authorities were lax and freely issued them, so these 'briefs', as pedlars called them, were often applied for as a cover for begging.[5] Beggars would stock themselves with some token array of small wares (laces, pins, matches and so on) and discreetly beg from anyone who stopped to look. This would confound any policeman in the vicinity who must actually see and hear the suspect soliciting alms.[6] The amount of stock pedlars might purchase from 'swag shops' (these were pedlars' wholesalers – in London they were generally Jewish-owned shops in Houndsditch) might be totally insufficient to make a living, but the last thing they wanted to do was to *sell* it. As Henry Mayhew explained in 1861:

> A poor half-clad wretch stands by the kerb exposing for sale a single box of matches, the price being 'only a halfpenny'. A charitable person drops a 1d in the tray and refuses to take the matches. In this way a single box will be sufficient for a whole evening's trading, unless some person should insist on an actual 'transaction' when the beggar is obliged to procure another box at the nearest oilman's.[7]

In 1931 Frank Gray, an MP with a deep interest in vagrancy matters, made a similar observation: outright purchases would annoy the pedlar, for he could easily otherwise make 15 shillings out of two shillings' worth of stock from sympathy 'drops'.[8]

Another dodge was deliberately to offer obviously and pathetically worthless objects for sale, to excite pitying drops. The pseudo-pedlar's outlay was then nothing, for items might include over-ripe fruit, picked up off the pavement at Covent Garden, or out-of-date newspapers,[9] cups without handles, old razor blades, the rusty works of a clock[10] and the like.

A beggar who happened to be in possession of a current 'brief', but for want of funds resorted to direct begging, was well advised to secrete his permit in his clothing, so if picked up by the police, his future legal pedlar's status would not be jeopardised. Conversely, it was a good ploy to meet a begging charge with the excuse that you were trying to raise money to purchase a 'brief' and so make an honest citizen of yourself. W.H. Davies mentions one beggar who took in a kind-hearted JP with his plea, the latter ordering that the requisite five shillings should be given to him out of the poor box![11] The Pedlar's Act exempted the sale of 'perishable' items from the need for a permit. It became a favourite beggars' trick to make up packets of 'funkum' (lavender) and keep them in their pockets. If approached by a suspicious policeman, they could always pull out the 'funkum', offered as a perishable, and needn't worry about a brief.[12] Crossing-sweepers were also often covert beggars, as well as look-outs for thieves.[13] In 1868 Alsager Hay Hill, a writer on vagrancy and the unemployed, called for some public regulation of crossing-sweepers, for 'in some places hardly a corner of our streets is free from some noisy and insolent representative of this class, who with threadbare pretence of service rendered to the public, demands his pence with all the importunity of the most accomplished beggar'.[14] In 1871 Dr William Guy bemoaned the fact that only one of London's local authorities had availed itself of powers under an Act of 1855 to employ paid crossing-sweepers.[15] F.S. Stuart in 1937 recalled seeing the last of the old-style crossing-sweepers at the turn of the century 'busily pretending to brush dirty roads for pedestrians whose vanity made them part with coppers for this purpose, though the good it did was more imaginary than real'.

In fact, veteran crossing-sweepers became in time an established part of the local scene, and might be summoned by local residents as messengers, odd-job men and the like, and even treated them as 'pets', with gifts of food and old clothes; even the police would protect their pitches from intruders,[16] and I have alluded to the problem juvenile sweepers had trying to break into the game. Some sweepers adopted colourful tricks of the trade to boost their earnings; dressing up in rumpled toff's clothes, complete with top hat, and bowing decorously at customers drew business from amused pedestrians,[17] and at least one sweeper used to don a farm labourer's smock, posing as an unemployed farmworker who had come to town for work, and was stranded.[18]

Street entertainers were not on the whole viewed as beggars under the Vagrancy Act, though the legal area is a little grey, for if the quality of the performance was so poor that it was an evident veneer for begging, then the Vagrancy Act would be invoked.[19] Thus in November 1911 a husband and wife were charged with begging at Westminster Police Court, when the husband whistled while his wife sang in the streets. Though they were leniently treated by the court, the *Westminster Express* was moved to comment sharply, and not without xenophobia, on their apparent victimisation 'when Teutons, armed with various instruments [i.e. German bands] – to say nothing of organ grinders, foreign and otherwise – are allowed to produce hideous sounds in our streets, in the hope of receiving money, even as this singer and whistler hoped. Begging? To beg means to solicit alms. What this means in the eyes of the law, goodness knows.'[20] The Metropolitan Police Act 1839 dealt with street performers by empowering householders or policemen to move them on for any 'reasonable' cause. Nowadays 'quality of performance' is irrelevant, for the police would charge for obstructing the highway.[21]

The term 'busking' in the mid nineteenth century meant peddling in pubs, seeking work as an entertainer there, or selling obscene songs in the street,[22] but by the late nineteenth century seems to have taken on its modern connotations of street entertaining. 'Griddling' or 'grizzling' was the specific term for street *singing* used in Mayhew's day and up to the 1930s (at least);[23] 'chaunters', according to Mayhew, were singers of the broadsheet ballads they were selling. 'Praters', as already noted, specialised in singing hymns and sacred songs.

Victorian entertainers were not confined, as they tend to be in modern times, to a few locales like cinema queues, the London Underground and a few market places; they could be found in any thoroughfare and side street, and were more varied than the modern busker, including Christy Minstrels, organ-grinders, jugglers, animal trainers, puppeteers and so forth, as well as the 'griddlers'. The singers would venture into quiet residential streets, and their renditions would bring (hopefully) a shower of coins from upstair windows; it was a good practice, it seems, to make a play towards a window from which a child was gazing out, for an amused child might induce a parent or nanny to throw down pennies. Often, we can be sure, the money was not a token of appreciation but a bribe to take the noise elsewhere.

A good voice was not always necessary to successful griddling; a feeble, cracked voice carried pathos and drew the money equally.[24]

Timing and location were all important. Crippled griddlers could do well in mining districts, where disablement was common – and Welsh mining communities, with their fondness for music, could be particularly rewarding. The pavements outside pubs were a good 'pad', too, for drunks could be mawkishly touched by the sound of vocal strains. The company of a child was very valuable, and into the 1920s at least the frequenters of common lodging houses were still hiring out their children to professional griddlers.[25] The Reverend Frank Jennings, the 'Doss House Parson', tried his hand at the game in the 1920s and affirmed that a 'respectable' appearance was best; people were moved by someone who had apparently come down in the world, whereas they would shun the dishevelled 'griddler'.[26] It would seem that the poshest areas were the meanest, and should be avoided. Laurie Lee, in the 1930s, found that pukka business gents were the most tight-fisted, whilst drunks and women were most generous.[27]

Victorian middle-class objections to street entertainers seemed to have been mainly directed at the disturbance they caused to quiet residential neighbourhoods, and in the 1860s there was an active campaign to suppress them, led by Michael Bass MP. The campaigners were unpopular with the lower classes, who saw them as stuck-up killjoys trying to take the bread out of the mouths of the poor, who were just trying to save themselves from the workhouse. Bass did get an Act passed in 1864 banning street entertainment that interfered with the domestic amenities of any household,[28] but it had no effect, and complaints about street entertainers – particularly French and Italian immigrant 'riff-raff' – continued to be voiced.[29] In 1911 the burghers of Westminster were running a 'Betterment of London Association' campaign to attack street noise, caused by traffic, street traders' cries and the 'Intolerable Nuisance of Organ Grinding by Aliens and by so-called "Out-of-Works" who prefer a lazy street-begging life to obtaining useful, honest work.'[30]

7 'Dens of infamy': thieves' kitchens and tramps' lodging houses

The historical shelter of the homeless and underworld elements of the population was the common lodging house, and I have mentioned their notoriety as nests of beggars and thieves. The Vagrancy Act perpetuated earlier legislation providing for periodic police searches of houses suspected of harbouring offenders under the Act. The houses, concentrated in the slum areas, were jam-packed with lodgers, with strangers sharing beds regardless of sex or age.[1] Lord Ashley in 1848 described them as 'haunts of pollution' (both physical and moral);[2] Henry Mayhew in 1851 branded them as 'wretched dens of infamy, brutality and vice',[3] and to Alsager Hay Hill in 1881, 30 years after the first legislative attempt to regulate them, they were 'seed plots of mendicity and vagabondage'.[4]

Early Victorian public health reports contain numerous descriptions of these human cesspits. Here is an account of Macclesfield's around 1851:

> In four small cottages, with two bedrooms each, there was an average of 188 persons lodged; they had a small yard, and the remains only of what had been two privies, all the ordure being in the open yard. . . . In another lodging house, there were three small rooms upstairs; in the first were 16 men, women and children lying together on the floor; in the second were 12, also on the floor; and the third room upstairs was used as a privy, the boarded floor being literally covered with human ordure.

In yet another house a woman was found in labour pains, 'by her side a man apparently asleep and 10 other men, women and children were in the same room.'[5]

Lord Ashley cited a first-hand description of the barbaric squalor: in one room 18 feet by 10 feet 27 men and women and 31 children (together with several dogs) were squeezed into 'a contracted den from which light and air are excluded'. Vermin plagued the place:

Figure 2   (a) *Cruikshank's quasi-romantic depiction of the revels of 'Jovial Beggars' in their 'padding ken' as compared with the squalid reality presented in*

I have entered a room, and in a few minutes I have felt them dropping on my hat from the ceiling like peas. 'They may be gathered in handfuls', observed one of the inmates. 'I could fill a pail in a few minutes. I have been so tormented with the itch, that on two occasions I filled my pockets with stones and waited till a policeman came up, and then broke a lamp that I might be sent to prison and there be cleansed, as is required before newcomers are admitted.'[6]

The inmates of such places were diverse: migratory workers, pedlars, the genuinely unemployed and their families, and sundry unfortunate flotsam mixed cheek by jowl with professional beggars, prostitutes and thieves. Early Victorian public concern about these 'netherskens' or 'paddingkens' was not, on the whole, prompted by indignation at the degradation that their inmates were forced to endure willy-nilly, but at the criminal and epidemic threats they presented to 'respectable' society.

The Royal Commission on the county constabulary in 1839 disclosed how lodging houses had become the urban bases from which criminals would launch predatory forays into the surrounding countryside. Indeed police often felt it was better to leave well alone unless they caused excessive public nuisance.

"THE KITCHEN, FOX COURT GRAY'S INN LANE.

(b) Henry Mayhew's London Labour and the London Poor *at the mid-nineteenth century. This lodging house reeks of villainy and vice. (Source: 'Jovial Beggars': George Smeeton,* Doings in London, *1826, 1840 edition. Source: 'Fox Court': Henry Mayhew,* London Labour and the London Poor, *Volume 1. Courtesy, Guildhall Library, London.)*

Edwin Chadwick's famous 'Report on the Sanitary Conditions of the Labouring Population' in 1842 contains much information.[7] The Medical Officer in Barnet Union reported on the routine removal of diseased lodgers to his workhouse infirmary: 'These unhappy beings are boarded and bedded in an atmosphere of gin, brimstone, onions and disease, until their last penny be spent, and their clothes pledged to the keeper of the house, when they are kicked out and left to the mercy of the relieving officer.' At Manchester, the dormitories were often housed in cellars. A Durham informant told how three or four lay on one bed of straw; the bedding was never changed, and human excreta lay indiscriminately about the place. And from Tain in Scotland Chadwick was told: 'I have been credibly informed that the bed-clothes have not been washed for the last five years!'

There was also concern about the lodging houses as a medium for corrupting youngsters into vice and crime.[8] *Oliver Twist* has made this folklore. In 'kid kens', gangs of youngsters – orphans and runaways – were housed and fed in return for the proceeds of their crimes, and while not yet in their teens were sexually experienced with girls of similar age and condition who were admitted to these establishments for debauches. Many youngsters forced into the common lodging house life-style were deeply unhappy. One lad, an orphan and pickpocket, who had fallen in with a gang when he hung about Billingsgate while unemployed, told Henry Mayhew:

> They are very bad places for a boy to be in. Where I am now, when the place is full, there's upwards of 100 can be accommodated. I won't be there long. I'll do something to get out of it. There's people there will rob their own brother. . . . They talk chiefly about what they've done or are going to do, or have set their minds on, just as you and any other gentlemen might do.

But he reluctantly conceded: 'Without such places my trade couldn't be carried on; I couldn't live.'[9] A girl prostitute told Mayhew of her background; how as a maltreated servant girl (she was also orphaned) she had run away and lived for a time in a lodging house by pawning her clothes. Then she was forced into prostitution, joining the ranks of the other girls in the house:

> They were all thieves and bad girls. I have known between three and four dozen boys and girls sleep in one room. The beds were horrid filthy and full of vermin. There was very wicked carryings on. . . . We lay packed on a full night, a dozen boys and girls squeedged into one bed.

In the heat of summer, some went naked, 'and would dance around the room that way . . . some were children, the boys generally the youngest'. The youths were already hardened ponces, sending the girls onto the streets and beating them black and blue if they did not bring enough money back.

Shelter in such places cost at mid-century anything from 1d to 4d a night.[10] At the lowest prices you might not get a bed, just a 'sit-up' space resting your head on a table, or sleeping space on the floor. A few pence more would give you a mattress, but the extra comfort afforded by these bug bags was dubious. The profits for proprietors were prodigious. Figures quoted to Mayhew showed that the net annual profit from an 80-bed house could be £300 or more. The owner of a group of 10 houses of varying sizes was reckoned to net some £2,300 a year around 1851.[11] Overheads were nominal. The properties were in the slum areas and often unfit to be anything but human cattlepens; rateable values were therefore low. Cleaning and laundry costs were minimal, and the wage bills of 'deputies' (lodging house managers) and other menials did not amount to much.

Some lodging house proprietors actively abetted the criminal pursuits of their clients, for it was in their own interests to see that they had the wherewithal to pay the rent. Owners of 'flash houses' acted as receivers,[12] and beggars' impresarios. At Llanfyllin around 1839 lived 'Old Peggy', a lodging house owner. The scrap food collected by beggars she took to sell to dog owners in payment of rent, and she often went to the local druggist to buy tar. When the puzzled druggist asked her what she needed it for, she replied 'Why, to make a *land sailor*. I want a hap'orth just to daub a chap's canvass trousers with, and that's how I make a land sailor, Doctor.'[13] 'Mother Cummins' of St Giles was one of the most notorious lodging house owners, brothel-keepers and fences of the early nineteenth century. A native of Ireland and a professedly 'devout' Catholic, she made good in the underworld. She ran a string of lodging houses in London, allowing the sexes to mix, and her charges seem unusually high at 6d to 2 shillings a night, no doubt reflecting the gains of her clientele. She trained young criminals, and her girls decoyed victims to her brothels, where they were robbed. At her death, the whole neighbourhood turned out to her funeral at St Giles Church.[14] In Chapter 4 I have mentioned 'Copenhagen Jack', the lodging house owner and 'captain' of his army of 200 professional beggars. Just over 100 years later in the 1920s there was a remarkably similar character in London called 'Jim Sullivan'. From his lodging houses he sent beggars out to allotted pitches, organised as 'Unemployed Miners' Choirs', 'Ex-Servicemen Songsters', 'timber merchants' (match-sellers) and so forth. His commission was 10 per cent of their take, and he employed 'crows' (watchers) who both protected the pitches and saw that Jim got his correct pay-off. Also, around 1914 a lady known as 'Maria' ran a women's lodging house, and hired out the babies of girl inmates to beggars at two shillings a day.[15]

Brighton, as a resort of the affluent, attracted a steady stream of cadgers to prey on them, and local lodging house owners were providing services for them in the 1830s. The keepers sold nick-nacks wholesale to pedlars who lodged with them, lent their auspices to robberies planned on their premises, and supplied newly-arrived beggars with lists of local 'soft touches' – all to boost their customers' incomes which they spent on rent and booze. The keepers gave departing customers trade cards to hand to vagabonds they met on the road heading towards Brighton.[16]

Of course, as there is no honour among thieves and beggars, the proprietors of netherskens were themselves liable to be robbed. George Smeeton tells how, at the beginning of the century, the kitchen gridirons, pokers and shovels had to be chained up. In the 1840s the rugs on the beds had 'Stop Thief' printed on them,[17] and Chadwick in 1842 told how in at least two houses in Birmingham '. . . a chain, fastened at one end by a staple and at the other secured by a padlock, was placed on the outside of the door at the foot of the staircase which led to the sleeping apartments'. It transpired that the mistress 'employed it to lock in the lodgers until she released them in the morning, as they would decamp and take away whatever furniture or moveables they could carry with them'.[18] The thieving cut both ways, though, for lodging house employees were not above pilfering from the customers, as they held the keys to the kitchen lockers.

Even if an absentee proprietor was not personally abetting rogues and vagabonds, his low-paid minions who looked after the houses often augmented their incomes by 'servicing' their shady customers. The houses were usually clustered in the labyrinthine rookeries, linked by secret passages and roof-top escape routes which could make it both futile and dangerous for policemen to enter even into the early 1890s, despite mid-Victorian urban re-developments and, by then, 40 years of police regulating powers over common lodging houses.[19] The lodging house dogsbodies would, for a tip, facilitate a fugitive's escape through the house, or conceal stolen goods among the lodgers' paraphernalia – pedlars' baskets, potato cans, costermongers' barrows and the like – clutter-ing the storeroom.[20]

Well-known thieves' kitchens became the immediate destination for any newcomer to a locality who was up to no good, for there he would find the local 'intelligencer', perhaps a retired beggar-thief, who lived permanently in the house and sold information useful to the brotherhood; he might keep a register of local notables with addresses, likely incomes, and details of family scandals, suscept-ibilities to beggars' approaches and so forth. Family wealth could be deduced from information sold by local tradesmen to the intelligencer, who also made it his business to know the vigilance or otherwise of the local police. 'Cadgers' maps', perhaps drawn by hand, showing the neighbourhood, with secret signs relating to begging or thieving prospects at marked residences, would be sold or pinned up on the kitchen wall for all to peruse.[21] (See page 55 for a Cadger's Map.)

The Victorian police did try to compute the total number of 'houses of ill-repute' in the country, and the numbers of people likely to resort to them, but the terminology is vague and confusing, and the figures unreliable. I make reference to them here only because readers are likely to be curious about vagrant-world statistics.[22]

The Judicial Statistics between 1857 and 1868 provided police estimates. The numbers of tramps known to the police in England and Wales in the 1860s hovered around 33,000 to 36,000, and the total of 'known tramps' lodging houses' in 1868 was 5,648. But 'known thieves and depredators' and 'suspected persons' are listed separately (of the latter some 55,000 were known in 1868). How

A CADGER'S MAP OF A BEGGING DISTRICT.

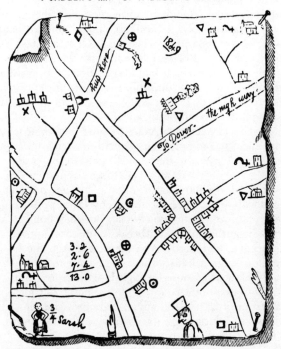

EXPLANATION OF THE HIEROGLYPHICS.

✗   **No good;** too poor, and know too much.

♌   **Stop,—**if you have what they want, they will buy. They are pretty "*fly*" (knowing).

⅄   **Go in this direction,** it is better than the other road. Nothing that way.

◇   **Bone** (good). Safe for a "cold tatur," if for nothing else. "*Cheese your patter*" (don't talk much) here.

▽   **Cooper'd** (spoilt) by too many tramps calling there.

□   **Gammy** (unfavourable), likely to have you taken up. Mind the dog.

◉   **Flummuxed** (dangerous), sure of a month in "*quod*," prison.

⊕   **Religious,** but tidy on the whole.

Figure 3   *'Cadger's Map' of around 1870. Maps like these were sometimes available in thieves' kitchens as a guide to local begging prospects. The column of figures near the bottom left might have been a totting up of a begging 'take', while ⁹⁄₄ Sarah' beneath might have been an actual lodging house character or the name of a dance popular in lodging houses. (Source: John Camden Hotten,* The Slang Dictionary, *1922 edition. Repository, British Museum; reproduced with permission of Chatto and Windus: The Hogarth Press.)*

can they be totally distinguished from tramps? And what was meant by a 'tramp'? Was a professional beggar with an income sufficient for a fairly regular bed in a lodging house a 'tramp'? (The 1906 Departmental Committee on Vagrancy indicated that only 10 per cent of London's lodging house residents were thought to belong to the 'vagrant class'.) Similarly 'houses of bad character' (brothels, etc.) are separately classified. Of the 5,648 tramps' lodging houses for 1868, 482 were listed for the Metropolitan Police area. Now, the 'Met' area then had about 16 per cent of England's population, yet this great stamping ground for beggars and vagrants is credited with only about 9 per cent of known tramps' houses, if the figures are to be believed.

Prior to 1851 local acts to regulate lodging houses in matters of disinfection and accommodation densities were few and far between. Ashley Cooper, by then Lord Shaftesbury, promoted the Common Lodging House Act of 1851 (to be strengthened in 1853) for the whole of England and Wales.[23] The principal acts empowered local authorities to frame byelaws prescribing bed densities and sanitary arrangements for lodging houses; keepers had to notify the authorities of outbreaks of disease, and also of the presence of beggars and vagrants in them. The Acts did not define what a common lodging house was, but it came to be convention-ally accepted in law as a house for nightly lettings for profit to poor persons sharing communal facilities.[24] A general Act for Scotland was not passed until 1897[25] and governed houses charging up to 6d a night; but with inflation this protection was to be progressively eroded in the twentieth century.

The 1851 Act was to be administered by the police in the Metropolitan Police area, and elsewhere by local sanitary author-ities. This early legislation was full of loopholes. It was not the lodging house premises that had to be registered with the authorities, but the names of keepers. These were just front men for the proprietors. If a keeper was struck off, the premises could remain open under a new keeper's name. The powers given to regulating authorities were only permissive, and even when diseases were notified, the authorities were not obliged to remove the victims to a hospital, and ensuing disinfection could legally be confined just to the victims' beds, rather than the whole house.[26] The great 1875 Public Health Act[27] did not define a 'common lodging house' either, but an important legal ruling in 1899 brought charitable shelters, not run for profit, within the ambit of the acts. This, as we shall see, was important, for the expanding efforts of the Salvation Army and other charities at the end of the century had led to a multiplication of shelters which for all the good intentions were often seriously sub-standard.[28] The continu-ing absence of a definition of a 'common lodging house' until the 1936 Public Health Act[29] aided legal evasion. Weekly instead of nightly letting exempted a house; and in Irish areas, where family inter-relationships were complicated and extensive, the keeper could confuse the authorities by claiming that the lodgers were his relatives, and outside the scope of inspection.

In the early years of the Shaftesbury Act enforcing authorities, both metropolitan and provincial, claimed great progress in clearing disease-nests, limewashing, reducing overcrowding and improving the moral tone by dividing the sexes in separate dormitories.[30] However, one academic has suggested that the keepers co-operated superficially to cover up the more criminal goings-on in their establishments.[31] Lodging house inspection certainly occupied a great deal of the time of the Metropolitan Police. Between 1851 and 1869 the Met's strength grew from 5,195 to 6,672 men while the Metropolitan Police Area's population grew from 2,500,000 to 3,500,000. In that period the police had made over 3,000,000 visits to lodging houses (over 162,000 in 1869 alone), though the 'Met's' annual report for 1869[32] does not make it clear whether these also included routine searches for suspects and wanted men. Figures for the numbers of common lodging houses in London can never be complete; two-thirds or more of all houses were never registered, it has been suggested. They were either 'tolerated' as being in the process of improvement prior to registration, or else unknown to the public at all,[33] tucked away in the back streets.

One figure in 1854 gave 1,441 registered common lodging houses in the Met area accommodating 30,000, with 3,276 known unregistered houses in the course of improvement accommodating 50,000 more.[34] In the 1870s when the population of London was rising on 4,500,000, the registered lodging house population was around 27,000.[35]

Though the police naturally put the best face on their efforts and achievements, for example, in virtually eliminating lodging houses as epidemic-sources, independent observers were less than complimentary. George Sims stated from first-hand experience in 1883 that police supervision was inadequate,[36] a view endorsed by Howard Goldsmid in 1886. Police determinations of houses' bed capacity were allegedly made in the less noisome atmosphere of their daytime visits. They did not sample the concentrated night-time stink when the dormitories were filled. Goldsmid heard second-hand from dossers that police took bribes from keepers. The regulations posted up in the dormitories were flagrantly ignored, he said, and the 1851 Act was a farce. Another criticism was that the police were only concerned with the good order in the houses to protect the rest of the community, not with the welfare of the dossers themselves.[37]

Indeed, the tolerance of disreputable houses was part of policing strategy, for then they knew the haunts of known criminals, and information received from keepers was the price for turning a blind eye; hence the already mentioned persistence of thieves' kitchens into the early 1890s.[38]

To be fair to the police, these statutory public health functions were really outside their line of country; their prime concern was, understandably, crime and public order, and they resented being used as instruments for regulatory needs connected with the homeless, for they had enough on their plate as it was.

Certain beneficial trends were evident under the police regime prior to the transfer of the Met's inspection duties to the London County Council in 1894. Whilst in the 1880s the number of beds in greater London's registered lodging houses exceeded 30,000, the number of houses had been declining from just under 1,300 in 1878 to around 1,000 in 1889, with a sharper decrease to 671 by 1894.[39] There had been a quickening trend towards shutting down the worst and smallest houses, and concentrating the dossers in easier-to-regulate, larger establishments. But conditions were still sordid, for though they were far less dangerous as pest-houses than in Chadwick's or Mayhew's day, they were only marginally improved as moral sinks. Whilst men and women slept in separate dormitories in the same house, they shared the common kitchen and ablutions facilities; and the so-called 'married beds' allocation was a legalised cover for casual consort or prostitution. The LCC applied new vigour to the job after 1894, and obtained increased powers under LCC General Powers Acts of 1902 and 1907. The former subjected lodging houses to annual licensing, and the latter made the appointment of 'deputies' (the lodging house managers) subject to local authority approval. (Chapter 9 will reveal how the character of the deputy set the whole tone of the house.[40]) The LCC increased the minimum cubic space allotted to each bed-occupant; inspectors called at 2.30 am; ventilation standards were raised, and, wrote an admiring observer in 1906, 'sheet changing once a month is no longer permitted' and there had been generally a 'remarkable improvement' since 1894.[41] The LCC motivation remained primarily the protection of mainstream society from disease. Smallpox was the great epidemic bogey in the late nineteenth century, now that cholera, typhoid and typhus had been brought under control, and we shall see later evidence of how dossers and disease went hand in hand.

8 Model lodging houses, the Sally Ann and Rowton's

There was a continuing rapid concentration in London's lodging house accommodation at the turn of the century – registered houses were down to 451 by 1904 – coupled with a slow but steady decline in the number of beds, from a peak of nearly 34,000 in 1890 to under 29,000 in 1904.[1] Unregistered, backstreet bug huts continued to operate, but the popular image of the doss-house in the first 30 years of this century was changing from that of the noxious bawdy-house to a bleak but superficially orderly human receptacle. The advent of municipal lodging houses and Salvation Army Metropoles strengthened the forces of rudimentary sanitation and good order, and brought a more austerely barrack-like character to the dosshouse scene.

It was Lord Shaftesbury's Labouring Classes Lodging House Act of 1851[2] that first empowered local authorities to build municipal lodging houses, but it was scarcely taken up. Huddersfield was an honourable exception, and its model amenities for lodgers from 1854 included the use of a reading room and a programme of temperance lectures; by the mid-1860s it had beds for 2,870 persons at 3d a night minimum.[3] Glasgow followed suit in the 1870s and by 1900 had seven establishments for 2,166 men and 248 women.[4] Later enabling legislation followed,[5] but the LCC only made a start after the Housing of the Working Classes Act 1890.[6] Even so, its performance compared with Glasgow's was dismal. Three hostels were built between 1892 and 1906 (the last being Bruce House in Westminster): in 1940 these were still all that was available, offering a total of 1,875 cubicles for men. No accommodation for women was provided by the London County Council on the grounds that it would be uneconomic, though Glasgow and Manchester had proved its viability before the First World War.[7]

Private Victorian good works had also tried to fill a gap on the 'philanthropy at 5 per cent' principle. The Society for Improving the Conditions of the Labouring Classes began opening model lodging houses in London from 1847; provincial initiatives followed suit.[8] By 1861 the SICLC in London was running nine model lodging houses (for men only); they were clean and not overcrowded, and charged 4d a night. But they were not reaching the labouring classes, as originally intended. John Hollingshead found the inmates, mainly artisans, clerks and shop assistants, 'all greasy faded men – men difficult to keep clean, who smelt of onions and were mostly out of work'.[9] George Atkins Brine tells of 'Watt's Charity' lodging house in Rochester for genuine labouring men, and how tramps would steal workmen's tools as 'credentials' to gain entry. Victoria Homes in London's East End was providing an excellent service for the homeless low-paid around 1906: for a shilling a day it offered a bed and three good meals – including roast beef, mutton, Irish stew and plum pudding on its varied menu.[10]

The Salvation Army appeared on the hostel scene in 1888. William Booth's interest in shelter is said to have been triggered one night in December 1877 when, crossing London Bridge, he saw a crowd of destitutes sleeping rough in the bitter weather. His commitment to sheltering the poor as a physical pre-requisite of spiritual upliftment was confirmed by a Salvation Army survey of the miseries of Embankment down-and-outs in 1890 (see Chapter 11). A network of 'Metropoles' was established around the country; the London ones had evocative names like 'The Ark', 'The Harbour' and 'The Lighthouse'.[11] Charges ranged between 2d and 6d a night in 1906; the penniless could earn shelter through work in the Army's Labour Factories or 'Elevators'. The 'Sally Ann' soon established its primacy in the field of philanthropic lodging houses in Britain. In 1931, of the LCC's common lodging house beds 4,600 were provided by philanthropic agencies, the Salvation Army alone accounting for five-sixths of these.[12] By then it was charging 7d or 8d a night, compared with 9d for a commercial lodging house.

Since 1899, as we saw in the last chapter, the Salvation Army Metropoles had been subject to the same inspection as the commercial lodging houses. What were conditions like, and how appreciative was the 'Sally Ann's' clientele? The universal complaint, before and after the First World War, was the religion forced down the throats of captive audiences by officers whose performance of Christian duty was cold, officious and distant.[13] W.A. Gape recalled enduring a sermon for an hour and ten minutes on the evils of gambling, drink and idleness. This atmosphere was made even more gloomy by walls adorned with gaunt religious homilies, which were lost on the weary derelicts. George Orwell remarked tartly in 1933: 'The fact is that the Salvation Army are so in the habit of thinking themselves a charitable body that they cannot even run a lodging house without making it stink of charity.'[14] Even Frank Jennings, himself a clergyman, wrote regretfully of the Salvationists' zeal for protracted bible-thumping punctuated by raptuous 'Hallelujahs' and 'Praise the Lords', which left their threadbare congregation dozing on the benches.[15] John Worby in 1937 recalled one occasion in a Sally Ann service when a fellow down-and-out sang a wry parody of the hymn beginning 'Just as I am without one plea':

> Just as I am without one flea
> If I stay here, how long will it be?
> For bed and food and one cup of tea
> O Adjutant, I'll come to thee![16]

Denis Crane, who sampled the Salvation Army's Petticoat Lane Metropole prior to 1910, judged the faults of the Salvationists more charitably, as they 'have themselves in many cases been raised from the gutter'.[17] And Mary Higgs, the Oldham-based propagandist of the female vagrants' plight, was positively complimentary about the patience of Salvationist officers towards the degraded specimens they took in.[18]

The physical amenities were less deprecated by the Army's critics. The consensus was that Metropoles were clean but cheerless, and George Orwell found that the main hall of one 'a great white-washed barn of a place, oppressively clean and bare, with no fires', where 200 customers sat on benches. At 10 pm an officer blew a whistle and they all filed upstairs to the clean but packed dormitories containing 60 or 70 beds each. Denis Crane in 1910 was satisfied with what he got for 5d a night – a warm hall, cleanliness, the hire of lockers for valuables, and a substantial meal for 2d including soup nicknamed 'Allelujah Stew'. However, W.H. Davies, who lived in 'The Ark' around 1908, found that the food though cheap, was poor, and the crowding in the dormitories intense: 'Men were breathing and coughing in each other's faces and the stench of such a number of men in one room was abominable.' Between 10 am and 1 pm the lodgers were turned out into the street, regardless of the weather, so that the attendants could tidy the place up.[19] Despite valiant efforts at hygiene, the Sally Ann could not always win against its customers' personal habits. Chris Massie in 1931 recalled going into one establishment clean and coming out verminous; and Thomas Callaghan around 1945 was sickened at the sight of men coughing up phlegm into the washbasins.

The type of berth depended on what you could pay. Around 1906 the Salvation Army was still offering 'coffin beds' (long boxes on the ground) for 2d a night.[20] But for the same price it offered a bunk in a women's lodging house; for 4d you got a bed with sheets, and for 6d a cubicle at the same period.[21]

The Church Army – the evangelical arm of the Church of

England – which, under its founder, Wilson Carlile, operated in parallel with the Salvation Army, ran (and runs) lodging houses but on a much smaller scale than the Salvationists. Whilst the latter set out to offer a mass-scale rescue mission to the destitute, the Church Army has traditionally been selective and more personal; its lodging houses were smaller, with a maximum of 25 beds each in the 1890s.[22]

Rowton Houses date from 1893, when Lord Rowton began building superior lodging houses as respectable working men's hotels, quite distinct in tone from the ordinary dosshouse. They proved a commercial success and this prompted the LCC to expand its municipal hostel accommodation.[23] By 1905 in London, Rowtons had five hotels with about 3,600 beds,[24] and was about to expand to Birmingham. Rowtons were considered showpieces in their day; indeed the courts had ruled that they were 'hotels' and not lodging houses by virtue of their catering arrangements, and so were exempt from the lodging house inspectorate. Soon after Tower House was opened at Whitechapel in 1903 it was graced by a visit from the Prince of Wales and church dignitaries.[25] Commentators up to the Second World War were all favourably impressed. W.H. Davies found the Rowton at Newington Butts to be 'a fine large block of red buildings with an imposing front, and a fine entrance, polished and clean'. Its facilities included dining rooms, a library, sitting rooms, baths and lavatories, all for 6d a night.[26] In 1906 T.W. Wilkinson enthused over the Rowton Hammersmith Road, with its dining room, smoking room and pleasant flowered courtyard as 'the best accommodation procurable in England for sixpence a night'.[27] By 1930 prices had risen to a shilling a night for a bed, and a decent dish could be had for 6d in the canteen. Frank Gray MP said in 1931 that on 17 shillings a week there a man could 'live in decency, comfort and health'.[28] George Orwell was complimentary, too, though remarking on the Rowtons' strict rules, for example against card playing.

Rowton Houses were models of efficient management at this period. (The LCC's Bruce House was slightly more expensive at 1/1d a night for a cubicle 8 feet by 9, and its standards in the early 1930s almost matched Rowton's.[29]) Between 1907 and 1931 the London Rowtons were offering just over 5,000 beds a night; this is to be set against the continued shrinkage of London's common lodging house bedspace from 27,000 in 1914 to under 17,000 in 1931.[30]

9 Lodging house society

In this chapter we will step inside the commercial lodging houses of the period roughly from the Golden Jubilee of 1887, to the late 1930s and glimpse the human menagerie within. The back streets of certain districts of later-Victorian London were notorious nests of sleazy lodging houses; Whitechapel and Spitalfields in the East End were particular examples. Flower-and-Dean Street in Spitalfields was the bottom of the pit. Of the street's 1,078 inhabitants in 1871, 902 lived in the 31 lodging houses concentrated there, and the unusually high proportion of women (about a third) suggests the strong links with prostitution. Jack the Ripper's East End victims in 1888 were denizens of such places.[1] Registered common lodging accommodation indeed catered overwhelmingly for men. In February 1905 there were 25,671 authorised beds for men, 2,450 for women and 422 for 'married couples' in the LCC.[2] Men formed about 90 per cent of London's lodging house population, and I shall look at homeless women's tribulations within this period in a later chapter.

Lodging houses varied in class, and you got what you paid for. Even in 1930 you could still go as low as the 'Twopenny Hangover', in which, Orwell tells us, you sat on a bench, leaning over a rope which was unceremoniously dropped in the morning by the attendant 'humorously called the valet'. For 4d, he found, you could still find coffin beds with tarpaulin covers, which were cold and full of bugs. Twenty years before the Reverend Zachary Edwards had found the cheapest type of lodging house in Preston, the 'Penny Sit-Up'. In a room 25 feet by 18, 30 to 60 men slept each night; there were no washing, heating or cooking facilities; and the shake-down was a space on the floor with a wooden block as a head-rest.

Scotland was possibly even worse than the English provinces, as its lodging house law was weaker in the long term.[3] In the 1930s places could still be found using oil lamps and candles, and with the coal just heaped on the floor by the fireplace.[4]

The LCC area's commercial lodging houses were more sanitary

(a)

"SINGLES" AND "DOUBLES" IN A COMMON LODGING-HOUSE

Figure 4   *(a) Apparently more orderly lodging house conditions, later Victorian period. The communal existence in the kitchen of the Spitalfields lodging house around the time of Jack the Ripper (late 1880s) comes over clearly. Note the kipper box on the table. Kippers and 'addicks' were invariable staples of lodging house fare. (b) The dormitory looks well-regulated; but the untrustworthy character of the clientele is indicated by the precautionary 'Stolen' mark on the bedclothes. The double bed inset was rented to any couple declaring themselves man and wife. (Courtesy, BBC Hulton Picture Library.)*

than their provincial counterparts around 1900. As we shall see, the London houses were not the originating sources of smallpox epidemics by then. But their accommodation, notwithstanding LCC regulations, was still abysmal. In 1909 Everard Wyrall, a journalist, described his visit to a cheap, licensed London dosshouse: 'I once had a peep into a room with four hundred outcasts lying asleep, or trying to sleep on "beds" placed next to one another. It was an awful sight, no less terrible than the stifling atmosphere of the room.' In 1906 Mary Higgs (see Chapter 15) found in the common room of one London lodging house (later shut down) dust and the remains of meals swept under the table, and gobbets of spittle everywhere. In another 'a notice was posted that "Gentlemen are requested not to go to bed in their boots". Nevertheless it was evidently not obeyed.'[5]

Zachary Edwards found in Lancashire in 1910 lodging houses where the genuinely hard-up mixed with thieves, as in Mayhew's day, and where the separation of the sexes was flouted by men bringing so-called 'wives' in and hiring a 'married' bed. This was winked at by the keepers who charged even more, if they suspected the couple. Around this time a scandal had broken in Cardiff regarding the town's lodging houses which catered to a large and multi-racial seafaring population.[6] The lodging house inspectors had admitted their inability to do their jobs properly through overwork. Keepers with criminal backgrounds or unsavoury habits were running many houses and girl servants were in moral danger. In one house, we learn, 'the bedroom of a servant girl communicates by means of a window with a room in which six sailors are permitted to sleep'. Racial dangers to young white girls are hinted at, similar to stories then current about Chinese opium dens. One house was run by a coloured seaman with a white girl who had had two babies by him, and whom he used to beat savagely. In another an English girl shared a house with 24 Chinamen. Overcrowding, in breach of regulations, was common, and at Neath tramps were found sharing rooms with married couples without partitions, and where the bugs dropped onto the beds from the ceiling. In one house, in a room for eight married couples 'there is not even a board or rag curtain to conceal them from each other. It is frequently the habit of tramps to sleep nude. In the centre of the room is a large battered tin pail.'

Unlike the municipal lodging houses and Metropoles the commercial houses were not purpose-built, just makeshift conversions, and their landlords could appear pillars of respectability. Thomas Wright in 1892 tells of a rags-to-riches story of one tramp who graduated through a deputy's job to becoming an owner and parish councillor. And Frank Jennings in 1926 observed that 'many landlords who own blocks of slum property take prominent position in civic religious affairs.'[7]

Figure 5   *Coffin beds in Medland Hall, an East End night shelter in London around the turn of the century. (Courtesy, BBC Hulton Picture Library.)*

A typical common lodging house would have a communal kitchen cum dining room cum day room in the basement; upstairs would be the dormitories. The ablutions and lavatories might be situated across a yard and could be appalling. Mary Higgs found one lodging house around 1905 with just one WC for 40 people, and its flush was not working. In 1933 George Orwell stayed in a house where the washbasins were in a cellar: 'I had a piece of soap in my pocket [evidently the house provided none] and I was going to wash, when I noticed that every basin was streaked with grime – solid, sticky filth as black as boot-blacking. I went out unwashed.' Later experience taught him that it was 'a fairly representative lodging house'.

At the front door was the deputy's office where you paid for your night's bed at a window, receiving a ticket or token in return. Your name was entered in a register and might be checked against a blacklist. Many lodging house keepers tolerated the use of their kitchens by day as an open house for any dosser type who cared to drop in, for they did not know who would be buying a bed that night. But at night when the whistle blew for the kitchen crowd to file upstairs, there was a ritual 'turn-out' of the non-payers. Bed-tokens were checked as the payers went up; however, with a hundred or more lodgers to be checked, 'bilking' (gatecrashing) was a perennial problem. Where deputies were keen tipplers, it was not difficult to slip into their offices to steal tokens while they nodded off, or to escape their notice as the lodgers trooped upstairs.[8] In the rougher establishments the staircase might be caged and locked to stop bilkers slipping in, despite the dangers in the event of fire. Many deputies knew they had to tread cautiously over ejecting bilkers, for the other lodgers tended to take their side, and an overzealous deputy might be set on by one and all. It was also unwise to call in the police, as this attracted unwanted attention to the place. Some lodging houses around 1900 employed ex-boxers as bouncers.

What were a deputy's necessary qualities? According to Joseph Stamper, who experienced many lodging houses when on the tramp as an unemployed ex-foundry worker in the 1920s, he 'has to be something of a business man, a touch of the bully, and a good chucker-out' and 'an atmosphere of dread and authority . . . stands him in good stead when he has to officiate as a chucker-out.' Alexander Paterson, the youth club pioneer and prison reformer, wrote in 1912 of the London deputy (whose appointment since 1907 in each case was subject to LCC approval and so was no longer a free agent) that he had to walk a fine line between the underworld whose custom he depended on, and the police who expected co-operation: 'Often his is the buffer between detective and lodger, forced to own that he does not know the baptismal names of Pat and Fishy, and yet fearing to drop a hint of their whereabouts. For prudence demands that he should win both the confidence of the lodgers and the good favour of the authorities.'[9] Before 1907 deputies had generally been shady characters,[10] and Paterson stressed how the character of a deputy, now on the upgrade since that date, could affect the whole tone of an establishment. Stamper encountered one mean specimen in the provinces, a 'surly, sordid avaricious brute, without the slightest flicker of humanity', who, during a flu epidemic refused to dole out a medicine issued to lodging houses gratis by the town's health department, unless the prostrate inmates paid for their dose. In fact, deputies had to supplement their incomes by other means as their wages were so low. Mayhew in 1851 gave a figure of 7 to 12 shillings a week[11] – roughly comparable with a farm labourer's at that time – but he would be living-in (his office might also double as his bedroom) perhaps with a wife or fancy woman, and there were many opportunities for 'perks'. In Chapter 7 I mentioned services to the underworld; lodgers also found it wise to tip the deputy on arrival, as W.H. Davies cautioned: 'Men that do not think of doing this must not be surprised if he accidentally overturns their teapots or shovels coke into their frying pans.'[12]

The deputy might employ lower menials – night porters and kitchen men – recruited from the ranks of the dossers, who, for a few shillings a week and a bed, would serve as bed-makers, sweepers-up, fire-makers and boiler-fillers.[13] They ran errands for lodgers in return for tips, usually tobacco, liquor or unwanted food, and in the late Victorian thieves' kitchens they covered the tracks of fugitive criminals. The vagrant low-lives, conscious of their own degradation, were apt to tread on anyone they had a semblance of an excuse to regard as inferior to themselves, and the kitchen-man fitted this role as everyone's dogsbody.[14] Kitchen men were usually misfits and oddities who did not hold the job for long. Thor Fredur mentions one, a Pole who had deserted the Russian army in the Crimea, who was so violent when drunk that one day the lodgers collectively threw him into the street; his successor was a certified lunatic whose career was also brief.

These menials correspond roughly to the 'narks' described by W.H. Davies a generation later.[15] They were dossers who had become 'regulars' in a particular house and made themselves useful to the deputy as odd-job men and informers about other inmates. Their reward was a free bed, and they lived by servicing the clientele as inexpert barbers, shoe-repairers, clothes stitchers, corn-cutters and the like. Lodgers found it was in their interests, much as they despised the nark, to get on his right side with gifts of tobacco, drink and clothing – and the nark was able to sell the surplus.

The kitchen was the social heart of the lodging house. Here, on the open fire the inmates did all their cooking, sitting before it chatting, and toasting or frying-up their morsels. It served also as laundry, drying room and cottage industry workshop combined. Men and women, strangers to each other, though segregated at night, mixed here in crowded contact. One long, bare dining table served all the inmates; and benches, not individual chairs, were the rule, partly because they were harder to throw in the event of a fight.[16] Lodgers might have to provide their own crockery and utensils, or else hire them.[17] Those without the money had to eat with their fingers from newspaper.[18] The kitchens, due to their general basement location, were dark, stifling and grubby. Howard Goldsmid, an East End welfare worker, stayed in 'Beehive Chambers' in Brick Lane, Whitechapel a couple of years before the Jack the Ripper murders, and described kitchen life. Haddocks, bloaters and sausages seemed to form the mainstay of the inmate's diet. The gloomy kitchen was like a pig sty. The resident menial nicknamed Bluegown washed the lodgers' shirts, and Goldsmid remarked that his work must really be cut out for him, considering his customers' squalor:

'Bless yer', returns Bluegown, 'there ain't a real dirty 'un – what I call a real dirty 'un – 'ere to-night. Some on 'em as I get to wash is covered with wermin. W'en I gets 'old o' some o' them

scaly-backed 'uns, as I calls 'em – haw-haw-haw! – I just lays
'em out on the flags and scrubs'em with a blessed long broom'.

At 'Cooney's' in Spitalfields drunken men and women thronged
the street outside swearing and fighting. Inside, the foetid,
blackened kitchen further suffered from an inrush of stench from
the conveniences in the yard whenever the door to it was opened.
Half a dozen cats had the run of the place to keep down the rats.
At the 'Little Wonder' he experienced the most squally kitchen
rows. In one incident a drunken termagant rounded on her
husband, who had been away a week, accusing him of going off
with 'flash girls'. He remained unmoved:

> 'Are you coming to bed?' was the reply, 'or shall I drag you
> upstairs?'
> 'Drag me upstairs! You can't! You daren't lay a finger on me
> an' I'll knife yer! I'll swing for you yet, you wretch!'

The husband went upstairs on his own. His wife, her temper at
full pitch, now turned fiercely on a surprised woman present,
accusing her of spreading gossip about her. Then the husband
came downstairs and fetched his wife, still snarling and snapping,
up to bed. The other lodgers sat indifferent during this drama:

> Some of them went on eating their suppers of whelks or
> 'addicks'; others sat moodily staring at the disputants; but not
> one of them seemed to care the proverbial two straws whether
> the man split his wife's head open, or whether the latter executed
> her threat of 'knifing' either or both of the objects of her rage.

Goldsmid had experienced the worst lodging houses, where, in
the grossly overcrowded dormitories, he was advised to sleep with
his clothes on as a precaution against theft, and not to let anyone
hear the chink of money. Although lockers in the kitchen could
sometimes be hired, this was no guarantee against theft, as the
attendants had spare keys.

Thor Fredur remarked on the dangers of violence. Female
pedlars in particular might be assaulted or even murdered for the
contents of their baskets. When very old lodging houses had been
demolished for redevelopment, skeletons had from time to time
been unearthed, sometimes showing marks of violence. Jack
London's uneventful stay in Whitechapel, some 16 years on in
1902[19] indicates some improvement. The pervading atmosphere
was one of dinginess rather than danger, and the lodgers did have
a recreation room with billiards and draughts. But the same
stifling, gloomy kitchen pall was there, and nothing seems to have
changed when Frank Jennings stayed in a lodging house a quarter

of a century later,[20] where two dozen down and outs were herded together, 'some . . . frying, some eating, some washing, some brooding, some chewing tobacco, some smoking it'. From the open fire, an amalgam of aromas from the sundry fish, meat and vegetables cooking away swirled about, trapped in the sealed room. Above them the ceiling was black as soot, and the walls endeavoured to 'hide their shame in stains and dirt . . . the atmosphere foul, disease-laden and suffocating . . . in a vile, putrid, accursed kitchen about twenty feet by ten feet . . .'

In the towns the common lodging houses were, it seems, inhabited overwhelmingly by 'regulars' who looked on the place as their home. Estimates of short-stay transients varied, but were not thought to exceed 10 per cent around 1906.[21] George Orwell in 1933 believed that improved orderliness had attracted a more settled population. Rural lodging houses on migratory routes by contrast had a preponderance of transients.[22]

Dossers prepared to exist at the most basic level could scrape by on the lowest subsistences calculated by the early sociologists, Charles Booth around 1890 in London and Seebohm Rowntree in 1899 at York. Booth reckoned 10 shillings a week as the poverty line for a single man, and Rowntree gave seven shillings a week as minimally necessary for an 'efficient subsistence'.[23]

Around 1905 the staple diet of lodging house types was herrings and bloaters, meat and potatoes when they could afford it; otherwise they fell back on bread and margarine. Cheap meat offcuts called 'block ornaments' were purchased from butchers. Tea was commonly drunk without milk, and the stewed leaves were given to the poorer lodgers to be infused again ('bulling the teapot'). The lodgers were very partial to alcohol. A London 'dosser' could live – bed and sustenance – on a shilling a day, and dossers' incomes then ranged between 3 and 15 shillings a week. Second-hand clothes at rock-bottom prices could be bought at Petticoat Lane. Female dossers had a somewhat harder time: beds were dearer, and clothes were more expensive, but it was reckoned that they compensated by clubbing together in food purchases and cooking more than men would.[24]

What was the social mix in such places? One great change between 1880 and 1930 was a decline in the professional thief element (though casual pilferage among dossers themselves was another matter). This was partly due to improved regulation, but Frank Gray suggested that the living standards of thieves, like those of the community at large, had risen in that time; successful thieves now enjoyed homes of their own, and only failed petty thieves fell back on the lodging houses. The decline in drunkenness and violence encouraged the settled element, which, as we shall see, was to be supplemented by old age pensioners.

Women were largely prostitutes or hand-to-mouth street sellers and out-workers. Among men low-paid casual workers were very numerous. In houses near Covent Garden one would find porters; in St Giles theatreland the sandwich-board men and 'supers' who hailed cabs; in Stepney and Bermondsey the dockside workers, together with sailors in passing – and so on.

Ex-soldiers were numerous. Traditionally, disabled war veterans (real or fake) had figured prominently in the beggar ranks, but even among the able-bodied there was a tendency to drift into the lodging houses, charitable shelters and casual wards. On completing their enlistment they generally had no saleable skills in civilian life. In 1892 of nearly 30,000 men leaving their colours, just under 21,000 were ex-infantrymen without a trade.[25] The small army pension, though not a subsistence, was just enough to disincline them to regular work, and following each quarterly payment the cycle was to drift downwards progressively to the casual wards and charity shelters till the next payment came through. For those who did want to be helped, regimental associations and agencies like the National Association for the Employment of Reserve Soldiers and the Corps of Commissionaires had developed from the mid-1880s. Thor Fredur in 1879 met one lodging house ex-soldier who lived in the summer by going on tramp and doing haymaking. Ex-soldiers were a fund of colourful yarns of far-off places and this fellow could earn a night's free shelter, food and beer by entertaining yokels in the local pubs. It is interesting to note that 'an old soldier' had become a pejorative working-class expression for a scrounger.[26]

Navvies were also frequent lodging house customers, for even when flush with money the migratory nature of their work precluded a settled home life. W.H. Davies[27] claimed that they were not popular with other inmates, as they tended to hog the cooking and washing facilities, but they were prime mugs for the cheating beggars they stayed with.

The introduction of old age pensions in 1908 enabled more and more old folk to stay out of the workhouse and just about survive in the lodging houses. George Orwell in 1933 referred to one who on 10 shillings a week paid 9d a night for a bed, and, allowing for haircuts and shaves, he was left with 4/4d a week for food and tobacco; bread, margarine and tea were his principal fare.

Alcoholic wrecks ended up in the lodging houses, and, more pathetically, labouring men like dockers who were worn out at 40 or thrown on the scrapheap by ruptures and other injuries and had no resources to fight for compensation.[28] Professional beggars abounded, with a strong professional pride in their cadging skills, displaying their daily take on the kitchen table to show off before their confrères.[29] The kitchen was a hive of cottage industries for the miscellany of pedlars, beggars, pavement gambling sharps, buskers, broken-down professional men – the odd struck-off lawyer or alcoholic doctor, for instance – and unemployed clerks. T.W. Wilkinson in 1906 described their arts and artifices:

> Paper flowers, sand bags, toasting forks, miraculous corn cures, 'novelties' of all kinds – such as the walnut thimble case – are made before your eyes. Old worthless seeds are converted in a twinkling into the 'sweet-scented lavender' of commerce. A pennyworth of scent from the chemist's effects the transformation. You can watch the pavement artist doing 'all my own work' by deputy, the begging letter writer studying his private directory and drafting a condensed tragedy on the back of a music-hall handbill, the broken-down journalist racking his brain for ideas that obstinately refuse to come at his bidding, the old soldier . . . coaching a comrade in the art of cadging from officers of his former regiment. Occasionally even a singing lesson may be heard in a kitchen. Not that 'griddlers' practise their hymns in a doss-house; they learn them at the 'ragged churches' on Sunday.[30]

Professional screevers were still in 1906 going the rounds of lodging houses, putting up wherever there was a demand for their services among lodgers.[31] Itinerant 'mush-fakers' (umbrella menders – 'mush' is short for mushroom) used the lodging houses as bases. 'Tattlers' came round selling second-hand clothes in the 1930s as they had in the 1830s,[32] and the 'translators' who repaired them for re-sale turned a corner of the kitchen into a tailor's or cobbler's workshop.[33]

Brine mentions going round the country fairs picking up cigar butts for sale in the kip-houses, and over half a century later in the 1930s there was still a doss-house industry making up new cigarettes from fag-ends.[34] These were variously nicknamed 'o.p.s.' ('other people's stumps'), 'Hard-up Virginia', or 'Bender's Mixture'. Tramps would pick up dog-ends in the street, or rummage through the dustbins of cinemas and theatres for sweepings and sell them to the dealers, known as 'Hard-up Kings'. In the 1930s these reconstituted abominations were selling in the doss-houses at 2d or 3d for 20.

White-collar dossers were found scraping a living, too. One struck-off lawyer, the 'Dossers' Solicitor', around 1900 was selling legal advice to the poor at 1d oral and 2d written and had an extensive clientele.[35] Unemployed clerks, who tended to be found in the better-class hostels – the municipal lodging houses and Rowtons – kept out of the workhouse by addressing envelopes for firms. 'Wrapper writers' could expect to earn a meagre 2/6d or 3 shillings per 1,000 at the turn of the century[36] and would be seen working all hours at the table.

Though forced into suffocatingly close contact with each other, in the kitchen the different social groups – the professional beggars, the casual workers and the frayed white collar element – tended to keep to their own circles within the kitchen and did not mix.[37]

On Sundays the kitchens could expect an invasion by 'slummers', the religious evangelists who saw the lodging houses as pagan wildernesses, ripe for missionary work. These 'slum saviours' were treated at most with amused tolerance, but they could expect barracking, too. Cynics ridiculed 'that Christ business', as John Law in 1891 witnessed in 'Darkest London'; one group of evangelists was rudely asked how much they made a week by their preaching and another dosser bluntly 'told them to "clear out", as they took away his appetite'.[38]

Dr Barnardo did his share of missionary work to rescue boys from the moral pollution of the lodging houses[39] and fondly described how boys would sit around him intently in the kitchens. He had one harrowing experience when he arrived in a house he had been 'working on' and was surprised by a bunch of fast girls who had been in the habit of visiting the place to consort with the boys. They were enraged that he should have lured their boy-friends away, and set about him furiously; he was saved from worse injury only by the timely arrival of the deputy, who saw them off.

George Orwell around 1930 also experienced a visit from the slummers, and described the rough music they got from the dossers – chattering, jeering, clattering of pots and pans and so forth while the service was in progress. The deputies had to let them in because the hallelujah brethren were well in with the police.

The presence of these gullible idealists could, however, be turned to advantage by crafty dossers. Sydney Hallifax tells of 'the Phoenix' in the notorious dockland Ratcliffe Highway which was visited by preachers each Sunday from the local Zion Chapel around 1900. A dosser who was co-habiting claimed he needed the wherewithal to marry and live as a decent Christian. The missionaries found him a room and furniture, and made all the marriage arrangements. When all was set up, the fellow, at the last minute before the ceremony, and with all outward display of grief, told them that he had just learned that his woman was already married to a sailor; in the meantime he had pawned the wedding dress and the furniture was 'distilled into drink'.

Could the crowded lodging houses ever have formed a serious breeding ground of radical or revolutionary discontent? Henry Mayhew found them anti-establishment, not surprisingly, hating the aristocracy and no lovers of monarchy, but their political temper he describes as 'Liberal-Tory', not revolutionary.[40] Later in the century, however, against a background of the rise of socialism, deeper fears were expressed about the revolutionary potential of these concentrations of have-nots. Howard Goldsmid in 1886 was

not alone in seeing an outbreak of looting by London's unemployed
the previous winter not just as spasmodic hooliganism but as a
portent of a 'REVOLUTION' (this is the last word, written in
capitals, in his book) debouching from the lodging houses.[41]
Similar views were expressed after the First World War, following
the Russian revolution; Reds were seen in the lodging house beds.[42]
However, such fears were chimerical. Whilst the dossers did talk
politics and groused, it was just a casual conversational outlet, like
the sporting and crime news they gleaned from the papers, as
Josiah Flynt observed in 1899. W.H. Davies makes no suggestion
of political activism, and both Jack London and George Orwell,
two committed socialists, convey merely a mood of dejection,
resignation and a preoccupation with just staying alive among the
doss-house netherworld.

Indeed, as we have seen, there was no homogeneous doss-house
society; mutual suspicion often prevailed over comradeship, for
pilferage was rife. Even if you could afford a cubicle, your
neighbour might, for example, hook your shoes away through the
gap underneath, or throw a hook and line over the top to lift the
jacket, remove any money and gently lower the jacket back into
place. The most slippery thieves were even known to hide
themselves under the beds of cubicle occupants, emerge in the dead
of night to steal and then open the door-catch from within to
escape.[43]

The more 'respectable' no-fixed-aboders gravitated towards the
better lodging houses which were more choosy about their clientele
and imposed stricter rules. To Bart Kennedy, an American
'literary tramp' in London in 1902, the LCC hostel off Drury Lane,
conveyed the same faded atmosphere as the debtors' prison in
Pickwick Papers: 'Here were men of all sorts – the actor, the
artist, the gentleman, the mechanic, the labourer. All with the air
of failure upon them.' All, he says, smelling mustily of yesterday,
for they had no tomorrow.[44] Some better lodging houses around
1906 had names, like 'Shaftesbury Chambers off Drury Lane' to
disguise what they really were, for clerks applying for jobs from
them would be blighted by an obvious lodging house address.[45]

Rowtons at this time at least had a more wholesome tone; the
clientele were more like paying guests, in gainful employment,
some indeed going out to work in smart clothes, even top-hatted.[46]
But even the Rowtons held their discreet substratum of petty
thieves and con-men, for as they were hotels and not lodging
houses the police had no automatic rights of entry.[47]

Whilst, as we have seen, Rowtons continued to enjoy a high
reputation for good management, cleanliness and civilised amenities, the social seediness seems to have become more evident
between the wars. W.A. Gape in 1936 said that their clientele
were predominantly old men, just waiting for the end: 'I have

heard these places referred to as "Abodes of Lost Souls" and I think it describes them well.' And Chris Massie in 1931 described some of the shady types he met in a Rowton, including professional beggars and a memorable con-artist whose speciality was walking into commercial premises dressed as a City gent and lifting commercial directories which he sold second hand.

But the Rowtons do not seem to have sunk to the level of the LCC's Bruce House by 1939. Despite the complimentary descriptions of it in the early 1930s, as noted in the last chapter, John Worby found the place rife with theft; someone filched his dinner while his back was turned and his shirt vanished while he was washing himself.[48] The 'cottage industries' were just like those of any dingy private lodging house, and Bruce House seems to have sunk still further by 1945, when its custom appears to have been sliding towards the 'Skid Row' wreckage familiar in contemporary times. Thomas Callaghan, who stayed there then, had to be on constant guard against theft; urine puddles covered the lavatory floor; the wash basins were used as phlegm bowls, so he found it safer to shave in running water; and he recalls being revolted by the sight of a naked man with a double hernia, 'the deformity so complete that the penis was barely visible'.

To round off this chapter, I will just say a few words about the singular and eccentric characters sometimes encountered in the common lodging houses. Occasionally there were the men of mystery no one could fathom, like the apparently destitute old man in a London house, late last century, so abject that the other inmates fed him. When he died £900 was found stitched in his clothing.[49] F.S. Stuart in 1937 tells of a cashiered army officer who was fetched from his doss-house by a carriage complete with flunkeys; and a fat, seedy man who wrote 'mysterious' cheques and left a fortune when he died. In other respects, the kitchen society could make a colourful mixture. There you would find the broken-down actor, the amusing versifier, the 'prater' with his Biblical cant, the viscount's son who sold phoney racing tips by mail order and dealt in quack medicines (made up in the kitchen), the dosser with his own valet, the deluded tramp who insisted that he had been swindled out of an inheritance by scheming lawyers[50] – these and other sundry tragi-comic cranks and crackbrains formed the variegated if frayed tapestry of doss-house society.

10   An outline of the casual ward system, 1842–1914

The casual ward system applied only to England and Wales. Scotland, because of its relative poverty and strong tradition of Kirk-based parish charity, excluded relief to all able-bodied men, settled parishioners and itinerants alike. However, many parishes did in time lay on crude sick shelters for the latter; but these were little more than sheds for the footsore and weary, and there was no régime of supervision or discipline as in England. Much of the overnight shelter for itinerants which in England was the duty of the casual wards in Scotland was performed unofficially by the police, who gave shelter and food in their station cells.

In England and Wales the casuals had to search out a Union relieving officer for an admission order.[1] They then queued outside the workhouse till admitted, usually from around 6 pm. The casual ward was separate from the main block; the principle since 1842 was to keep itinerants – who might be diseased – strictly segregated from the resident paupers, and though technically they were entitled to ask to see the workhouse medical officer, in practice they were usually snubbed. Casuals were supervised by a Task Master, a paid official, who in turn employed the Tramp Major and porters for menial tasks. The gate porter checked each applicant and the vagrants were at the mercy of this lowly but officious and brusque personage – himself sometimes just a resident pauper – who enjoyed an unofficial power to refuse entry. Technically, he had no right to do this; admission was at the relieving officer's discretion, and even if you made a habit of using a particular ward, after 1871 the penalty was a longer dose of detention and work tasks, not exclusion. But it should be remembered that the porter was himself under strict instructions to discourage applicants. Meaner workhouses had other tricks, though. Misleading 'Full' signs might be posted up, and there was one instance of cold water being poured on the miserable queue outside.

Once inside, the casual was searched for money and personal luxuries, like tobacco, which were removed (the money offset the cost of his stay). He was stripped for a bath and his clothes 'stoved' (i.e., baked to destroy vermin). The bath-house was likely to be an unheated chamber with bare lime-washed walls and a stone floor, while the water, if there was any warmth left in it, was probably already grimy from previous users, as one filling did for a whole batch of arrivals. The casual was given a grubby, worn night-shirt and a 'meal' of a morsel of cheese, a chunk of bread, and gruel or plain water. This was standard fare, supper, breakfast or (for the detained ones) dinner. He was then led to the dormitory. The bedding was primitive, perhaps straw mattresses laid on the floor, or coffin stalls, with rugs for covering. Elsewhere there were hammocks, or a wooden resting platform sloping down from each wall to a central gangway. The general feel was that of a cattle shed, and the inmates were locked in for the night, with perhaps a single bucket as a communal lavatory.

Next morning the compulsory work task was allotted. Task masters had discretion whether to waive the task in the case of the aged or infirm or those claiming they had jobs to start early in the morning. For men, the standard tasks were stone-breaking or stone-pounding, wood-chopping, corn-grinding, or oakum-picking; for women, oakum-picking or cleaning up around the place. Children were not given tasks but stayed locked up till their parents had finished. Breakfast often followed the task, which thus had to be performed on an empty stomach. With stone-breaking rocks had to be cracked down to chippings that would pass through a sieve, or a grille in the wall of a stone-breaking cell; two inches appears to have been the standard gauge. Stone-pounding was far more severe; here the rock was pounded to grains and powder. A journalist who experienced it first-hand in 1909 described it as 'ghastly': four-foot bars with square ends, so heavy 'that only men in good health can use them properly', were used to bash the stone; no protection was given for the eyes, and after half-an-hour he was exhausted, with sore and bleeding hands.[2] In 1923 the Magistrates Association condemned it as barbarous and cruel, especially as so many of the sufferers were war veterans, now forced into vagrancy by the depression.[3]

The labour shed often had no walls, just an open-sided roofed structure exposed to all weather. No work was given on Sundays, but the inmates were left locked in their sleeping quarters all day with no recreational facilities; all they could do was talk, brood and pick vermin from their bodies (perhaps caught from the bedding). The work was performed in the casuals' own clothes, so that this, combined with the crumpling effect of stoving, left them looking more dishevelled when they came out than when they went in.

When fully developed, the poor law Unions provided a national network of wards about 10 miles apart. The idea was that they would be within a day's walking distance from each other, as an amenity to the job-hunting migrant. However, the wards were

Figure 6   *The 'Penny Sit-Up'. The unfortunates would sleep resting their arms and heads on the back of the bench in front. (Courtesy, BBC Hulton Picture Library.)*

located within the workhouse precincts which were often well away from the main highways, and the newly-arrived traveller, having exhausted himself hunting out the relieving officer, then had to trudge off his route to find the workhouse.

I have given a generalised picture of the casual ward system. In practice there were very wide variations. Rural casual wards were generally more primitive, dirtier and more laxly run than those in large towns. Many wards dispensed with the bath and stoving altogether, and the work task for many others was either non-existent or an unsupervised formality; the inmates were left to make a token poke at work for the requisite detention period. The motive was not humanitarian, but to save the administrative costs of laying on raw materials and supervision; each Union just wanted to fulfil its minimum obligation at minimum cost and move the vagrants on as quickly as possible.

This brings us to the quandaries faced by the central poor law authority in casual ward administration: how should one distinguish between the genuine wayfarer and the scrounger, so as to exclude the latter? If they could not be distinguished, should the casual ward régime be penal for *all* users, even though the innocent ones suffered? What penal measures were best? How did one try to achieve uniformity of treatment among Unions and bring the backsliders into line? Did the very existence of casual wards encourage vagrancy, and should we copy alternative methods adopted by some Continental countries?

Between 1842 and the turn of the century poor law policy veered one way and then another as it groped for solutions. The 'Hungry Forties', with trade recessions and the Irish Famine influx, witnessed a rapid rise in the numbers of casuals relieved. At Stafford Union, for example, in the year ending March 1844, 3,178 vagrants were relieved; in the year ending March 1848 the figure was 11,108, and the pattern was repeated elsewhere.[4] The 'Buller Memorandum' of 1848, issued by the President of the Poor Law Board to all Unions, laid down stricter guidelines for admitting casuals. Among the able-bodied preference should be given to those carrying a certificate from some 'reliable' person confirming that they were seeking work, in which case they should be admitted into the main workhouse block. The casual ward would remain a dump for the uncertificated ones. Selection by relieving officers must now be the universal rule, and Buller recommended the use of policemen as assistant relieving officers, on the assumption that their knowledge of the criminal classes would make them sharper spotters of scroungers and professional tramps. Over the next 20 years police forces, including the Metropolitan Police, were recruited into this role; participating constables received a small remuneration on top of their salary. However, certainly in the Met the duty was not popular. The police resented being the jack-of-all-trades for vagrant control.

A policeman was no shrewder judge of the word of an itinerant stranger than any civilian relieving officer. Police stations became the focal point for lengthening queues of smelly and verminous vagrants, repugnant to the officers and distracting them from their regular duties. The Met began issuing admission orders indiscriminately and in increasing numbers; in 1864 it issued 2,159 orders and refused 18, and in 1869 it issued no fewer than 443,974 and refused 11,239. It dropped the job in 1872.[5] Over the year ending July 1849 the national nightly casual ward intake fell dramatically from 13,714 to 5,662. An upturn in trade in that time no doubt played a part, but an ebbing of Irish immigration and the general tightening up following Buller took chief credit at the time.[6]

However, the hardships caused by 'strict discrimination' had led to a change of heart by the early 1860s. 'Buller' was an excuse for many Unions to evade their obligations altogether. London Unions in 1863 had only 997 casual beds, when the capital's tramp population was estimated at 12,000.[7] A circular from C.P. Villiers, President of the Poor Law Board, in 1863 marked a 'softening' of 'Buller', with its emphasis on the obligation to help the genuinely destitute. Two Acts for London in 1864 and 1865 were aimed at encouraging each Union to do more by making the cost of casual relief a London-wide charge, payable by the Metropolitan Board of Works; no London Union need now fear that an extra effort on its part would be attended by an unfair share of the burden. The policy worked, for by 1866 London's casual ward beds had more than doubled compared with 1863, but, as some Unions had sharing arrangements with others, vagrants could still find they had a long, miserable trudge to a shelter.

During the 1860s vagrant relief was increasing again; 'Villiers' was probably a major cause, though the sharper rise between 1867 and 1869 also coincides with a trade recession then. The Poor Law Board was under pressure to tighten up, and in 1868 prescribed a return to 'Buller'[8] and urged the adoption of waytickets to distinguish the wayfarer from the cadger.

The wayticket was a document issued from the vagrant wards or by the police certifying that the bearer was en route to a specified destination to seek work. It was endorsed by the superintendent at the last casual ward visited, so long as this was on the stated route, and the ticket would only be respected and endorsed at further wards along that route. Possession of a 'good ticket' would ensure favoured treatment, for instance exemption from work tasks and early discharges to meet deadlines.

A ticket presented at a ward off the route would be 'bad', and the bearer would have to endure the full discipline before being issued with a completely new ticket from that ward. The ticket would thus benefit the true workseeker, heading for a particular destination, and penalise the vagrant who wandered at will. It might also be combined with a breadticket; this was issued from the vagrant ward upon departure and entitled the bearer to a basic food ration at specified bread stations (police stations or food shops) along his stated route to the next casual ward. This was an added inducement to stick to the route, and was intended to remove any excuse for begging.[9]

Berkshire was a pioneering wayticket county from 1871, but lost enthusiasm (as did other counties who tried it) owing to non-co-operation from some of its own poor law Unions and lack of continuity into neighbouring counties. By 1906 only Gloucestershire and Wiltshire retained it county-wide. The Departmental Committee on Vagrancy that year ascribed the waytickets' indifferent success to patchy adoption nationally, for a vagrant could deviate freely once he reached a non-wayticket authority; also the professional vagrant did not mind the occasional detention on a 'bad' ticket, for the clean ticket he would then be issued with would see him through for as long as he cared.

Nonetheless, waytickets took on a new lease of life after 1906. Sussex, Surrey and Kent had adopted them by 1912, and in 1913 the Local Government Board gave them its blessing and

STONE POUNDING MACHINES

For Task Work in

CASUAL WARDS, etc.

Do you wish to clear your district of the professional tramp,

then use

THE GENUINE LOOSE BOTTOM STONE POUNDER.

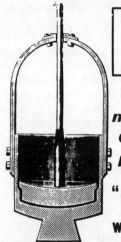

> **It is impossible for the Hammer to be used as a Weapon.**

Hundreds of our machines are in use in Casual Wards in all parts of the country.

"THE BEST IS THE CHEAPEST."

Write for Illustrated Catalogue.

PATENT STONE POUNDER CO.

Patentees and Sole Makers,

POOLE, DORSET.

Figure 7   *Advertisement for a stone-pounding machine for casual wards, 1914.
(Courtesy, Public Record Office, H045/19657/224947, File 41.)*

encouragement.[10] County Vagrancy Committees took up the idea and by 1920 45 counties in England and Wales had wayticket and meal ticket schemes.

From 1871 the government had also tried another tack. Detention powers under the 1842 Act were to be developed, so that vagrants who made repeated resort to a ward would be liable to extended detention; frequency of usage became the criterion of unworthiness in place of 'strict discrimination', and it had the more humane-seeming merit of keeping the homeless *in* shelter rather than shutting them out. In fact, workhouses were now to be turned into administrative prisons; the hapless vagrants, unrepresented and untried, were to be kept locked up in conditions worse than those for convicted criminals on the principle that their return to a ward at least twice in a month made them presumptive parasites.

The Pauper Inmates Discharge Act of 1871 provided that such returnees were to be detained till the morning of the third day after arrival. The work tasks performed after the first day were to be penal; thus, for example, while a maximum of three hundredweight of stones were to be broken on the first day, this rose to anything from five to ten hundredweight on the subsequent days – all on a diet of bread, cheese and gruel.

There was a temporary fall in vagrants' applications; by 1875 the numbers relieved were less than half those of 1870. However, as these intervening years were an economic boom period, it is not possible to disentangle that effect from the Act's. The rise in applications after 1875 may conversely have been due to the recession setting in then, or a fading of the Act's deterrent impact.[11] The Casual Poor Act of 1882 turned the screw tighter; first-time applicants were now detainable till the morning of the second day after entry, and 'habitual' users, as defined in 1871, could not leave till 9 am on the fourth day. London wards were deemed to be a single unit; thus the use of any ward in the Metropolitan Board of Works area counted anywhere else in the same area, and Local Government Board inspectors regularly toured the London wards trying to identify faces. Even this apparent hardship to London vagrants failed to have the hoped-for effect. Between 1865 and 1905 London vagrant ward standards, for instance in regard to bathing and bedding, had improved markedly and overall were the best in the country. The capital had bred a tribe of vagrant ward roundsmen, who lived by mooching from ward to ward as 'regulars' hardened by long practice to the rigour of the work tasks.

One modification was made in 1892, when casuals were made dischargeable at dawn at the workhouse masters' discretion to enable vagrants to take up jobs that day.

The detention and work task of the 1871 and 1882 Acts remained the theoretical foundation of casual ward discipline and deterrence up to the Welfare State take-over in 1948 (and in a diluted form in the nationalised Reception Centres till 1980). But the administrative reality was very different; laxity and variations of practice bedevilled and vitiated the casual ward system till new approaches through County and Joint Vagrancy Committees were tried in the early twentieth century. If one Union conscientiously applied strict rules of detention and work task to deter vagrants from its neighbourhood, it could be totally undermined if they passed through en route to a neighbouring Union that was slack. Whilst the casual ward system remained fragmented, each Union's impulse was to send its casuals on their way as soon as possible and to avoid the expense of building extra room for detainees and organising the work tasks; the central authority's efforts to establish uniformity by regulations just fell flat. Take, for example, the cell system. In 1865 separate cells had become obligatory for prisons, and the Poor Law Board Circular of 1868 wanted them applied to casual wards to replace dormitories, as this would isolate the vagrants who looked on the casual ward as a club and made trouble there, and also separate young itinerants from the hardened old lags. Individual Unions, most notably the rural ones, complained that cell construction was too expensive, and did nothing. By 1896 only about half the workhouses in the country had any kind of cell system, and less than half detained inmates in the wards for more than one night.[12] Even by 1910 only two thirds of the workhouses had cells.[13]

Given these administrative failings, it *did* look by the mid-1890s as though the casual wards were encouraging public scrounging. The numbers of all poor law dependants (that is 'residents', both indoor and outdoor, and casuals) hovered around 1,000,000 between 1865 and 1810 and was just below this in 1905, and had therefore remained roughly static on a 62 per cent population growth, but the numbers of casuals alone had *doubled* between 1865 and 1905, to about 8,000–9,000 a night (on 1 January).[14]

The first half of the 1890s was a period of recession. Casual ward figures were on the increase, from under 5,000 on 1 January 1884 to 8,300 on the same night in 1894. Poor Law Unions approached the Local Government Board for an enquiry into the system, but received a dusty answer; its 1896 Circular recited the Unions' failings I have just discussed and told them to mend their own ways if they wanted to stop the rot. The Unions enjoyed a respite during a prosperous spell from 1897, and potential casual ward inflow was also siphoned off into the army during the Boer War. On 1 January 1900 casual ward figures were down to less than 5,600. The end of the war in 1902 saw a return of ex-soldiers; another recession was setting in, and the wards began filling up again. This time the government relented and appointed an Inter-Departmental Committee on Vagrancy in 1904, whose study in

1906 is encyclopaedic and seminal to any historical research into vagrancy.

It was being recognised more and more by local authorities that only by widening vagrancy regulation beyond the individual poor law Union to county-wide or even region-wide units could the hitherto unattainable dream of uniformity be achieved. Before 1914, County Vagrancy Committees were beginning to be established, combining Unions on a voluntary basis, and laying down common régimes on a mutual support basis. This de-parochialisation made for broader-mindedness, and some Committees were to begin assuming a more positive welfare and rehabilitative responsibility towards vagrants, for example by keeping tabs on child vagrants, and encouraging senile tramps to settle down permanently as workhouse residents. By the mid-1920s County and Joint Vagrancy Committees (the latter covering groups of counties) embraced the majority of England's poor law Unions, and the government was actively encouraging their formation.[15] London had gone the same way when in 1912 its Union casual wards had been taken over by an overall authority, the Metropolitan Asylums Board, which began rationalising them and establishing greater uniformity.

Curiously, the Departmental Committee Report of 1906 did not see the potential of CVCs, and fell back instead on the unwilling shoulders of the police with a recommendation to transfer the whole casual ward administration to the county police forces, both as larger units than the Unions, and as supposedly more knowledgeable detectors of scroungers. The police protested to the Home Office, and the proposal was still-born.[16]

The whole problem of the Vagrancy Act and the casual wards was that they sought to deter the vagrant, purely negatively and quite vainly, by locking him up for short periods. Since the later nineteenth century more and more interest was shown in the labour and detention colony systems operated in some Continental countries, like Belgium, Switzerland and Germany. The former took in vagrants who voluntarily committed themselves to rehabilitation and training in a camp; the latter were compulsory centres for those convicted by the courts, where they spent up to three years in a prison-camp régime of farm or trade work. They were extolled by British observers, and were recommended as a long-term replacement for casual wards by the 1906 Departmental Committee. Labour colonies and labour homes had already been set up by some British charities; most notably the Salvation and Church Armies had labour homes, where, by wood-chopping, paper-sorting and the like, down-and-outs would pay their way in their shelters, and (an idealistic hope) relearn the habit of work. They both ran rural colonies. The Salvation Army, for instance, bought a 1,500 acre site at Hadleigh in Essex in 1891 as a colony for selected volunteers, and it was both Armies' firm conviction that rehabilitation followed by emigration to the colonies was the answer to Britain's vagrancy problem.[17] However, there was a high rate of premature self-discharge from Hadleigh and no conclusions can be drawn about its success.[18] Whilst British admirers praised the freedom of Continental streets from beggars thanks to the detention colonies, the reality was not so clinically perfect at all. Visitors who sampled German tramp life at the turn of the century found the country rife with vagrants who found their own ways of hoodwinking the authorities that they were genuine work seekers.[19] The '*Kolonie-Bummler*', or colony-loafer, who actually preferred life in a camp to self-dependence, was a known German type and we should remember that the Americanism 'bum' comes from the German *Bummler*.[20] In fact the same reprobates turned up again and again in the Continental detention colonies, whose main use was in clearing the streets but not changing their captive leopards' spots.

The Home Office was not unreceptive to the detention colony idea but no action was ever taken in Britain.[21] The probable unspoken reason was a deep-seated aversion to forced social reconditioning not so much for specific crimes as for a particular way of life; it jarred with Anglo-Saxon notions of personal liberty.[22]

The 1906 Departmental Committee had also recommended that casual wards and police stations should be developed as labour exchanges. Local labour exchanges, both voluntary (like the Salvation Army's) and municipal, already existed,[23] and it seemed anomalous in the age of the telephone that men should have to go on tramp as ostensible work seekers. A national system of labour exchanges was set up in 1909, and with the advent of national insurance in 1911 (to a limited range of occupations) it was thought that the possession of a national insurance card, stamped as proof of recent employment, might serve as an updated wayticket, entitling the bearer to preferential treatment in a casual ward; but we shall see in Chapter 18 that this was itself to become an instrument of profit to wily cadgers.

11 'The vicious shilling': indiscriminate charity and its enemies, from 1860

Begging, as a habit or profession, fed on impulsive charity. The severity of the Victorian poor law and the bogey of the workhouse made people respond readily to appeals for alms to keep the supplicant from 'going on the parish', and commentators on mendicancy observed that if the public had confidence that humane poor law relief was available to the destitute, indiscriminate charity would cease, and begging would wither on the vine.[1] The Howard Association for Penal Reform waxed censorious about indiscriminate charity, and in 1882 quoted one poor law guardian's opinion that 'The money given at cottage doors to habitual mendicants in a single year probably exceeds twentyfold, to put it at a low figure, what the working classes contribute to real charitable and beneficent objects.'[2]

Notice that it is the working classes who get the blame here, for they were presumed most susceptible and least capable of discretion, especially the womenfolk.

Victorian charity, whether as casual street tips or organised philanthropy, was very big business. Howard Tallack in 1869 retailed that £7,000,000 was given away in London alone each year, and that nationwide at least £1,300,000 went into the pockets of professional scroungers.[3] In 1905 Sir Eric Buchanan of the London Mendicity Society thought that anything from, £100,000 to £300,000 had been given the previous winter to the capital's street beggars,[4] adding wryly: 'It would be no exaggeration to say that probably 90 per cent of persons who pity the lot of the street beggar simply give him the money to relieve their personal feelings, without troubling themselves whether the case is helpable or unhelpable.'

There was a multitude of local charities for doling out bread, fuel and clothing to the needy. They were run by local clergymen and Lady Bountifuls, operating in complete ignorance of the activities of other local charities, and so opening the field for the 'charity hound', the professional 'overlapper' who went the rounds of the charities with hard-luck stories appropriate to each. The Reverend

J. Hornby Wright told in 1871 of one woman he used to arrange gifts of winter coal for, till he became suspicious and stopped. At her death sackfuls of coal were found in her house together with a haul extracted from other charities, and she was able to afford a lavish funeral, complete with hearse, mutes, plumed standards and coffin furniture of the finest materials.[5]

W.A. Gape told of a charity hound of a later date, one 'Lady Dorothy', who approached one committee passing as a seaman's widow in straitened circumstances. The committee was not convinced, but 'Lady Dorothy' knew of a pub that one of the committee men customarily visited. While he was there, but pretending not to see him, she loudly and tearfully poured out her grievance, and the gentleman, much embarrassed, offered to review her case and the rapprochement led to her spending the night with him; an indiscretion she then exploited as blackmailing leverage on the indiscreet committee man.[6]

A favourite form of charity to the down-and-out was the night shelters and their allied benefaction, the soup kitchens. The latter appear to have had a longer history, at least in London. A London soup charity in the depressed winter of 1797 was feeding 10,000 persons a week till the summer.[7] The capital's first charitable night shelter seems to have been the Houseless Poor Asylum in Playhouse Yard, Cripplegate (the 'Ouseless', as it was familiarly known), founded in 1819,[8] and was the largest by far of London's seven night refuges in the mid 1860s. The leading five boasted about 1,000 beds, and the 'Ouseless' alone had 600.[9] Among provincial cities, Liverpool and Manchester had established night refuges by the 1830s.[10] These places were commonly open only in the winter months.

The soup flow rose to a flood in the heyday of Victorian philanthropy, and religious missionaries realised that a full stomach was an essential prerequisite of spiritual receptiveness (or at any rate, a semblance of it) among the 'grateful' poor. London's 'Model Soup Kitchen' distributed 150,000 free meals in 1869, while among the night refuges that also provided free food, the Providence Row Refuge gave 140,000 breakfasts and 140,000 suppers between 1860 and 1869,[11] and in 1904 alone gave over 47,000 free meals.[12]

Probably the most sympathetic commentator on this type of charity was Henry Mayhew who furnished a lengthy description of the Houseless Poor Asylum in his *London Labour and the London Poor*.[13] The building was a converted hat factory, and offered separate accommodation for men and women. The beds were of the rudimentary 'coffin' type with mattresses of hay stuffed into waterproof bags. Mayhew gives the impression that the place was kept clean, though this must have been an uphill task, considering the abject, sometimes squalid condition of its clientèle. He described them as '400 and odd creatures utterly destitute –

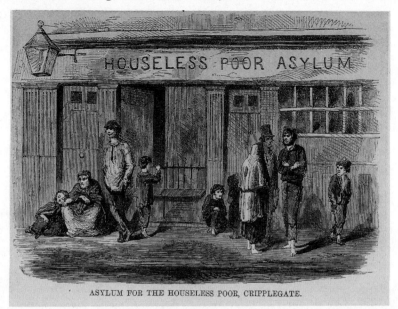

ASYLUM FOR THE HOUSELESS POOR, CRIPPLEGATE.

Figure 8   *Down-and-outs waiting for the charitable Houseless Poor Asylum to open its doors, 1950–60. (Source: Henry Mayhew,* London Labour and the London Poor, *Volume 3. Courtesy, Guildhall Library, London.)*

mothers with infants at their breasts – fathers with boys holding by their side – the friendless – the penniless – the shirtless, shoeless, breadless, homeless; in a word, the very poorest of this, the very richest city in the world'. They made a miserable spectacle as they queued up for the door to open at 5 pm – a parade of sickness and infection – the 'flu-ridden and feverish, the rheumatic and ulcerated, the ruptured, the dropsical, and those with diarrhoea and bowel pains, the bronchitic, and those spitting blood'. The inmates ranged from respectable unfortunates to the dregs, and many had piteous stories to explain their predicament, like the unemployed railway navvy and carpenter who had had to sell their tools and were reduced to beggary; the former laundress who had burst a blood vessel after lifting a heavy pail and was reduced to peddling; and the American negro sailor who had arrived at Liverpool and had tramped to London to find another ship and was reduced to sleeping under the butchers' stalls in Whitechapel in freezing weather.

However, the night refuges had their bitter critics. It was alleged that they gave shelter and food indiscriminately without a work task and actually encouraged beggary, bringing hordes of undesirables riddled with disease into the neighbourhood.[14] The Mendicity Society claimed that when the Houseless Poor Asylum opened its doors in the winter, the Society suffered the side-effects, and the numbers it had to relieve shot up, only falling when the Asylum shut again;[15] but this may have been a natural winter peak, irrespective of the Asylum's existence. On the other hand, it appears that the Liverpool refuge was due to shut in 1848, as it was attracting prostitutes and low-lives, and the Cardiff police were then complaining of an increase in vagrancy in the city since a night shelter had opened – even before the Irish famine influx.[16]

Of course, while casual ward accommodation was inadequate common humanity inevitably inspired private ventures to fill the gap, and once London began expanding its casual wards after 1865 (see Chapter 10) it is said that some night refuges did indeed shut.[17] But the casual wards themselves put the poor law Unions in a Catch-22 situation: if their régimes were lenient or slack, they laid themselves open to the same objections as the night refuges; but if they were strict and succeeded in deterring vagrants, then the consequent hardship prompted the reopening of those self-same refuges! A classic instance of this happened in Manchester where a large, purpose-built casual ward was opened at Tame Street in 1897. The régime was strict; work tasks were rigidly enforced, and the number of casuals 'gratifyingly' dropped off. But there was a simultaneous increase in sleeping rough, and philanthropists duly opened a night shelter. The influx of vagrants this brought not only rapidly filled up the shelter, but spilled over into the casual ward and numbers began rising there again. This brought pressure to close the shelter, which was duly done. With the onset of a recession after 1900 the numbers sleeping out rose alarmingly in the city, as men would not go into Tame Street. Finally, after appeals from the police, the régime there was relaxed from 1903, and the numbers relieved there nightly doubled between 1903 and 1907.[18]

The public emergency relief appeals launched in times of economic distress or severe winters could also degenerate into a welter of indiscriminate charity (and a new dimension was added from the late nineteenth century when newspapers publicised their own appeals among readers). In London, the Lord Mayor's Mansion House Appeals, dating at least as far back as 1819,[19] were very effective fund raisers but imprudent distributors; likewise, during the acute winter of 1860–61 when thousands of dock workers were laid off, a London relief campaign brought a tremendous response, but the money was doled out haphazardly through the magistrates' courts, and cheating was rampant. The 1864 Select Committee on Poor Relief recorded:

> We hear how applicants often obtained relief from one police
> court in the morning and from another in the afternoon; that
> there was no co-operation between the Guardians and the police

magistrates, so that in many cases duplicate and even triplicate relief money may have been given without the possibility of detection. . . . Sums as large as £50, £80 and £100 were often distributed in handfuls of silver to crowds of applicants, the sole qualification being a display of dirty hands. Bread, which was given in relief, was taken to public houses and exchanged for beer, and then sold by the publicans at reduced rates.

During the Cotton Famine in Lancashire, the £2,000,000 relief aid raised between 1861 and 1863 was distributed through local distress committees, which did attempt some liaison between different agencies, but there was still much fraud. In Manchester a quarter of the claims were allegedly fraudulent, for example through misrepresented earnings and claims for offspring borrowed, in fact, from neighbours.[20]

The relief raised for London's East Enders during a slump in 1867–8 was also partially squandered on cheats who went the rounds of different distribution centres, and the beggars even coordinated their cadging circuits.[21]

The most notorious episode of misdirected charity was the Mansion House Appeal fiasco of 1886, followed by the Trafalgar Square scroungers' beano of 1887. A severe depression in 1885–6 had prompted a new Lord Mayor's Appeal and £80,000 was rapidly raised. This was free-handedly disbursed and the spongers came flocking, from within London and from the provinces, to partake of this bonanza. The Lords Select Committee on Poor Relief was told in 1888 how the 'drink following the distribution of the Mansion House Relief Fund was something fearful'; one woman was drunk for three weeks on her rake-in, though her husband was actually in work.[22]

By 1887 the Fund was exhausted, but the recession continued. In the summer there was widespread sleeping out in Trafaglar Square and St James's Park by the unemployed, but the police did not interfere. With the onset of winter a renewed Mansion House Appeal failed miserably as the scandal of its mismanagement became public knowledge.[23] But individual philanthropists tried to fill the gap, moved by the plight of the down-and-out, and they converged on Trafalgar Square to hand out personal bounty. Hot coffee and bread (the latter in cartloads by accounts) were blithely doled out, and an American was 'reported to have scrambled loose silver among the crowd'.[24] Trafalgar Square became a happy hunting ground for down-and-outs whose numbers swelled from the usual 20–25 to some 300–400. But the side-effects spread out further, for central London so teemed with vagrants that the West End casual wards were swamped. Strand Casual Ward had to start issuing tickets to lodging houses; St George's Hanover Square's ward suffered a minor riot, and at Kensington the overflow had to sleep in the dining room.[25] It was this experience that prompted the Charity Organisation Society to conduct a survey among night refuges and central London casual wards over the next year or two, and it concluded that only a minute fraction of the inmates were worthwhile cases.

The failings of emergency relief schemes were firstly the lack of co-ordination among charities, causing duplication and giving the 'charity hounds' a field day, and secondly their discontinuity; the schemes were wound up once the crisis was passed and no experience of case work and assessment could be built up. The organisers tried to compensate for their ignorance of case backgrounds by requiring relief work from applicants as a test of genuine destitution. Labour yard tasks were offered in winter by many workhouses to tide over the seasonally unemployed as a condition of outdoor relief, but this bore the poor law stigma. From the time of the Cotton Famine, relief work was also offered through the charities and municipal authorities to the unemployed in times of crisis, free of the workhouse 'taint', and from 1886 the government actively encouraged local authorities to provide relief work at a subsistence wage in times of depression. As a method of separating the sheep from the goats relief work was a failure. The crude labouring work offered, such as stone-breaking and earth-moving, suited the calloused labouring types who formed the mainstay of the casual wards; clerks, and artisans used to fine work, could not cope so well and tended to be elbowed out of the queues by the rougher breed. The work had to be rationed out among the multitude of comers, and so was part-time, and irregular; it started later in the morning than normal jobs, and suited the lay-a-beds; it was paid in money and bread according to family need, not output, and was a boon to slackers. Although the local distress committees under the scheme were supposed to co-ordinate charitable, poor law and municipal relief and to vet applicants, in practice the sheer weight of numbers reduced this to a travesty, and lenient authorities like Poplar in London's East End reputedly became a Mecca for an army of ragtag and bobtails.[26]

The Embankment crisis of 1910–11 brought ultimately a more sophisticated official response. After the Boer War ended in 1902 the economy had been shaky and there was a noticeable increase in sleeping-out on the Embankment. Since their construction in the 1860s the London Embankments had become a traditional haunt for down-and-outs, attracted by the makeshift bed space on the benches and under the bridges, while the proximity of West End theatres and restaurants afforded the chance to earn coppers as beggars and cab-touts.[27] In addition, cooks and waiters would sometimes bring left-overs to the unfortunates in the Embankment Gardens, and Fleet Street printers were known to be generous to tramps when they left work.[28] In 1890 William Booth commissioned a survey of Embankment down-and-outs on behalf of the Salvation Army. In one night in July 368 were found sleeping there in a mile stretch between Westminster and Blackfriars. Their case histories made pitiable reading – some had been made unemployable by cataracts, bronchitis, rupture and other ailments; others had congenital defects, like feeble-mindedness; then there was the man with the withered arm; while others owed their downfall to drink.

The Embankment became a focus for charity work. In 1905 the Church Army opened its 'King Edward's Labour Tents' on a Strand redevelopment site, to offer relief to Embankment down-and-outs in return for wood-chopping. (Edward VII had donated £100 towards the Tents and allowed his name to be used; they were set up each winter until 1914.)

The Church Army, true to its ideal of selectivity, put up a signboard overlooking the Strand urging people not to tip beggars but to offer Church Army work tickets instead.[29] The Salvation Army each night came down to issue tickets to its labour centres for soup and a 'kip' in return for wood-chopping. The jockeying among the roughs in the queues drove the meeker ones to the back, and the Salvationists started issuing tickets from the rear end.[30] A Mr Eustace Miles Barrow had started a charity which by 1911 was issuing 800 free meals a day on the Embankment, and a Thames Embankment Relief Fund issued free tickets to lodging houses. The *Morning Post* newspaper ran an Embankment shelter, requiring work tasks.[31]

By 1909 the tramp throng was said to vary from 500 to 1,200 a night.[32] Sheer numbers alone made it impossible for the Salvation Army and other charities to discriminate, so the Church Army kept away from the Embankment itself, offering tickets instead more selectively (through the police) around the West End streets.[33]

This Embankment largesse was attracting the scroungers; it was claimed that people slept at home by day, and came down to the Embankment at night for hand-outs.[34] One journalist saw recipients of Salvation Army tickets who had already eaten during the day selling them to others for up to 2d each.[35] John Burns, the President of the Local Government Board, went down to see the situation for himself, and was himself offered a meal by an undiscriminating charity worker![36] The congregation of down-and-outs struck another worrying note in some, for where the have-nots massed they were feared to be potential tinder for 'socialist agitators'. The same applied to marches of the unemployed; it was alleged that they were latched onto by spongers not only as a cover for begging, but also for any opportunities offered by disturbances provoked by left-wing trouble-makers.[37]

The Charity Organisation Society spelled out the problem: indiscriminate and duplicated charity compounded by lack of liaison with the casual wards aided the Embankment scroungers; and as the tramp ward bed space was not available where it was most needed, the public relief system under-functioned. On the night of 18 February 1910 the LCC homeless census counted 969 literally on the streets, but while 1,107 slept in the casual wards, these still had 685 vacancies, and 161 free lodging house beds were unoccupied.[38]

Early in 1911 the Social Welfare Association (an umbrella organisation of charities and poor law authorities) met at the Mansion House to work out a scheme for better co-ordination and liaison, and the upshot was the formation of the 'Metropolitan Homeless Poor Committee' in 1912, composed of charities, police, and poor law officials, as a general advisory body; whilst a central register scheme for the names of charity recipients and casual ward users had already been agreed. The Metropolitan Asylums Board took over London's casual wards in April 1912, and was able to start rationalising them. The 28 wards in April had been reduced to 17 by December 1912; this slimming down was aided by the MAB's new 'Night Office' on Waterloo Pier from October.[39] Applicants were screened in an interview and directed to the most appropriate shelter;[40] the Office had telephone contact with charities and casual wards, and could pay travelling allowances. Those deemed most 'helpable' were sent to charitable shelters; 'regulars' were directed on the whole to the casual wards. The Night Office was credited with solving the Embankment crisis, and as early as December 1912 J.S. Oxley, a Local Government Board Inspector, wrote in relief how 'By clearing this place a most fruitful recruiting ground of vagrancy has been closed'.[41] The fall, not only in the numbers 'on the streets' but also in the casual wards, was very dramatic after 1912; on 9 February 1912 there were 983 homeless persons on the streets; on 14 February 1913 this was down to 491. Casual ward occupancy averaged about 1,000–1,100 a night just before April 1912; by December it was down to 600 and by 1914 had dropped to 300.[42] Now, while the upturn in trade from 1912 would have contributed to this fall,[43] the Night Office must receive its due as well, for its screening procedure not only ensured more efficient placement but seems to have deterred the casual ward habituals as well. Two pieces of evidence point to this. Firstly, even in the depths of the post-war depressions homelessness never reached anything like the pre-war levels. Thus, on one night in February 1930 the LCC counted 79 on the streets; a year later 78, and in February 1932, 87.[44] Secondly up to 1914 the Night Office was directing half its applicants to the casual wards as the less worthy types, the 'helpables' being assigned to the charities. This proportion fell steadily, and immediately after the First World War only a fifth was directed to the casual wards, as most applicants were now genuine victims of the depression. The incidence of non-arrival among those *directed* to casual wards was much higher than among those directed to charities, so the lead-swinging vagrants (who might have had enough money to afford a lodging house bed after all) were presumably disappointed and ducking out.[45] After the mid-1920s, as the depression bit harder, London's casual ward intake rose above the 1914 level, but at around 600–700 a night in the worst years it was still well below the levels prior to the Night Office's inception.

So far I have concentrated on the problems of indiscriminate public relief in times of economic or winter crisis. But what efforts were made to discourage day-to-day casual alms-giving? The earliest were through the Mendicity Societies, a topic I broached in Chapter 3. The London Society was the longest-lived, but from the 1860s it went into gradual decline for it was hard to maintain the momentum of public interest, and large individual donations ceased after the 1860s. Its efforts to curb the public's charitable impulse proved an heroic failure, as its director, Sir Eric Buchanan, acknowledged before the 1906 Vagrancy Committee: he had recently circularised the newspapers about his society's work, 'and what do you think we got in return? Four donations amounting to £2–12–6d.'[46] An article in *The Times* in 1905 paid tribute to the Mendicity Society, which, it said, 'deserves much greater support than it now receives'.[47] Whilst in the late 1860s it could average 703 arrests of beggars a year (about half of whom were convicted) in 1910 it arrested 42 and in 1913 79, with constables now reduced to three.[48] It was more successful in the begging letter department, and the income it received for its services here helped keep it solvent: 'We have to do it for the King and all sorts of big people', Buchanan told the Vagrancy Committee.[49] Prior to 1914 it was dealing with some 1,400 to 1,800 begging letter queries a year. The First World War reduced its constabulary to one, and its 1919 Annual Report, a century after its foundation, showed intriguingly that history was repeating itself. Just as in the post-Napoleonic period, beggars in the guise of war veterans 'are coming back to town and resuming their former occupation of preying on the public, and the number brought before the metropolitan magistrates is gradually increasing . . .' Whilst the number of arrests each year remained well below 100, the Society constable spent much time in court giving evidence in hundreds more cases each year. Begging letter investigations, at up to 1,300 a year to 1931, still remained its predominant activity, and its subscribers were then issuing some 2,000 food tickets a year. The Society was wound up in 1959, but annual reports after 1931 have been mislaid by the British Library. The last reference to it I have found is a comment in the LCC Annual Report for 1934 that the Society was helping the LCC to follow up alleged cases of those receiving outdoor poor law benefits who were improperly making extra by begging in the street.[50]

In 1869 the Bread Ticket scheme was inaugurated to discourage alms-giving. It seems to have been pioneered in Dorset, where the local Mendicity Society operated it through the police and poor law. Subscribers to the scheme could issue bread tickets to wayfarers, redeemable for food at bread stations (such as police stations or bakers) scattered throughout the county. The object was to remove all excuses for begging and as public confidence in the adequacy of the scheme was essential to its success, the county was placarded with posters urging people not to give alms to beggars.[51]

Other counties adopted the scheme, only to drop it later. By 1906 only three other counties apart from Dorset were operating it. Dorset stuck to its guns in claiming that bread tickets *did* diminish indiscriminate charity and reduce vagrancy offences, but other counties that had tried it were less enthusiastic, perhaps because it was difficult to sustain public interest over a long period.[52]

In 1914 the Local Government Board made obligatory what some Unions had already been doing unofficially, namely the issue of a packed meal to casual ward dischargees, to see them to the next ward; alternatively they were to be supplied with a meal ticket redeemable at food stations en route. Whilst intended to check begging, it led to mean-minded cheating by contractors, who sold the hapless ticket-holders short but benefited from the tickets' full value. This happened to George Orwell around 1930, when, equipped with a ticket from 'Romton' casual ward, he looked in at a coffee shop in Ilford; the waitress turned very frosty on seeing his and his companion's tickets, and gave them both a 4d snack for their 6d vouchers, knowing full well that they could not take their custom elsewhere.[53]

The Charity Organisation Society was formed in 1868 in the wake of the recent winter East End relief scandals, and as a response to the chaotic multiplication of overlapping charities. It was a co-ordinating and vetting network, whose procedure entailed careful preliminary enquiry (with home visiting) before reference to an affiliated charity. It pioneered systematic casework and dossier-keeping, and originated the profession of social worker. Its principle was to steer the 'deserving' towards charities, whilst leaving the residue to fall back on a severe, almost penal poor law.[54] It condemned indiscriminate charity, and its especial targets were the night refuges and soup kitchens. In 1870–71 it conducted enquiries into them and the mischiefs they allegedly caused.[55] Soup kitchens, it found, became an actual pretext for begging, for cadgers would appeal for pennies in the street to buy a cheap meal and rake in many times the actual price of the dinner. Night refuges, it urged, should screen applicants, and instead of being mere temporary dumps of misery should develop into voluntary labour homes and actively try to set inmates on their feet. (We have noted in Chapter 10 how some charities, notably the Salvation and Church Armies did, subsequently put this idea into practice.) Soup kitchens should be merged into a single charity, buying food cheaply in bulk and selling meals at a low but economic price; free meal scroungers would be cut off, and unified management would end overlapping.

Nonetheless, refuges and soup kitchens remained a favourite subject of charity, even, as the 1906 Vagrancy Committee pointed out, among those who *otherwise* deplored indiscriminate relief. In London's East End the Providence Row and Medland Hall shelters were very much part of the local scene; and the Salvation Army Whitechapel Shelter gave over 50,000 free meals in the first half of 1904 alone. Until a court ruling in 1899 made charitable shelters subject to the same regulation as common lodging houses, they could not be touched unless they became a positive public health threat. As they were run on a shoe-string, standards were lower – tiered bunks were common, for instance – and the applicants were the dregs; the Vagrancy Committee commented that 'Vagrants who frequent shelters and the cheaper common lodging houses appear to belong to a lower class than the casual pauper and are much less clean.' It concluded that shelters and soup kitchens, by their lack of discrimination, 'constitute a serious evil' and should be licensed.[56]

The Charity Organisation Society also checked out begging letters, and W.H. Davies experienced COS methods around 1908 when he wrote to the Surgical Aid Society, from his lodging at the Salvation Army's 'Ark' Metropole, for a new wooden leg. He subsequently received a visit from a COS Officer and was invited up to their office to be interviewed about his background and income.[57] His fellow dossers warned him off, for the COS was in their experience probing but tight-fisted, and this was Davies' own impression; but he acknowledged that the Surgical Aid Society did lay itself open to begging letters, for applicants had to obtain written endorsements from subscribers in a list distributed by the Society.

12   The freedom to itch, and the itch to be free

In this chapter we shall examine the physical and mental constitution of the tramp, and the public's popular image of him.

Drunkenness appears to have been first and foremost a cause and a condition of the tramp's existence in Victorian and Edwardian times. Alcoholism in society at large was rife; the death rate from cirrhosis of the liver in the late nineteenth century was nearly five times the rate in the 1960s and 1970s.[1] Scotland had an even worse record than England, for the drinking vice there was exacerbated by the Scots' greater partiality to spirits,[2] and in the 'shebeens' or illicit drinking dens of the Glasgow slums around 1870 a knockout mixture of whisky and methylated spirits was a favourite tipple.[3]

There are numerous Victorian and Edwardian references to the role of alcohol as a cause of the slide into vagrancy, and to the numbers of drunken wrecks in the lodging houses and the casual wards.[4] Josiah Flynt, the American sociologist and tramp-life sampler, reckoned in 1899 that alcohol lay behind 90 per cent of the vagrancy in England, and a Metropolitan casual wards inspector in 1906 similarly estimated that 95 per cent of casual ward users were drunkards;[5] and vagrants not infrequently rolled up to the workhouse intoxicated, indicating that their lodging-money had been pre-empted by the pub.[6] A LCC survey of lodging houses in 1903 showed a much higher death rate from alcoholism among their habitués than among the population at large; for example, among males aged 45–55 it was 80 per cent higher than among males of the same age group in the community as a whole.[7]

Short jail terms for drunkenness offences were manifestly futile, for prisoners, deprived of their tipple, just went on a 'bender' again on release; one attraction of the detention colony idea was that alcoholic vagrants could be weaned off drink over a long term.[8] A limited version of this was attempted under the Inebriates Act of 1898 under which habitual drunken offenders instead of going to jail could alternatively be committed to certified Inebriate Reformatories for up to three years. In practice those who ran them, like the Church Army, found the inmates too far gone and difficult to handle; assaults on staff were not uncommon.[9] In fact, compulsory detention of drunkards at a time when therapeutic techniques were virtually unknown proved a failure and the reformatories were all shut by 1921.[10] The inter-war period witnessed a dramatic and spontaneous fall in alcohol consumption, a salutary long-term after-effect of the severe restrictions on drink sales during the First World War. Drunkenness offences, which had hovered around 200,000 a year in England before 1914, were down to 30,000–40,000 a year by the 1930s; Scotland followed the trend, though at a higher relative level. But any beneficial effect this may have had on vagrancy was offset by the impact of the Depression.

What of the tramps' comparative intelligence? Was it below that of society in general? The tricks and dodges of the professional cadgers certainly show that a proportion of the vagabond netherworld was very acute indeed; Victorian tramps' slang even had disparaging terms like 'half-sharps' and 'dozeys' for the simpletons among their number.[11] Dr James Pearce of Wiltshire, in a report to the Royal Commission on the Feeble-Minded in 1908, opined that 'a man who lives on the road must live by his wits, and the feeble-minded are thereby barred from this method of livelihood'. This statement is *too* sweeping but the acuteness of many lodging house residents was also attested to by Dr Charles Melland of Manchester, after extensive conversations with dossers on political and social topics. He concluded that they were 'fully up to the average of respectable working men in intelligence. Loafers they are almost without exception . . . and in a large proportion, perhaps 90 per cent, the yielding to drink has been the starting point of their degradation. But feeble-witted they were not.'

W.H. Davies had many anecdotes about the quick-wittedness of tramps. To take just one example: a character called Bony could turn any situation to advantage. On one occasion he saw a crust of bread on the ground just as a couple approached. He promptly picked it up, pretending to eat it, and the couple were so moved that they gave him money. On another occasion when knocked down and shaken, but not hurt, by a cyclist, he acted up this 'injury' and his impaired job chances so convincingly that the cyclist gave him 10 shillings and asked him to keep in touch, so Bony was able to tap him for more funds later.[12]

Some idea of the level of tramp mentality may be gauged from their conversation. Their staple seems to have been 'each other, the police, prison, favourable and unfavourable "spikes", good "dosses", tobacco, beer and the latest murders'. To which sport and politics may be added.[13] Frank Gray found their interest in crime not just prurient, for tramps were often themselves the first suspects of crimes in a neighbourhood. Furthermore, he found that their conversation was more varied than the ordinary working man's, for they were mentally in less of a workaday groove, and had more leisure to peruse the newspapers. The presence of ex-soldiers in a casual ward was bound to enliven the talk, for they were a fund of anecdotes about exotic places and war experiences. Occasionally, casuals proved well read and showed a knowledge of verse and literary classics, which they discussed while locked up on a Sunday; at the other end of the scale, though, inmates also had to put up with the babblings of schizophrenic tramps.[14]

Formal statistical surveys confirmed that whilst most tramps were up to the intelligence of the rest of the population they had a higher proportion of mental defectives within their ranks. Thus a Salvation Army survey of London casual wards in 1905 found 82.3 per cent of the inmates 'mentally fit'.[15] The Royal Commission on the Feeble-Minded found that while 0.46 per cent of England's population was feeble-minded, among casual ward inmates this amounted to 5.3 per cent. The 1913 Mental Deficiency Act provided that the feeble-minded (that is mentally above the imbecilic) could be compulsorily committed to institutions, but many vagrants escaped the net. A sample survey of workhouse casuals by Dr E.O. Lewis in 1929 showed that 15.7 per cent were mentally subnormal in different degrees (compared with 0.73 per cent for the population as a whole); 5.4 per cent were 'insane' (mostly senile dementia among aged vagrants 'wandering to their own hurt') and a further 5.7 per cent suffered from psychoneurotic disorders, some of which dated from shellshock in the War.[16]

Tramps were perennial and notorious disease-carriers, and there have already been scattered references in the book to their infestations. Typhus was probably the most feared tramp-borne contagion before the 1860s. It was largely brought in by the Irish, and in Scotland during typhus epidemics attempts were made to quarantine incoming Irish on the Clyde, but they slipped ashore.[17] The lodging houses became hot-beds of disease, and George Atkins Brine (see Chapter 4) found it wise to steer clear of them during the great epidemic of 1847–8 that followed the Irish Famine influx. During the cholera epidemic of 1831–2 police in the West Country kept a closer watch on vagrants' movements – steering them to approved lodgings and then seeing them on their way next morning,[18] while in Scotland fear of cholera impelled parishes to ship any Irish vagrants they picked up back home.[19]

Within the workhouse precincts casuals were strictly segregated from resident paupers to avoid contagion; this was one reason why on Sundays casuals were barred from religious service in the workhouse chapel.[20] A secondary case for the proposal for geographically separate District Asylums for vagrants in London in the 1840s was that they would distance workhouses from tramps' diseases.[21]

The casual wards did have powers to clean up tramps. George Atkins Brine has left a graphic description of the sulphur treatment he was subjeted to at Shepton Mallet tramp ward when he arrived there with the 'Scratch' (scabies). He was shut into a large box with a neck hole:

> A flat iron pan full of brimstone was slided in and set fire to. Of all the sensations ever I felt that was the worst. I thought I would choke as the fumes of the sulphur filled the room but the porter only laughed at me and I was utterly helpless. There I sat in that accursed thing for about ten minutes and was then let out. Every other morning for a week I had the 'tramp torment' as some wag had styled it and cut it in the box deeply with a knife.[22]

From 1848 casual wards were given stronger powers to search and cleanse new arrivals.[23] A bath was (supposed to be) compulsory, and clothes were liable to be removed for fumigation ('stoving'). However, no medical officer was routinely present while the men stripped for a bath, and a casual's chance to see a workhouse doctor was remote. Now, after the mid nineteenth century (when typhus was rapidly fading as an epidemic threat) smallpox was the most widely feared tramp-ward contagion, but the cleansing procedures were calculated positively to fuel any outbreak of this highly infectious disease. Whilst casuals stripped for a bath their clothes might be piled up together, 'a beautiful scheme for the spread of vermin', as Jack London sardonically observed in 1902 after his visit to Whitechapel casual ward. Furthermore, new arrivals shared the same bath water:

> There were two ordinary tubs and this I know: the two men preceding had washed in the same water, and it was not changed for the two men that followed us. . . . I am certain that the twenty-two of us washed in the same water. I did no more than make a show of splashing some of this dubious liquid at myself while I hastily brushed it off with a towel wet from the bodies of other men. My equanimity was not restored by seeing the back of one poor wretch a mass of blood from attacks of vermin and retaliatory scratching.[24]

Nor was there any guarantee that the piled-up clothes would be stoved, for not all casual wards had the facilities; and as bathing supervision was lax (and attendants were even known to waive baths in cases where men's bodies were so disgusting that the other inmates would refuse to use the same water), unbathed, infested men would be using bed coverings that were changed around the ward without washing.[25] The sharing of bath water still persisted, certainly in the more rural casual wards, into the early 1930s.[26]

A pioneer in the study of tramps as smallpox spreaders was Dr Henry Armstrong, the Medical Officer of Health for Newcastle-on-Tyne. During a national smallpox epidemic in 1893 he found that two tramps who had come into Newcastle workhouse from Liverpool, were carrying the disease. This triggered off an interest in the tramp factor, and in 1894 a broad survey he conducted into large cities and other districts, indicated that smallpox outbreaks had originated, in over half the returns, with tramps. A sanitary conference of local authorities was held following Armstrong's report, and certain recommendations were made to the Local Government Board, for example that medical inspection of casual ward arrivals should be routine and compulsory; vaccination be made compulsory, if necessary, in lodging houses and casual wards, and local health officers be empowered to detain infected persons in those places. But no action was taken.[27] In 1901–3 there was another national epidemic. The Medical Officer for the West Riding of Yorkshire stated in his 1903 annual report: 'Last year there were 144 cases of the disease in the West Riding. In nearly every centre affected, the tramp was responsible for its introduction.'[28] There followed another sanitary conference in London in 1904, reiterating the earlier recommendations and this time adding for good measure that vagrants be isolated in detention colonies.[29]

It was all very well for health officers to look to central government to tighten the régime, but there was far more that the local authorities could have done with their existing powers. In 1897, for example, the Cleansing of the Person Act empowered London boroughs to establish disinfecting stations where people could go freely without recourse to a casual ward; but very few boroughs took it up.[30] However, the LCC lodging house inspectorate could claim a good job done since taking over from the police in 1894, for in the smallpox outbreak of 1901–3 it was found that smallpox for the most part was imported into the London lodging houses from elsewhere, and did not originate there; and only a fortieth of the lodging house population were affected by the disease.[31]

The 1906 Vagrancy Committee, while agreeing with many of the sanitary conference recommendations, jibbed at the compulsory vaccination of vagrants as being too authoritarian; they should be covered in a national vaccination programme instead. Some authorities had already begun offering financial inducements to tramps, or a week's free stay in a lodging house, to have themselves vaccinated, but this was abused, for tramps were going back for repeated vaccinations to multiply the reward.[32]

What was the general stamina of the tramp around 1900? Was he a sturdy, leathered vagabond, or a mess of bodily corruption? The evidence is conflicting. Body vermin were less in evidence than earlier; louse-borne typhus had all but vanished; and while typhoid was still quite common, cholera had not raged since 1866. The Salvation Army survey of London casual wards in 1903 found that 70.3 per cent were 'physically fit'. Dr Shirley Murphy, the LCC's Medical Officer, however, found that among London's male lodging house population around 1903–4 he was surveying a landscape of physical wreckage. For example, among the 45–55-year-olds the death rate from consumption was five times that among males of the same age at large; from pneumonia it was two times, and bronchitis four to five times;[33] their alcoholic debilitation I have already discussed.

Nevertheless, several witnesses before the 1906 Vagrancy Committee testified to the robustness of the vagrant; those who hung about the East End were said to be particularly well-nourished, as the working classes were notoriously generous to those apparently worse off than themselves. East End tramps were said to turn their noses up at the casual ward fare they were offered, or even refuse it because they were already full up![34] On a casual ward diet of bread, gruel and cheese a veteran vagrant could sail through a work task breaking 10 hundredweight of stones. Charles Simmons, a Local Government Board inspector, was amazed to see a 'casual' doing just that:

'Could you break stones on that?' he was asked.
'Yes sir, and he is a lazy devil that cannot do it. There is plenty of food enough to break stones on. I have done it for years and I have done it to-day and there it is.'[35]

Josiah Flynt observed that almost all the tramps he met appeared well fed; and W.H. Davies in 1908 claimed it was a myth that tramps were dirty. They got used to regular baths in the casual wards, and were forever washing themselves and their clothes in the lodging houses; indeed dirty tramps would not be admitted to a lodging house or even a Salvation Army shelter; only the mentally deranged ones were unkempt, and a decent appearance was a necessary begging aid. Davies was a lyric tramp who certainly deodorised, even romanticised, his portrayal of the lifestyle he had chosen. Against his defence of the tramp's attention to personal hygiene should be set W.A. Gape's observation how, around 1914 in Trafalgar Square, it was the filthiest tramps who seemed to get most charity.

What sort of social animal was the tramp? The 1906 Vagrancy Committee described him typically as 'unsocial and wretched': 'He has no object in life, and his very contentment with his miserable surroundings renders any improvement in his condition practically hopeless. It may be truly said that he exists "poor, nasty, mean, solitary, brutish". . . . , W.H. Davies, however, was never short of companions on the road, and Frank Jennings, a quarter of a century later, found them gregarious and fond of the company of their own kind.[36] But the writings of Brine and Davies indicate that tramps did not form permanent bonds; at some stage they would drift off on their separate ways.

The public's image of the tramp was oddly ambivalent. He could be an object of sympathy, but he was also an object of fear. The bogeyman tramp, the shaggy, rampant menace to women and children, haunted the public imagination. All sorts of local crimes were popularly ascribed to tramps: rick-burning (supposedly by disgruntled tramps, refused alms at the farmhouse door, or by careless tramps who had not put their fires or pipes out), assaults, intimidation of people at isolated houses, and rapes. Any tramp who was coincidentally in the neighbourhood could expect to be the prime initial suspect. In 1882 C.E. Trevelyan told the Howard Association how the fear of tramps in Northumberland had reached such a pitch that 'the women often lock themselves up or keep loaded guns at hand as a protection against the intrusion of tramps'.[37] Victorian and Edwardian newspapers readily splashed accounts of tramp roguery. For example, the account of the trial and imprisonment of two tramps at Skipton, Yorkshire in 1903 after going on the rampage at Kidbrook to raise drink money: 'The prisoners fairly took the village by storm. They were singing and shouting and swore at women who would not relieve them. One of them kicked a door . . .' They went off to the pub, drank their fill to the terror of the barmaid, and went off to 'beg' some more.[38]

Were they really a potential threat to women? W.H. Davies insisted that tramps were misogynistic by nature, and tended to avoid women, a point also made by Frank Jennings.[39] However, George Atkins Brine is unusually frank for a Victorian writer in admitting that the opportunity to consort with loose tramp women was one of the attractions of the vagrant life. The free and easy moral atmosphere in harvesters' camps, where the sexes mingled uninhibitedly, was also a draw for seasonal farm labourers. George Orwell in 1933 stated that tramps must learn to live without sex, unless they are in funds and can buy a prostitute. Sexual frustration, he acknowledged, might provoke occasional rapes, but was as likely to lead to homosexuality, and Orwell himself was once the object of a feeble homosexual advance in a casual ward.

The 1906 Vagrancy Committee was in fact satisfied that public fears of tramps were much exaggerated, and that they were generally responsible only for minor local offences.

The sexual fear of tramps magnified them into supposed mass breeders. The Edwardian period marked the peak of the Eugenic movement. The faster fall in the birth rate among the educated classes than among the lower orders had inspired fears of progressive racial degeneration, and the élitist Eugenists were then

mooting schemes, some of them with disturbing (though uninten-
tional) fascist overtones to us today, with a view to curbing
procreation among the unworthy. The tramp was visualised as an
unbridled sexual animal by some. In 1911 during the Embankment
crisis, one Minnie Taylor wrote on behalf of an unnamed women's
group to the Home Office urging that 'the maimed, the diseased
and the half-witted degraded creatures who swarm and promiscu-
ously reproduce their miserable degenerate kind upon the Embankment, should be removed and placed under proper supervision'.[40]
She evidently imagined a seething heap of copulators on the
pavement, going at it until the soup arrived! In 1913 Thomas
Holmes likewise wrote of feeble-minded down-and-outs mating and
saddling society with their defective progeny. As early as 1886
Robert Giffen, a senior Board of Trade official, had proposed that
such economic liabilities to society should be barred from breeding
and segregated in labour colonies.[41] And Dr Henry Armstrong
was just expressing a strand of Eugenic thinking when he suggested
to the 1906 Vagrancy Committee that tramps be castrated![42]

In fact, as tramps were overwhelmingly male and single[43] the
opportunity to mate and reproduce would have been very limited;
the circumstances of any infant's birth would not have been
conducive to its survival chances, and the 1906 Vagrancy
Committee pointed out that women tramps, once they took to the
road, rarely appeared to give birth. Scottish tinkers, who lived in
family groups, were exceptionally prolific it is true, and there was
the near-vagrant class of resident workhouse pauper 'ins-and-outs',
some of them feckless and feeble-minded single girls who left and
re-entered the workhouse at will, often pregnant on their return.[44]
But the bugbear of uncontrolled propagation among tramps was a
myth and I cannot help wondering if there was a Freudian element
in it – the 'King Kong' syndrome of projecting one's own repressed
libidinous urges in the form of some external monster-figure.

At the same time there was in the Victorian and Edwardian
period a sentimentalised treatment of the tramp that gushed out in
the wealth of Victorian and Edwardian parlour songs on the
vagabond theme. Space permits only a token selection here. They
can be broadly divided into celebrations of the freedom of tramp
life, and mawkish personal tragedies. Robert Louis Stevenson's
poem, 'The Vagabond', was put to music by several composers,[45]
and falls into the former category:

> Give the face of earth around
> And the road before me.
> Wealth I ask not, hope nor love
> Nor a friend to know me;
> All I ask is the heaven above
> And the road below me.

'The Tramp' of 1908 defiantly vaunts the carefree vagabond spirit:

> Go stick to your towns, ye city clowns
> Like rats within a cage,
> And rattle your chains as you count your gains
> Poor slaves of a weekly wage. . . .
>
> O'er vale and hill I roam at will
> I come at no man's call;
> A fetterless tramp with the world for a camp
> Monarch and lord of all. . . .[46]

Of the latter category, 'The Tramp's Story' (1893) tells of a tramp who knocks at a door seeking a crust of bread. He tells how he has been searching ages for his darling 'little May' who was lured away by a seducer from his farm.[47] 'The Tramp' (1892) watches the swells passing by in their carriages:

> Drive on my Lady fair drive on;
> Your pleasant smiling face
> Reminds me of my own lost love
> Whose name (and form) was Grace . . .

His 'lost love' was dead, and he was now desolate:

> Tramping, tramping on life's road I go
> No time for grief I cannot weep
> As tramping on I go.[48]

The music hall made a speciality of humourising ordinary folks' problems to make them bearable. The real tragedy of down-and-outs in Trafalgar Square was burlesqued in the famous song 'I live in Trafalgar Square', written in 1902, when the recession following the Boer War was setting in:

> I live in Trafalgar Square, With four lions to guard me.
> Fountains and statues all over the place
> And the 'Metropole' staring me right in the face!
> I'll own it's a trifle draughty
> But look at it this way you see,
> If it's good enough for Nelson,
> It's quite good enough for me. . . .[49]

Between the wars 'Underneath the Arches' (1932) wistfully captured the resignation of the down-and-outs:

Pavements is my pillow, no matter where I stay,
Underneath the arches I dream my dreams away.[50]

In prose, too, before 1914 there was, it seems, a vogue for 'down-and-out' romances: 'Everything had to be painted against a background of stainlessly blue sky. To get in prison was a big lark; to go hungry full of exquisite humour.'[51] Such was the curious dichotomy of public attitudes to the tramp; at some times he was the menacing wild man of the woods, at others the enviable personification of freedom.

13 A statistical capsule: tramp levels, trade and seasonal cycles

Tramp figures in the 1860s, as given in the Judicial Statistics (see Chapter 7), when set against contemporary Poor Law Board figures for casual ward usage, suggested that numbers in the wards formed about a sixth of the total tramp population of the country, and this became enshrined as the conventional formula for gauging tramp levels into Edwardian times.

The 1906 Departmental Committee on Vagrancy reckoned that in England and Wales there was a hard core of 20,000 to 30,000 permanent vagrants in a population of some 34,000,000. If the numbers of migrating work seekers were added, it estimated up to 40,000 on tramp altogether in good times, and up to 80,000 in times of recession.[1]

Scotland was relatively more tramp-ridden than England. Scotland had a regular twice-yearly tramp census conducted by the police from 1859 to June 1915.[2] The compilation has puzzling features,[3] but different statistical constructions around the turn of the century definitely pointed to a proportionately higher level of vagrancy north of the border, for which the presence of a conspicuous tinker element was partly (but only partly) responsible. Thus, in Scotland in 1893 over 9,600 vagrants were counted, but the population at 4,200,000 was only a seventh that of England's.[4]

Can we automatically assume a firm correlation between levels of casual ward use and trade cycles? In the last chapter I made several references to possible, or probable links, but suggested that other factors may have been involved as well. Some more examples should further undermine over-confident assumptions about such a correlation. In the bad year of 1861, when the cotton famine was beginning to bite, tramp ward figures were lower than in the improving years of 183 and 1864. In the period 1884–6 there was an increase of usage, and this admittedly was a period of depression; but the immediate impact of the 1882 Casual Poor Act (see Chapter 10) may have been wearing off, too. In the aftermath of the Boer War from 1902 there was a rise in vagrant ward use; on the night of 1 January 1902 7,840 occupied the wards, and on 1 January 1908 10,436. This was an economically parlous period, to be sure, but just as the vagrant ward numbers are likely to have been previously reduced by recruitments into the Boer campaign, so a returning flotsam of war veterans after 1902 doubtless contributed to the reversing trend.

The fluctuations in casual ward use were far narrower than the variations in unemployment, which were estimated to range between 200,000 in good years and up to 1,000,000 in slumps in the nineteenth and early twentieth centuries.[5] This and the 1906 Vagrancy Committee's estimate of tramp number limits indicated that only a tiny proportion of unemployed workmen ever left home to go on the road. W.H. Dawson in 1910 said that there was 'no prima facie justification for supposing that trade depression causes any number of genuine workmen to join the highway population'. This relative lack of fluidity suggested that the tramp wards were populated by a hard core of habituals, regardless of trade conditions, according to the Metropolitan Poor Law Inspectors in 1916.[6] The vast majority of unemployed stayed at home where they could get some kind of poor relief, and where their chances of finding work again in areas where they were known, whether skilled shipyard workers or unskilled dockers, seemed best. In sum, while there appears to be a link between casual ward usage and trade conditions, this is by no means hard and fast.

Nor was there any consistent national pattern of seasonal fluctuations in casual ward use. The 1929 Departmental Committee on Casual Poor Relief did state that, broadly, December was a low month, and that figures rose towards May. Usage fluctuated thereafter, though August and September were peak months. The interpretation of this is that tramps were leaving winter quarters to go on the roads in the warmer weather, and migrant seasonal farm workers swelled the numbers in the late summer harvest months.[7] The 'cuckoo tramps' who stayed in their local workhouse as winter resident paupers, and ventured forth each spring,[8] were said by the Committee not to amount to many. The Committee acknowledged that local factors could alter the pattern. Thus, Yorkshire, with its collection of racecourses, at Pontefract and Catterick for example, felt the swell of vagrants in the racing season between April and September; in south Lancashire the 'heavy' months were December to March, possibly because the vagrants who followed the holiday-makers to the Lake District returned to their winter haunts in the industrial towns.[9]

14 Men's tramp ward underlife to 1939

In 1847–8 a Poor Law Commission inspector, W.G. Boase, was assigned to a field survey of vagrants travelling the main route between south Wales and London, via Bristol. This was, as already observed, a time of a worryingly escalating resort to the casual wards, and Boase's brief was to ascertain the vagrant types and their exploitation of the casual wards. His report in 1848,[1] together with those of other regional inspectors, forms the earliest depiction of tramp ward life; we have to wait until 1866 for another set of inspectors' reports, most notably that of Andrew Doyle, for comparable colour.[2] That year also marked the publication of the earliest undercover 'investigative' exposés of the casual wards by private fact-finders: James Greenwood's article 'A Night in the Workhouse', published in the *Pall Mall Gazette*, and Dr J.H. Stallard's pamphlet, 'The Female Vagrant and her Lodging'.

The findings of 1848 revealed widespread laxity and abuse. Boase classified tramp ward types as first the seasoned professional beggars; then the young semi-criminal 'idle apprentice' types, who in hooligan gangs, often accompanied by female hangers-on, terrorised the casual wards with their disruptive behaviour, window-breaking, swearing and bawdiness. Next came the Irish as a rapidly swelling element. In Inspector Grenville Piggott's region along southern England between Sussex and Dorset, the casual wards had relieved 16,135 English, 2,009 Irish and 389 Scots in the six months to 30/9/1846. In the six months to 30 September 1847 the figures were 32,683, 11,548 and 706 respectively. Whilst the Irish were here as refugees from the famine and as harvest workers Boase criticised their eagerness to avail themselves of any public relief on offer.

Eighty per cent of all tramps, he found, were male: ninety per cent of casual ward patrons he classed as 'undeserving'. There may have been, of course, a degree of prejudice in this; though Andrew Doyle's later survey brought him to precisely the same conclusion, and a Metropolitan Police investigation into casual relief seekers in 1869 also considered 90 per cent to be scroungers and wasters.[3]

110

Boase found the confiscation of valuables and luxuries to be widely ignored. The porter dogsbodies who would have to do this risked assault and felt that the game was not worth the candle. In any case the tramps were masters of guile. They would 'bank' valuables with shopkeepers and marine store owners before applying, and habitually lied about their means and identities. If workhouses became awkward towards any vagrant who stayed at the same ward on successive nights they risked having their windows smashed. (Remember that county constabularies did not become mandatory till 1856; rural workhouses were very vulnerable.)

Casual ward accommodation was very primitive. Usually, said Boase, the wards were one-storey buildings: 'In general they have brick floors and guard-room beds with loose straw and rugs for males, and iron bedsteads with straw tics for the females.' Washing facilities were crude: sometimes a pump had to suffice, and no soap or towels were provided. The wards stank from the tramps' bodies; they tended to stuff up whatever ventilation there was (presumably through lack of heating). Tramps were riddled with body vermin and VD. At Newbury Base Boase found that the women slept in the workhouse coach house where the hearse was kept, and had wattle hurdles strewn with straw to sleep on; the men slept in the stables. At Bath the tramp room was directly beneath the workhouse fever ward, and at Marlborough 32 tramps were found sleeping in a room 16 feet by 9. Typhus, the 'Irish fever', a side-effect of the famine influx, was then raging; and tramp wards helped to spread the disease among resident paupers, too.

Work tasks were half-heartedly enforced; rural Unions in particular were only too keen to see potential troublemakers on their way and did not want to provoke disturbances by enforcing discipline. This in turn added to the attractions of casual wards to scroungers, it was alleged, and Sir John Walsham's Report for East Anglia and the East Midlands illustrated the salutary deterrent effect of work tasks. At North Witchford Union supplies of oakum ran out and work tasks were discontinued temporarily. The 'telegraphic despatch' among the vagrant fraternity brought a surge in applications there from 20 a week to 75 within three weeks, the numbers falling off again when oakum-picking was later resumed. This is paralleled by an even more dramatic instance at St Saviour's Union in London in 1842. The Union had recently become over-liberal in admitting vagrant applicants for fear of falling foul of the Poor Law Commission's strict circular of 1839 warning of disciplinary action if destitutes were turned away. Within a few weeks the numbers relieved each week had risen from 549 to a peak of 4,281. In desperation the Union introduced compulsory stone-breaking. In the three weeks prior to its introduction 11,111 persons were relieved. In the three weeks after, the figure was 776![4]

Nearly 20 years later in 1866 inspectors' reports conveyed much the same picture. In Dorset and Hampshire nearly a third of the Unions imposed no work task. In others it could be as little as half an hour, and this was typical nationwide.[5]

Andrew Doyle, reporting for the West Midlands and Welsh borders, explained that it was administratively cheaper for each individual Union to backslide and let vagrants go on their way 'than to provide stones or oakum and to pay a task-master, without whose aid the labour test is merely make-believe'. As 20 years before, the rural Unions were at risk from refractory inmates if they tried to impose a work task. Doyle believed that three-quarters of tramp ward habitués were 'thieves of every sort, deserters from the army, bad characters discharged from the army as such, runaway apprentices and idle vagabonds of every kind, who will not work'.

The master of Newport (Salop) Union told Doyle of his experiences with inmates who deliberately tore their clothes to get issued with replacements. He stopped this by impounding their clothing on admission and standing over them while they dressed in the morning. In June 1862 he had been instrumental in getting two tramps a fortnight in jail for refusing a work task. In January 1864 they arrived again, and when introduced to their task 'they deliberately threw two blocks of wood through a window, smashing three squares of glass'. For this they got 21 days' jail.

The casual wards were used as venues for plotting crimes, and as hideouts for criminal fugitives. The same workhouse master had sheltered two tramps who, he learned later, had burned down a haystack in revenge for the farmer's refusal to assist them when they came begging at his door; and more recently some youths had arrived on the run after stealing some workmen's tools.

The master of Runcorn workhouse had a narrow escape from one violent inmate in March 1862:

> John Law, aged about 30, was taken before a magistrate for refusing to pick his oakum. While in court he threw an open clasped knife at me (stiletto fashion); I only saved myself by ducking behind the witness box; he then rushed out, seized the knife again, and was pushing at me when he was secured by the police.

Different sources fed Doyle the same stories; of vagrants turning up dead at night, roaring drunk; of foul jokes and obscene singing; of vandalism, clothes tearing and insolence; of the swapping of information about the relative attractions of different tramp wards; of the boasting of crimes; of the raggedness and vermin. Sexually they were unrestrained and even tried to force their way into the women's ward. The master of Walsall workhouse related an incident when a man arrived enquiring whether a particular girl, a prostitute, was staying there. The porter said 'yes'.

'Where is she?'
The porter replied 'upstairs'. He said, 'I am going to sleep with her'. The porter said, 'I am sure you are not'. He said, 'I shall' and was impertinent, and I was fetched. . . . He was very abusive, and said he would have his 3d, as he gave her 3d before she came in, to sleep with her. I sent for the policeman but he left before the policeman came.

The walls were strewn with graffiti. Tramps had a compulsion to leave their mark, or to use the walls as notice boards for passing on messages and friendly warnings:

'Londonderry Ginger was here on the 7th October 1865 bound to Cardiff for the winter . . .'
'Madman was here on the 3rd June 1865, bound for Bangor . . .'
'Beware of the Cheshire tramps, Spanish Jem, Kildare Kem, Dublin Dick, Navvy Jack, Dick Graven, the shrewd Cheshire tramps . . .'

Some were comments on the merits of different workhouses. One scribbler, 'Bow Street', was a prolific contributor. He wrote favourably of Seisdon Union tramp ward at Trysull:

> Certainly the meals are paltry and mean,
> But the beds are nice and clean;
> Men, don't tear these beds, sheets or rugs
> For there are neither lice, fleas or bugs
> At this clean little union at Trysull.

Of another Union he is far more critical:

> The room is large, but the windows are small
> But that don't matter much at all, at all.
> A pint of skilly [gruel] for your supper to drink
> But of sleep you cannot get a wink.
> You may lay on the boards or the chilly floor
> About as warm as a North American shore.
> The old bed is full of fleas all alive:
> I killed in number about five times five. . . .

Later in the century, a witty mock epitaph was found, inscribed by a self-confessed 'Weary Willie':

Here lies a poor beggar who has always tired
For he lived in a world where too much is required;
Friends, grieve not for me that death doth us sever
For I am going to do nothing for ever and ever.[6]

James Greenwood also conveyed the sordidness of the vagrant
ward when he went in the guise of a tramp to Lambeth workhouse
in 1866, a year or so after the legislation promoting the expansion
of London's workhouse accommodation. He was obliged to bath on
entry in water the consistency and colour of 'weak mutton broth'.
His clothes were bundled, and he was conducted in a nightshirt to
a dormitory 30 feet by 30 with no ceiling, for the roof tiles, 'furred
with the damp and filth that reeked within', were exposed above.
The walls were dingy and whitewashed and the flagstone floor was
'so thickly encrusted with filth that I mistook it at first for a floor of
natural earth'. The beds were hay-filled bags. Like Doyle he tells of
the villainousness of the other inmates and their immoral talk, but
he also emphasises that among the gathering there were harmless,
pathetic types who cringed from the villains they were forced into
close quarters with.

After a breakfast of bread and bitter skilly, they were put to
corn-grinding. Supervision was perfunctory and the men lounged
about when not watched. They were openly rude to the miller who
oversaw them, singing to the tune of 'John Brown's Body':

We'll hang up the miller on a sour apple tree . . .
And then go grinding on
Glory, glory hallelujah [etc.]

In *The Wilds of London* in 1874, Greenwood's chapter on
'Mr Bumble and his Enemy the Casual' bitterly attacked the
blinkered officiousness of the task-masters who put genuine
unfortunates in the wards to the same hard labour as the
scroungers: 'it is on the novice at oakum-picking, the tender-
fingered worn-out tailor, the decayed clerk, or worker at a trade
requiring mental rather than muscular exertions that the full
weight of Mr Bumble's whip falls', while the hardened casual ward
veteran takes it all in his stride.

Under Mr Bumble were the petty tramp ward officers, the
tramp-major and the porter, figures who were hated and feared by
casuals, and were recognisably the same stereotypes in the early
1930s as in the 1870s. The tramp-major was a vagrant who in
return for basic bed and board in the workhouse was employed on
the poacher-gamekeeper principle as the workhouse master's
minion. To the other tramps he was a nasty, lickspittle renegade,
'invariably a man of the bully type',[7] 'scab-casual' and 'lower than
a snake's belly' are other printable epithets[8] and Hippo Neville's

book *Sneak Thief on the Road* (1935) contains a heartfelt inscription he found on a casual ward wall:

> O Lord above
> Send down a dove
> With wings as sharp as a razor
> To cut the throat
> Of that dirty goat
> Who calls himself the tramp-major.

It was the tramp-major who supervised the bath, took the clothes, handed out the nightshirts, escorted you to the worktask and dished out the bread and skilly. Casuals found it wise to tip him a penny on entry; for this he might waive the bath, give you a larger slice of bread or find you a better 'kip'.[9] The tramp-major and the porter rough-tongued and intimidated the new arrivals. Frank Jennings in 1932 wrote of one porter who greeted the wretched applicants with the snarl: 'You're a precious lot of lazy lubbers. If I had my way I'd crack a few of you on the head with a hammer'.[10] George Orwell had a similar experience at the hands of a 'great bawling ruffian of a porter . . . who treated us like cattle', and mentions an incident when one morning a feeble-minded tramp who had just been discharged refused to go and clung to the railings, protesting he was too tired, 'until the tramp-major had to dislodge him and start him with a kick'.

In 1929 Thomas Mason, a 61-year-old 'confirmed tramp' prepared a semi-literate but keenly felt statement about tramp ward treatment for the Governor of Exeter Prison to present to the Departmental Committee on Casual Poor Relief: 'there is a lacky knocking about the workhouse what they call a Tramp-Major . . . he is a dirty Broot as a rool he stops in for a month for doing part of the Porter's work for a Bit of tobacco.' He told of how men soaked to the skin came into the wards and were turned out again next day with their clothes undried, and of a personal incident when he caught a tramp-major going through his trouser pockets while he was bathing, and struck him. Pilfering from tramps, he alleges, was common among these petty officials – 'these masters is all on the get rich quick'.[11]

Mason was not the only worm who turned. A much more serious eruption took place at an unnamed but particularly vile casual ward somewhere between Watford and London, as described by W.A. Gape in 1936. Its skilly he described as looking like 'billposter's paste touched up with a little washing blue, smelling like stale washing water and tasting strongly of soap'. The cells stank; there were no beds, only blankets; soap was not provided and the washhouse towels were dirty and wet. A 'skilly revolt' had broken out there. An inmate poured the indigestible mess over the assistant master's head, and his companions gave him a leg-up over the workhouse wall before he could be arrested. When the porter ordered the men back to their cells he was punched in the stomach, and a 70-year-old veteran went up, spat in his face, exclaiming 'Ten long years of torture I've suffered through you. . . . Take that!' and kicked him in the ribs. This brief insurrection was followed by a mass break-out, before the police could arrive.

Sometimes, however, a friendly bond developed between ward attendants and the regulars. Frank Jennings in 1926 recorded a jovial exchange he overheard in a London casual ward:

> 'Hullo Shiney! You've called again?'
> 'Yus I 'ave,' came the reply, 'an' quite time too. Look at the blinkin' wevver outside! Safe 'ome at last for me!'
> 'Well,' went the porter, 'get ready for your bath. I know you like them.'
> 'Not ser bloomin' likely! I 'ad one last year!'
> 'Aw right, 'ave yer own way agen! It's spoilin' good water, though!'

A common lay-out of cellular wards was to have, in place of a communal labour yard, individual stone-breaking cells, a few feet square, leading directly from the dormitory cell through an intercommunicating door. There at the bottom of the outer wall would be a grille giving onto the courtyard. The inmate worked in isolation, breaking the stones and pushing them out through the grille, which served as a gauge.[12] Late Victorian and Edwardian casual wards ranged from bleak to the barbaric, and in the rural Unions were generally at their most primitive and lax in the matters of bathing, 'stoving' of clothes and work tasks. C.W. Craven, a bookseller in Keighley, Yorkshire, thought he would sample his local casual ward in 1887. After the usual preliminaries he was given four ounces of 'Tommy' (bread) as supper and ushered into a pitch-black dormitory: 'My bare feet slipped on what I afterwards found was vagrants' spittle on the stone floor, and the sensation was cold and slimy. . . . I felt glad when my hand touched the boarding on which my limbs were to rest for the night.' He was naked, and his 'bed' consisted of bare planking with a wooden pillow and rugs for cover. There were half a dozen others in the ward. Though the combined body odour was unpleasant he found that they were decent types – all working men with trade skills down on their luck. They talked of their experiences. One spoke of Skipton casual ward, where an enormous rat had carried off his bread. Another suffered from acute diarrhoea, and whereas at Wakefield he had been given medicine, here his pleas to see the workhouse doctor had been ignored 'and the only effort made to relieve the pain was by giving him a tin of warm water to drink'.

Next morning they were roused at 6.45 and Craven had a chance
to see the facilities. The dormitory wall was whitewashed, though
scribbled over. At one end was a passageway leading to a bath, a
lavatory tub and a towel on a roller. After a breakfast of bread and
water they were allotted their day's labour task of monotonous
corn-grinding (for most), but were allowed no water to drink whilst
cranking, despite the thirst they worked up. Craven's opinion was
that, allowing for the shortcomings of the vagrants themselves, 'the
lowest of mankind deserve better treatment than that accorded to
pigs, dogs and other animals of creation'.

A similar grim picture was painted over 20 years later in 1909 by
the journalist Everard Wyrall who went in disguise to sample three
casual wards, including a 'notorious' London one. He has been
accused by one academic of deliberately selecting the worst
examples to furnish himself with lurid copy.[13] The horrendous
work tasks he describes were, it is claimed, not typical, as so many
casual wards were slack, but be that as it may, this does not
detract from its value as an insight into the tramp wards at their
worst.

At the first Ward he visited – he does not say where – there was
the usual routine of waiting in an outhouse until admission,
bathing (the water was at least warm, though there was no
privacy) and the issue of a thin nightshirt. The first night was
spent in a cell; its amenity he describes as 'A low wooden bench,
four evil-looking blankets, a hunch of bread, all dimly outlined in
the fitful glare from one small gas jet in the centre of the passage
outside, and a window a few inches square, iron-barred'. Next
morning, after a 'breakfast' of a wedge of bread, the inmates were
allotted their work tasks by the tramp-major whom he summed up
in suspiciously stereotyped terms as 'a sour looking man with the
face of a bully and a coward, one who knew he had the whip hand
and meant to use it'. Some were given timber sawing, but the
majority got stone-breaking, on a meagre ration of bread, cheese
and water. One lame man so assigned asked to see a doctor, 'but
he was talking to a brick wall'. Another casual, an ex-soldier,
protested against being treated this way after serving his country,
but was browbeaten into submission by the tramp-major. The
latter, on returning later, expressed dissatisfaction with the amount
of work done by the ex-soldier and summoned a policeman to have
him arrested for wilfully refusing to perform his task. The
policeman tried to be sympathetic: 'Come quietly, mate . . . You'll
be better in chokey than this 'ere 'ole. Chokey's all right compared
with this . . .'

Wyrall records that regulations authorised stone-breaking for
men up to 70 if so directed, and witnessed a pathetic character in
his sixties who could not undertake it being brusquely turned out
by the callous tramp-major. His description of stone-*pounding* – a

far more punishing task – has been cited in Chapter 10.

This particular ward – as was common among those with cells – transferred inmates to a dormitory after the first night of detention. (Cells were employed more as a precaution against physical than moral contagion, and once the officers felt sure that a newcomer would not start an epidemic he was transferred to the dormitory.) This was a dubious privilege for Wyrall. His hammock smelt so badly that he chose to sleep on the floor, and he spent a restless night disturbed by the noises of other inmates.

In the next tramp ward he visited the 'beds' were rows of tarred boxes on a platform 18 inches above the floor; again he received the same curt treatment from officialdom. At his last ward, in London, he insisted that the work task was to break half a ton of granite!

What sort of people were generally found in the casual wards? We saw in the last chapter that only a minute fraction of the genuinely unemployed ever seem to have gone on tramp, even in times of depression. The skilled artisan was the type of tramping workseeker least likely to end up there. Early trade unions gave travelling members overnight shelter in local lodges; pubs were commonly used as venues, hence inn signs like the 'Carpenter's Arms' or 'Bricklayer's Arms'. Later they offered travelling allowances; and with trade unions' own unemployment benefit schemes and labour bureaux by the end of the nineteenth century, the skilled worker at least could feel fairly cushioned from the casual ward.[14]

Migratory thieves and professional beggars on their seasonal circuits used the wards as a convenience. Ragged school attendances slumped in the spring as youngsters ventured forth to Cheltenham, Bath and other spas, seaside resorts and race meetings; anywhere, in sum, where the gentry congregated and pickings were to be had.[15] Scenes of excitement and disturbance, or a public spectacle, would also bring the tramp-beggars in hordes; London experienced such an influx during the great Chartist manifestation in 1848.[16] They were only too visible a presence on the country highways. In 1882 Henry Fletcher MP complained of the vagrant armies that made their seasonal journey along the south coast towards Wales and then back east: 'Day after day, week after week, he had seen these men tramping along the roads, being nothing but a nuisance to the labouring classes whom they jeered at as they passed, asking why they should work when bed and board could be had for nothing.'[17]

By the Edwardian period when conditions were probably more settled, it was by and large only the failed thieves who were found in the casual wards, for the successful ones used the lodging houses.[18] But they were still possessed of much low cunning. Wily tramps now had to use subterfuge, not open defiance, to cock a snook at casual ward rules. Diverse were the tricks to outwit the search for contraband: pre-arrangements with mates outside to throw tobacco in over the walls; the concealing of cigarettes in slots in linen collars, or under a trilby hat band, pressed flat; the stowing of money in packets of tea and sugar, which they were allowed to keep; and in one case at least the concealment of articles in a hollowed-out compartment in a crutch. The attendants, indeed, were not uncommonly armed with hooked rods to probe the toe-space of vagrants' shoes.[19]

Many vagrants were out of circulation from the wards since they swelled the prison population as petty offenders. Discharged prisoners looking for shelters and rehabilitation did at least have the help of the Discharged Prisoners' Aid Societies which had been given statutory recognition in 1862.[20] By the 1890s both the Salvation Army and Church Army had DPA schemes as part of their workshop and labour home network.[21] In 1891 the 61 recognised DPA societies helped over 18,000 released prisoners.[22] It was sourly noted among down-and-outs that the DPA Societies were more interested in helping 'real' criminals than those convicted for short spells under the Vagrancy Act, and the 'Bath Herald' quoted one cynical tramp: 'Don't go to prison for begging; steal, you'll be better treated and stand a chance of being helped when you come out'.[23] The DPA Societies, it seems, found the real criminals more worthwhile to help as they had more enterprise than shiftless vagrants[24] who just drifted back from the prisons to the casual wards.

Seasonal farm workers filled the casual wards on their itineraries, and when they reached their destinations they lived in communal semi-shanty conditions on the farms. The free and easy moral atmosphere was quite an inducement for footloose young men and girls.[25] The hop-pickers from London's East End made the seasonal exodus southwards to Kent and Sussex, and they converged in late summer on London Bridge, carrying or towing their belongings, trailing their children, and piling into the cut-rate 'hoppers' trains'. The south-eastern counties braced themselves for this annual invasion by beery Cockneys looking for work, and the casual wards were at the sharp end. By 1906, however, 'hopping' was becoming a more civilised excursion: farmers were tending to pre-arrange work by correspondence with known families, and assured shelter on their land made it possible to avoid the casual wards.[26]

Casual wards were also populated by 'local' non-migratory tramps. Sometimes, even where a notorious vagrant had a legal settlement in a particular parish, the workhouse would not allow him the use of the main body of the house. However, other Unions allowed themselves to put up with the irritating 'ins and outs', regular paupers who came and went from the house as they pleased.[27]

London with its endowment of casual wards, charitable refuges and soup kitchens bred its own species of localised vagrants, the roundsmen who lived by circulating around the casual wards and shelters.[28] Though liable to longer detention in the casual wards after 1871 as 'habituals' they become inured to the work task régime and looked on the London wards as 'home'. In 1880 of about 40,000 adults relieved in London's casual wards 16,000 were 'habituals' (that is, using them twice or more in a month).[29] The 1906 Vagrancy Committee remarked on the distinctiveness of these London roundsmen. By then the casual wards had sufficiently improved to make them more attractive than the charity shelters, which the roundsmen disdained to use;[30] Wyrall's granite-hewing ward must have been a gross exception to the rule! They were a particular administrative nuisance, for at each return the same procedure of bathing, medical inspection and stoving of clothes had to be repeated, even if discharged the night before.[31] The 'roundsmen' were also a phenomenon in other great urban centres like Birmingham and Manchester; unlike the casuals found in the rural wards they did not even *pretend* to be on their way somewhere.[32] The Charity Organisation's Society's survey of St Giles and Wandsworth casual wards in 1887–8 revealed only a miniscule proportion deemed 'helpable'[33] and several witnesses told the 1906 Vagrancy Committee that genuine workseekers formed two to three per cent only of the London wards. The remainder were casual and intermittent workers plus a hard core of cadgers and petty thieves. Contrast a *rural* Union cited by the 1909 Poor Law enquiry: between 1905–7 of about 1,600 casuals relieved a year, 1,000 were 'navvies' or 'general labourers'; the remainder was made up of a miscellany of occupations – masons, carpenters, seamen, grooms and the like – and only 50 were thought to be professional tramps.[34]

Among occupational groups, navvies and seamen made the most regular use of casual wards, as the nature of their jobs made travelling unavoidable.[35] When they had the funds they preferred the common lodging houses, but navvies were notoriously heavy drinkers and might find themselves without the resources for the latter. Navvies were also generous to down-and-outs, who clung to them like camp followers as they travelled from one construction project to another, sharing the casual wards.[36]

In Chapter 9 I referred to the conspicuous presence of ex-soldiers in doss-houses and casual wards. Tramp ward censuses of 1896–7 revealed that a quarter of the inmates claimed to be ex-soldiers, though only a fifth of this proportion could prove it – the implication being that many possibly gave false information to appear less disreputable.[37]

15   The 'perambulatory dustbin': homeless women and their shelter to 1939

Adult females formed only a small proportion of all 'tramps'. Between 1833 and 1843 of all vagrants taken into custody by the Metropolitan Police, only a quarter were female.[1] In 1845 casual wards outside London totted up 247,337 cases of relief of males against 39,539 female cases,[2] and the Judicial Statistics in the 1860s indicated that among the over-16s women accounted for between a quarter and a third of all known tramps.

There seems to be some evidence that the proportion of women was in long-term decline. Thus in London casual wards in 1880 30,874 adult males were relieved as against 8,633 adult females.[3] On 1 January 1891 there were 4,204 men and 553 women in the casual wards of England and Wales, and on the same night in 1908 the figures were 9,272 and 986 respectively.[4] Women, as judged by casual ward use, appear to have fallen to 11 or 12 per cent of the total. But was there a higher percentage of women in the common lodging houses, or sleeping rough? Although W.G. Boase in 1848 reckoned that male tramps sent their womenfolk into the casual wards for 'security' while they went to the lodging houses (if they could afford it), Edwardian observers suggested the reverse: that the men put their women and children into the lodging houses, holding any money while they went into the casual wards.[5]

Perhaps this was because lodging houses were by now better regulated and safer. A Gloucestershire police survey between 1878 and 1886 indicated that the female percentage (all ages) in common lodging houses was slightly higher than in the casual wards – 28 per cent as against 21 per cent.[6] On 18 February 1910 in the LCC's registered and municipal lodging houses, 18,111 men's beds, 1,415 women's and 177 married couples' were actually occupied.[7] Moreover, the proportion of unoccupied beds was highest among 'single' women's. Does this further indicate the relative fewness of female vagrants, or was the higher price of women's beds (as we shall soon see) a deterrent? If the latter were true we should expect to find a much higher proportion of women

121

sleeping rough. The LCC homelessness censuses from 1904 provide some indication (though the street searches were of limited scope). Thus, on the night of 10 February 1910 2,510 men and 220 women were found in the streets and in rough sit-up shelters. On that night also 1,405 men and 194 women were in Salvation Army and Church Army Labour Homes.[8] Thus even among the out-in-the-colds women formed only a tiny percentage of the male figure. It is true that after 1911, with an improvement in the trade and a rationalised, centralised placement service for London down-and-outs operating from the new Embankment Night Office, the numbers of male sleepers-out did fall more dramatically than their female counterparts; on 14 February 1913 there were 522 men to 127 women. Of those who did seek free shelter in the casual wards the fall in numbers was sharper than among men. Thus on the night of 15 January 1909 there were 1,001 men and 184 women in London's casual wards; on 24 October 1913 the figures were down to 352 and 46 respectively.[9]

The apparent decline in female vagrancy both absolutely and in comparison with male vagrancy since the 1840s may have had something to do with the fall in Irish immigration, most specifically the practice of Irish seasonal workers of leaving their womenfolk to follow them separately.

But why should vagrants have been overwhelmingly male? Men were more venturesome and footloose, and women more home-rooted; women tended to put up with home stresses, whereas men were more likely to walk out, and Mary Higgs suggested that women had an income from prostitution to fall back on when desperate.[10] This might explain a statistical puzzle. Police estimates in the Judicial Statistics of the 1860s showed that below 16, girls accounted for nearly half of all juvenile tramps; above 16, as noted, this fell to below one third. Allowing for the unreliability of police figures and the fuzziness of their distinctions between 'tramps' and 'prostitutes', this might be accounted for by maturing girls shifting to the category of 'prostitutes' in the police returns. Also, women overwhelmingly more than men came to the poor law as 'settled' paupers rather than as vagrants. As women were lower-paid and had the care of children they received more official sympathy when it came to outdoor relief (that is, relief at home as opposed to the workhouse). Thus on 1 July 1882 there were 13,095 able-bodied men on out-relief compared with 61,600 able-bodied women; 6,301 and 11,948 respectively were on indoor relief.[11] On 1 January 1907 2,528 men and 59,712 women were on outdoor relief.[12] G. Boase in 1848 found the female element in the casual wards largely composed of low-grade Irish, prostitutes and young teenage runaways, but he believed that the proportion of sympathetic cases was higher than in the male wards. He described one pathetic case, a recently widowed mother of an infant who was on her way north, where her child could be cared for while she found a job. By contrast with the dirty Irish women and their dysenteric children, she tried to cling to the shreds of decency: 'She asked for some water to wash her infant and I shall not readily forget her look of disgust at being offered the only vessel, a dirty broken basin, just used by the Irish mothers for the same purpose'.

Andrew Doyle in 1866 was also told of the conspicuous prostitute element among female casuals – the hangers-on of the tearaways described in the last chapter. The sheer physical squalor of the life-broken and degraded physical specimens in the London wards of that time emerges in the first under-cover exposé of women's casual wards by 'Ellen Stanley' on behalf of Dr J.H. Stallard, a noted campaigner for improvements in work-house infirmaries.[13] The conditions at Newington and Whitechapel casual wards (probably the worst) were horrific: bedding of straw-filled canvas bags laid in wooden troughs, crawling with vermin in overcrowded, ill-ventilated wards; a single latrine bucket in the ward, with women queueing all night with cramps and diarrhoea (1866 was the time of a national cholera epidemic); no washing facilities, soap or towels; skilly and almost inedible black bread as a meal; and the oakum-picking work task interrupted by women picking vermin off their clothes and bodies. Stanley was shocked by the physical condition of the inmates. At Newington she encountered a filthy ragged woman who had not washed for weeks: 'there she sat, tearing her skin to pieces, and on her back were sores as large as your hand. . . . The stench was terrific'. Generally she found the women plagued with scabies and 'Pharaoh flights' (fleas). At Lambeth (where there was at least a bath, though the bedding was verminous) one inmate advised her that it was healthier to sleep rough in the summer when infestation in the wards was at its highest, and to come in only in the winter.

At the turn of the century the campaign to improve accommodation for homeless women was associated with the name of Mary Higgs (1854–1937), the wife of a Congregational minister at Oldham. Her welfare work in Oldham brought her face to face with the problems of female down-and-outs; she helped to found a local YWCA and a 'model' women's lodging house, and in 1903 went with a friend, disguised as tramps, on a fact-finding mission, subsequently published as *Five Days and Five Nights as a Tramp* and *A Northern Tramp Ward*.[14] (Her other publications before and after the First World War, are listed in the bibliography.) Her concerns covered women's lodging houses, and the plight of the young homeless of both sexes struggling in the post-war depression. Her theme was the need for more charitable and municipal hostels for women where they would be morally better protected. The squalor of the women's casual wards, she claimed, was peculiarly demoralising to women. Women more than men needed to keep themselves looking neat to find work; in the casual wards work tasks had to be performed in their own clothes, making them even shabbier when they were discharged. Her recommendation before the 1906 Departmental Committee on Vagrancy was that women's casual wards be shut, and that female vagrants should be admitted directly into the more salubrious main body of the workhouse where the issue of a uniform would protect their own clothing; this was endorsed in the Report, but was not implemented. (Frank Gray in 1931 criticised this proposal as exposing resident paupers to the risks of disease.) Her experiences of her tramp ward tour were retailed before the Committee. She found that the male attendants were apt to bully the down-trodden women and even make improper advances. At Dewsbury workhouse the porter leeringly propositioned that she was 'Just the right age for a bit of funning; come down to me later in the evening', and tried to kiss her companion. A woman there told Higgs of another workhouse where the women tramps were at the mercy of a male attendant who 'did what he liked with them'. At Tame Street, Manchester, casual ward, the porter 'bullyragged' and insulted the applicants to deter them. 'You've no business to be here imposing on the rates', he snapped. 'Do you know I could give you three months for it?' Though Mary posed as a respectable married woman, he insinuated she was a bad character, and warned her before grudgingly letting her through: 'See you don't come here again. I shall know your face and it will be the worse for you if you do.'

The wards she visited varied in detail, but the following gives a representative idea of the conditions she encountered. At Tame Street she was allowed to bathe in six inches of water. Whilst at Dewsbury there was no stoving at all (and casuals' clothes were stored together in a cupboard at Tame Street). At Tame Street blankets and night dresses were stoved but not cleaned after use, and were rotated round the ward. Wire mattress mesh beds she found particularly uncomfortable, as the metal drew the body heat from below; elsewhere she had to sleep on bare wooden planks. The latrine might just be a bucket in the ward. One interesting contrast she made was that while in the lodging houses you have the opportunity to clean your clothes but not your body, in the casual ward it was the other way round. Bed was at 7.30 pm, though late arrivals would disturb the sleep, and they rose at 5.30 am.

For work tasks like scrubbing the wards they got bread and gruel. The latter varied in quality; some times it was sour from having been prepared the previous day and allowed to stand; and it really needed to be washed down with water or tea (not provided). The food was inadequate. Tramps who had been on the road for a considerable time, having to submit to several nights' detention at a time on this diet and forced to do work tasks each day, should, she surmised, suffer from malnutrition.

Higgs met some desperately sorry characters in a northern tramp ward. There was 'Granny' for example, an aged and rheumaticky wreck with bandaged legs and a bad cough; a widow whose unemployed son could no longer keep her so she was reduced to tottering between tramp wards, begging for a living; and another who lived by charring and selling bootlaces. All in all a pathetic collection of worn-out doormats, some the worse for drink, the perpetual objects of bullying and insolence, drifting helplessly till the final quietus of a pauper's grave.

Commercial lodging houses presented their own problems and dangers to women. Women's beds were on average more expensive than men's. Thus in 1905, whilst most men's beds in London were below 6d a night, women's were 6d or more. Sydney Hallifax's *Annals of a Doss House* in 1900 tells of one tragedy in consequence. A girl named as 'Ellen S—' had, through an accident at work, been reduced to peddling for a living and descended to a lodging house existence. One night when queuing outside the 'Phoenix' with 6d for a bed, she was told there were only 'married' beds left at 8d. An umbrella mender in the queue propositioned her over this, but as a virtuous girl she refused and slept out. She was arrested for vagrancy, and the shame of her short spell in Holloway jail so brazened her that she finally agreed to take up with the umbrella mender for the sake of a bed at the 'Phoenix' – where she was later found murdered. Mary Higgs went undercover to sample the lodging houses, as she had the casual wards. In her *Three Nights in a Women's Lodging House* (1905) she told of a house where most lodgers were prostitutes. Around 10 pm they were making themselves up to go out on the streets; many girls came in very late, drunken and singing. This 'slatternly, dissolute-looking' collection socialised in the kitchen, 'smoking cigarettes, boasting of drinks or drinking, using foul language, singing music hall songs, or talking vileness'. Another lodging was even worse. Here a men's and a women's establishment adjoined each other, and 'through the open door we caught a glimpse of a girl who was dressing, and who attracted some attention from passers-by, by her condition of half-undress'. In the women's kitchen two large tins did universal service for washing kitchen utensils, laundry and feet. The women were tarted-up and evidently prostitutes; their conversation was lewd, and men from the house next door sometimes hung about in the passage.

In *Where Shall She Live?* (1910) Mrs Higgs highlighted the scandal of the so-called 'married couples' beds. The shortage of single beds for women (as she maintained) *forced* women to take a double, and 'It is well known that a woman is often told that she cannot come in unless she "brings her man".' And she quoted a marine engineer, speaking of seaport lodging houses: 'I have slept in a bedroom containing four double beds, and I can without fear of contradiction state that seven men and four girls occupied those beds, the girls' ages ranging from 15 to 17. Ask the prostitutes where they became what they are and 90 per cent would answer: "I was [a] servant in a boarding house and was compelled to sleep with seafaring men".'

It was not only married couples' beds that were frequently concentrated in one dormitory, for though the bylaws required single men and women to be berthed separately, often token partitions in the *same* chamber were the rule, for lodging houses were laxly inspected. Mrs Higgs was shown into a dormitory with no partitions at all: 'The landlady told us not to mind the man in the next bed, for he was blind. He slept there, and so did his dog'.[15] The women's lodging houses catered for the economic substratum of charladies, street pedlars, and outworkers like label stickers and paper flower makers, and it was women's low wages combined with the shortage of beds and their high prices that forced women into prostitution, claimed Mary Higgs.

To meet this problem the National Association for Women's Lodging Houses was formed in 1909 as a campaign and umbrella organisation for private initiatives like the British Women's Temperance Association, the Girls' Friendly Society, Dr Barnardo's, the YWCA and the Salvation and Church Armies.[16] London was not alone in the dearth of women's accommodation; in 1912 Birmingham had only 90 beds for women in the city's registered commercial houses. As noted in Chapter 8 Glasgow and Manchester contrasted with the LCC in providing municipally-run 'model' accommodation for women; the Salvation Army tried to fill the gap in London before the First World War with its Metropoles for women, whose beds at 4d to 6d a night were comparable with the rates for men's beds in commercial houses.[17]

The LCC for its part insisted that the paucity of women's beds in the commercial houses was due to lack of *demand* and there was no significant vagrant problem among working class women. A 1927 LCC Report considered that the lodging house 'is not, and never has been, the habitation of the ordinary working woman or girl. The figures show that the modern woman of the working class, in spite of her character for independence, lack of domesticity, etc., does not normally leave the domestic circle.'[18] In 1927 only 1,944 of the LCC's 17,543 licensed beds were for women; one third of the women's beds were provided by philanthropic agencies, the rest commercially. The report stated that while there was a 92 per cent occupancy rate compared with 85 per cent in the men's beds, charitable emergency shelters for women showed considerable capacity to spare, and the total unoccupied bed space in all forms of women's institutions was greater than the numbers of women actually found homeless in the streets, according to the LCC censuses. (However, these surveys only covered selected spots in the heart of London – railway termini, the Embankment, Trafalgar and Leicester Squares, for instance[19] – and, as we shall see later in the book, independent post-1945 surveys of homelessness have shown official counts to be very limited and incomplete.) There is other evidence to show that shortage of supply rather than lack of demand was the operative factor. Both W.H. Davies and T.W. Wilkinson before 1914 attested to lodging house proprietors' reluctance to service female demand.[20] Women tended to get in the way by making a home of the place, staying in the kitchens gossiping, sewing, cooking and so forth, while men preferred to be out and about during the day. When quarrelsome or drunken they were, it was claimed, more troublesome than men. Mary Higgs claimed that women were unpopular because of their greater insistence on cleanliness,[21] but the 1927 report, confirming that women cost more to lodge because of their greater demands on fuel as they stayed in, also referred to the greater 'damage' they caused to bed sheets, a delicate reference probably to lack of menstrual precautions (though women lodgers were decidedly less verminous than men).

A 'very considerable proportion' of female lodging house habitués were still prostitutes in 1927, and it was *this* consideration, not the alleged economic unviability, that was really behind the LCC's refusal to provide municipal hostels for women, according to Mrs Cecil Chesterton in 1926. Like Mary Higgs, Mrs Chesterton had gone 'undercover' as a charwoman immediately post-war to ascertain the plight of London's poorest women – so many were widowed by the war – especially in relation to their problems of shelter. Her book *In Darkest London*, published in 1926, caused such a stir that with funds raised from public subscription she was able to start up a 'Public Lodging House Fund', and founded the Cecil Houses (named after her dead husband). Her later book, *Women of the London Underworld* in 1938, developed the theme of the moral dangers to unattached girls in the metropolis due to the shortage of decent accommodation.

In the 1920s whilst men would expect to pay 9d a night in a London doss house, a woman would expect to pay 10d to 1/2d a night.[22] Mrs Chesterton found only one women's house in Holborn for the whole of central and West End London. The post-war housing shortage and the rise in rents for private lodgings compounded the wretchedness of unsupported women, who, said Mrs Chesterton, were reduced to begging in the streets, and risked NSPCC-instigated prosecution for neglect of their children. She, too, dwelt on the high proportion of prostitutes in the doss houses, but in one respect the moral atmosphere by 1927 in the licensed lodgings had improved since Mary Higgs' investigations. Thanks to strengthened child welfare legislation since 1908 far fewer girls under 16 were now found in them,[23] and the LCC attributed this achievement in part to the 'valuable work of the women police' (who were very new on the scene). Physical amenities, it was claimed, were on the upgrade, too, with a trend towards separate houses for women instead of separate dormitories in the same premises. But basement kitchens, and ablutions in chilly out-houses were still found; bedding, while on the whole 'good', could at its worst still consist of straw sacks on sheets of corrugated iron. Nonetheless, claimed the LCC, the gap in standards between men's and women's lodgings was by 1927 narrowing. Mrs Chesterton pointed out that apart from the houses known to the LCC there abounded dirty unlicensed houses in back streets for the lowest end of the market.[24] (This still left out of account the dead-enders, the verminous, filthy, alcoholic and mentally crazed cases who would not be admitted to any lodging house. They ended up in makeshift night shelters run by charities like the St Crispin's Dormitories.)[25]

In the late 1930s girls working in London at the bottom end of the employment market, as waitresses, usherettes and in 'sweated' trades were earning 18 to 20 shillings a week; for them there were crowded, dingy 'digs' which drove them out to seek a little life and glamour in the West End, where they were vulnerable to pick-ups. If they could not afford private rooms, women's lodging houses at a shilling to 1/6d a night might be found where poor working women might rub shoulders with some shady types who opted to stay there for anonymity – like shoplifters, begging letter writers and pro-curesses – together with other oddities and eccentrics.[26]

It was the diminution of female vagrancy, as officialdom saw it, after the First World War that appeared to justify the reduction of women's casual ward space in London to just one centre at Southwark. Mrs Chesterton claimed, however, that this was really to create extra room for more consideration-worthy ex-servicemen who might find themselves down-and-out in the post-war de-pression. Female casuals were Cinderellas, she complained. Whilst the LCC laid on a training and rehabilitation scheme for worthwhile male casuals, for women there was nothing; men were served hot tea first, and women got the cold dregs. A shabby unemployed man was the object of sympathy, but his female counterpart was unconsidered: 'Too often she is regarded as a perambulatory dustbin, and packets of bread the worse for wear, mouldy potatoes, cheese rind are thrust upon her, thus clearing the pantry and poulticing the faint sense of reproach that sometimes attacks the amply nurtured'. At Southwark she met Kitty, a seasoned casual ward user who epitomised the dish-rag way women down-and-outs could occasionally be treated. The master at Tonbridge workhouse had tried (illegally) to force her to do his *private* laundry as a work task. When she refused he had her charged before the court for refusing to do her work task (its private nature was not revealed) and she got 14 days' jail. Inmates were by now entitled to hot tea instead of gruel in the morning. The master later, out of spite, gave her cold gruel, but Kitty successfully appealed over his head. Other workhouses served up gruel alone if they thought they could get away with it. Mary Hughes JP (daughter of the author of *Tom Brown's Schooldays*) herself sampled vagrant ward life in disguise. She found skilly served up to the women, but when she led a protest and revealed her identity, the proper breakfast of a hot drink and bread and butter was laid on thereafter.[27]

Female use of the casual wards nationwide became miniscule. By 1926, for example, while London's average male intake had been rising to 693 a night, the women's average had fallen to 12,[28] and female vagrancy was higher in London than in the provinces.[29] By 1930 conditions in women's wards nationwide had generally improved thanks to the inspectors' efforts; but the poor law was still not doing enough to encourage aged women tramps to settle down as permanent residents in the workhouse proper. In 1932, however, the LCC established special rehabilitation centres to minister to the minute numbers of its female casuals.[30]

16 Child vagrancy to 1939

The idea of reformatories for wayward children, to rehabilitate them instead of committing them to futile and corrupting short stretches in jail, had developed on a very limited scale since the late eighteenth century and on a voluntary, unofficial basis. Some magistrates would hold the threat of jail over convicted youngsters as an inducement to go to a reformatory 'of their own choice'. These were residential establishments, but in 1841 Sheriff William Watson of Aberdeen pioneered the first day industrial school for street urchins who were *likely* to get into trouble with the law. The police would haul them along to the school and warn them to stay off the streets, while the offer of a free meal served as a positive attraction. In the evening the children returned home. Great success was claimed for its reduction of the number of juvenile convictions.

Ragged Schools were a parallel development to rescue waifs from the streets, as we have seen in Chapter 5. Though most worthy in concept[1] there is doubt whether they did any lasting good (apart perhaps from the movement's emigration schemes). Henry Mayhew and his journalist associate, John Binny, debunked the illusions of the schools' supporters. In the classes, they maintained, novices mixed with the hardened delinquents who played up to idealistic teachers while using the schools merely as a convenient shelter and source of free meals; juvenile delinquency, as measured by police arrests, had been increasing, to 1848; and the schools were offering non-practical pedagogy, not the trade training the ragamuffins needed to lift themselves from the gutter.[2] In Chapter 5 we saw Ashley Cooper's own description of the youngsters' exploitation of the schools, and in June 1848 he admitted in Parliament how summer attendances shrank dramatically as the pupils went begging and peddling; while the high migration rate in poor districts made the attendance turnover very high.[3]

Ashley Cooper (by now Lord Shaftesbury) saw the need to detain juvenile beggars in a reformative institution for a prolonged period, and in 1853, with the lodging house legislation under his

130

belt, he promoted a bill making children under 10 found begging in London liable to committal to a workhouse, to be maintained (where possible) at the parents' expense.[4] As a pioneering proposal for an official reformatory system it failed, mainly because of the inappropriateness of a poor house for custodial court sentences, but it did spur government to action: in 1854 the voluntary reformatories received statutory sanction, and juvenile criminals between 7 and 16 could officially be committed there. In 1857 Industrial Schools (also initially private foundations) were recognised for 7-14-year-olds who were *in danger of* slipping into crime.[5] In 1866 the laws relating to the two types of school were consolidated in two separate acts,[6] and it is the Industrial Schools that are most relevant to this chapter. Any child under 14 found begging or wandering without a home 'or proper guardianship' because of orphanhood or the parents' detention in jail, or found frequenting the company of known thieves, was liable to committal to an Industrial School till 16 years old. The Industrial School population of Great Britain grew steeply from 1,668 in 1864 to over 22,000 in 1898,[7] and the schools' preventive work was largely credited by the Royal Commission on Reformatories and Industrial Schools in 1884 with breaking up the gangs of juvenile thieves and the reduction in juvenile crime since the 1850s.

Under the 1870 Education Act the power to institute proceedings against potentially delinquent children was extended from the police to school inspectors (the new public school boards could also set up their own Industrial Schools). The 1876 Education Act made school attendance virtually compulsory between 5 and 10 years old, and with it came the Truant Schools and Day Industrial Schools for defaulters. But in practice the school boards were loathe to arrest and commit eligible children to Industrial Schools, especially if transients, as they would have to bear the costs of maintenance; this is another instance of the way small, fragmented authorities tended to shut their eyes and hope that the problem cases would 'move on'. The amalgamation of school boards into the larger borough and county councils in 1902 should have helped deparochialise these attitudes.[8]

Even though the education system was now harnessed to the fight against child begging, there remained the considerable problem of street trading and peddling by juvenile 'moonlighters' at the turn of the century; around 1900 nearly 10 per cent of London's schoolchildren were reckoned to be working outside school hours.[9] Many large provincial towns had armed themselves with local powers to suppress juvenile street trading from the 1880s; Manchester claimed to have driven it off the streets by 1905.[10] A succession of laws between 1894 and 1933 progressively restricted the age and the time of day at which children could trade; the Children and Young Persons Act of 1933 barred the under-16s, unless they were assisting their parents.[11]

Suppose that a vagrant child arrived in a neighbourhood accompanied by a parent or 'guardian': would the 1866 Act empower the courts automatically to remove that child to an Industrial School? Whilst the Home Office intended that the phrase '. . . not having . . . proper guardianship' should relate not just to orphanhood but to morally unfit guardianship, magistrates, conscious of the costs of a committal to local ratepayers, were taking the narrower view.[12] (Cost-conscious JPs, late in the nineteenth century, were still sometimes committing young offenders to short jail stretches instead of juvenile institutions for the same reason.[13]) The Children's Act of 1908 settled this by stipulating that the children of persons who 'habitually wander from place to place' and are thereby deprived of education were removable to an Industrial School.[14]

Industrial Schools law was designed primarily to rescue the children from the streets rather than punish the parents.[15] But from 1889 a succession of Prevention of Cruelty to Children Acts, culminating in the aforementioned 1908 'Children's Charter' played a complementary role by punishing parents for various forms of abuse that included causing their children to beg or entertain as a cover for begging; the parents were liable to fines and/or imprisonment, and their children might be entrusted to the care of some relation or 'fit person'. The latter in practice meant a NSPCC sanctuary or orphanages like Dr Barnardo's, the Church of England Waifs and Strays Society and the National Children's Home. Whilst children could be sheltered in a workhouse pending the parents' trial, workhouses were not classed legally as 'fit persons' for fostering children,[16] and Industrial Schools likewise lay outside this law's ambit.

Dr Thomas John Barnardo's work in rescuing orphans and waifs began in 1866, arising out of his work as a Ragged School teacher in Stepney and his introduction to a group of homeless urchins sleeping rough in Houndsditch by one of his pupils.[17] His first Home in 1866 took in just 25 boys; by 1907 Barnardo's Homes had 7,891 currently in care. Prior to the 1889 Cruelty Act, Dr Barnardo had had no legal grounds for removing children from physically or morally unfit environments and he had resorted to illicit 'philanthropic abductions'; this had started with a chance meeting with two pathetic, rain-drenched girls in Drury Lane. It transpired that they were charges of one 'Mother Brown', a crone who bought unwanted children and hired them out to beggars and street singers. After visiting her filthy hovel to attend, in his medical capacity, the girls' neglected and ailing younger brother, Dr Barnardo later returned when Mother Brown was out, and on impulse carried the children off. In 1886 Howard Goldsmid, in writing of the conditions in which children in London's East End lodging houses lived, the squalor, the lewdness they were exposed to, the beatings and neglect, stated that Dr Barnardo then could scarcely scratch the surface of the problem; and the truancy men scarcely dared penetrate the dangerous warrens like Flower and Dean Street. The 1889 Act, itself the product of a burgeoning public interest in child welfare, probably had much to do with the Barnardo Homes' rapid spurt in operations from 1890. Between 1866 and 1890 over 17,000 children had been 'rescued' but a further 48,000 were so helped between 1890 and 1907.[18]

Although workhouses could not foster the children of parents convicted for cruelty, separate Acts of 1889 and 1899 gave poor law authorities quite distinct adoption powers which had potential bearing on vagrants' children.[19] Boards of guardians were entitled to assume quasi-parental rights over the children of 'maintained' paupers who were unfit parents, for example, through mental deficiency, alcoholism, or 'vicious habits or mode of life'; once an adoption order was secured the paupers could not, say, take the children away with them if they left the workhouse. Legal opinion was cloudy over the extent of guardians' powers in relation to the children of casuals in the tramp wards,[20] but it was almost academic, for the guardians rarely bestirred themselves over non-locals who, hopefully, would be here to-day and gone to-morrow, and for whom a conscientious concern was financially unpalatable to the ratepayers.[21]

Even a willing authority would find itself frustrated by the procedures. The guardians, with whom the adoption proposal rested, met usually once a fortnight, and there was nothing to stop the vagrant decamping with the child before the next meeting, for the workhouses had no special powers of detention whilst cases were referred for consideration.[22] The most immediate step the workhouse master could take would be to call in the NSPCC or the police if the child showed evident signs of maltreatment under the Cruelty Law, or if the child's life-style and denial of schooling warranted action under the Industrial Schools and Education Acts. And once the parent was taken into custody he ceased *ipso facto* to come under the workhouse's jurisdiction altogether, and any 'adoption' plans automatically lapsed.

This is a pointer to a drawback of the three areas of law I have discussed, namely Industrial Schools (and Education), Cruelty and Poor Law Adoption. They were all mutually exclusive, and this tied the magistrates' hands as to the disposal of the vagrant's child. If processed under the Industrial Schools law, for example, the child *had* to go to an industrial school, and the JP could not send him to Dr Barnardo's or to a willing workhouse for 'adoption' even though a subsequent fostering in a private home might be best for that child's needs; and a decision in a Cruelty Law case likewise excluded the workhouse and Industrial School options. Another drawback in the eyes of some people prior to 1908 was that it was no punishable offence *per se* for an adult to wander with a child; a wandering child could be removed under the Industrial Schools Act, but the parent could not be punished. Wandering and cruelty in fact often went hand in hand, and the first prosecution undertaken by the recently-formed NSPCC following the 1889 Cruelty Act was that of a tramp who had walked from Nottingham to London with two children under 12, both in agony; one had two ruptures and died subsequently, and the other had an eye infection and also died later.[23] The NSPCC actively pursued vagrants who maltreated or neglected their charges, and the early decades of its journal, the *Child's Guardian*, contains numerous cases. To take just two at random: In 1893 a mother was jailed at Burnley after tramping for three months with her 'wretched' and 'ragged' children, including a consumptive girl,[24] and in 1897 at Birmingham the vagrant foster parents of a child were prosecuted for dragging a child around with them and forcing her to beg; the guardians were drunkards who beat the child, who was found ravenously hungry and covered with mud,[25] Robert Parr, director of the NSPCC, told the 1906 Vagrancy Committee of another particularly shocking case. A woman beggar was jailed at Edinburgh for exposing her one-legged six-year-old daughter to beg. A one-armed male tramp of the mother's acquaintance had wanted to take away the child for his own purposes, and with the mother locked up he had his chance. He took her tramping all the way from Edinburgh to Bolton, where a NSPCC inspector happened to see her in pain, and rescued her. The man was arrested, and it later transpired he had also 'outraged' the girl.[26]

Nonetheless, maltreatment was not invariable. Some tramps found a wholesome-looking child a useful begging aid, and being a tramp did not always denote callousness towards one's offspring.[27] The NSPCC's own campaign probably improved the tramp children's lot by the early years of this century. In 1899 the poor law inspectorate urged workhouse officials to report *all* instances to the NSPCC of vagrants entering the casual wards with children as a matter of routine, so they could be followed up when they came out and action taken where necessary.[28]

Some workhouse officials by the turn of the century were reporting a dramatic fall in the numbers of vagrant children coming into their wards, and a marked improvement in their physical condition.[29] As we shall see soon, official statistics do show that child vagrancy in the casual wards, at any rate, had fallen to very low levels in England by this time; but the NSPCC surely cannot be credited alone with such a trend, for the existence of the Scottish SPCC does not seem to have reduced the far higher incidence of child vagrancy north of the border.

Even in the absence of palpable cruelty, the very idea of being able to wander with a child with impunity was such an affront to some reformers that it prompted a series of Vagrant Children's Protection Bills between 1899 and 1906; they proposed to make simple wandering with a child punishable, and to give magistrates much greater flexibility of disposal of a child, whatever law it was summoned under. They also provided that the cost of maintaining an adopted child should be spread over the county, to reduce the burden to any single poor law Union and so encourage the practice of adopting vagrant children.[30] The proposals had to wait upon the recommendations of the 1906 Vagrancy Committee, which came out against penalties for wandering with children on the principle that it interfered excessively with individual liberty. The NSPCC was lukewarm to punishment without evidence of cruelty, and the Home Office felt that existing laws were adequate, if they were properly enforced.[31]

The 1908 Children's Act consequently contained only a highly diluted concession to the proposals of 1899–1906. Parents who 'habitually wander[ed] from place to place' so as to deprive their children of an education were liable to a fine (the earlier Bills had proposed imprisonment); their children were removable to Industrial Schools only – there was no flexibility allowed here – and there was no provision for adopted tramp children to be supported by a county rate.[32] Experience was to show just how ineffectual this new provision was, for it was very difficult to prove that a transient had been wandering 'from place to place' when there was no record of his earlier movements.[33]

Nonetheless, the physical condition of vagrants' children continued to improve after the First World War. The incidence of reported prosecutions in the *Child's Guardian* rapidly tailed off after January 1924, and the 1929–30 Departmental Committee on Casual Poor Relief admitted that vagrant ward children were 'seldom ill-nourished, badly-clothed or ill-treated' though it deplored the life-style they were being raised to. Some of the more progressive Joint Vagrancy Committees were by now taking voluntary initiatives to encourage poor law adoptions by defraying the maintenance costs on individual Unions' behalf, and had even petitioned the government for legal powers to detain vagrant children; but the Ministry of Health refused in 1927 on the grounds that the numbers of vagrant children in the casual wards were too insignificant to warrant any further measures.[34]

What, then, were the levels of juvenile vagrancy in the nineteenth and early twentieth centuries? The Judicial Statistics between 1858/9 and 1868/9 indicate that the proportion of under-16s among the 33,000 or more 'tramps' known to the police in England and Wales fell from 23 per cent to 17 per cent – a disturbingly high level, though the decline perhaps reflects the effects of the Reformatory and Industrial Schools legislation. Some statistical fragments between 1866 and 1880 suggest that the under-16s averaged around 1 in 13 to 1 in 17 of the casual ward population (and this was a fall since the 1840s).[35] They almost certainly formed a higher proportion of the lodging house habitués; in 1876 Dr Barnardo estimated that among the 27,000 or so dossers in London's registered houses alone some 6,000–7,000 were under 16, out of a supposed 30,000 homeless youngsters in the capital, sleeping rough or in casual wards or in *all* lodging houses including the unregistered ones.[36]

It is clear that there was a healthy fall in child vagrancy in England from the late nineteenth century. They formed about five per cent of the casual ward population in 1890 and two per cent by 1904; on 1 January 1891 there were 164 under-16s in all the country's casual wards; on the same night in 1907 there were 98, and in the 1920s the figures fluctuated around 40 to 80.[37]

Whilst there was a somewhat higher proportion of child vagrants outside the casual wards, even this was gratifyingly falling away. The NSPCC itself reckoned in 1906 that children now formed only three per cent of all tramps.[38] Children in common lodging houses were now very much rarer (at least in the registered houses); on one night in June 1897 a census showed only 139 children among London's dossers, and in the early 1900s the figures were dropping into the tens (allowing for seasonal variation).[39] In the 40 years since Dr Barnardo began his work the gangs of wretched youngsters sleeping rough in improvised shelters seem to have disappeared. On the night of 29 January 1904 of the 1,797 persons sleeping rough or walking the streets in London only 50 were children (46 of them boys) according to the LCC homelessness survey. Despite the limited scope of the LCC surveys, it does show a radical transformation; on the night of 13 February 1914 only five childen were found sleeping rough in London, and thereafter LCC censuses recorded no instances of shelterless children.[40]

How do we explain this steep and happy decline in child vagrancy from about 1890? A declining birth rate and consequently fewer children to trail about may be part of the explanation. The Industrial Schools and the rapid expansion of children's shelters and orphanages must take much of the credit. The dwindling opportunities for seasonal workers with increasing farm mechanisation affected the tramping 'scene' in the early twentieth century. And the NSPCC's pursuit, with the workhouses' co-operation, of itinerants towing children, *perhaps* had some effect on numbers as well as the physical welfare of those children.

But this does not explain the contrast with Scotland, where child vagrancy traditionally obtained at astoundingly high levels – in a country where vagrancy as a whole was more prevalent than in England – right up to the Second World War. In June 1909 the regular Scottish police tramp census counted 1,539 children under 14 among the 10,474 total;[41] and under-14s before the First World War generally amounted to a sixth or a seventh of the tramp population. During the war tramp levels fell sharply, but rose again after 1918, and although adult tramp figures were somewhat lower than pre-war, child levels remained comparable, so that in the mid-1930s children formed over a fifth of all Scottish 'tramps'![42]

Now, gypsies and tinkers were included in the police counts, and Scotland has traditionally had a conspicuous tinker population. Their living standards were primitive, to say the least; caves and rough-made tents were common habitations.[43] They lived by umbrella-mending, tinker work and begging; they were given to drunken squabbles, and their children were illiterate and ragged. There was a much higher proportion of children among tinkers than among the Scottish vagrant population as a whole.[44] In the mid-1930s tinkers formed perhaps a quarter of all Scottish vagrants, but even making a generous assumption that half the tinkers were children, I still estimate that children formed over a seventh of the non-tinker tramp population.

It would require a specialist study to explain the contrast with England. Perhaps it had something to do with the laxer enforcement of the vagrancy laws in Scotland.[45] The Scottish SPCC battled before 1914 to get vagrant children permanently settled, and to receive a full-time education, but the inter-war statistics show how little it succeeded.

17 Vagrancy Act enforcement to 1914

What patterns and trends in the application of the 1824 Act to begging and sleeping rough are evident up to 1914? One distinct difference in prosecution patterns for the two offences was that while the first was very sensitive to trade fluctuations, the latter was less reactive. Thus, in 1869, a depression year, there were 17,541 begging prosecutions and 5,323 sleeping out (technically 'wandering abroad . . .') prosecutions in England and Wales. But whereas begging prosecutions fell to around 9,000 a year in the prosperous period 1870–75, sleeping out prosecutions remained steady at 5,500 a year.[1] In 1900, a 'boom' year, begging and sleeping out prosecutions were 11,339 and 7,452 respectively, but in the depression years 1904–7, whilst begging prosecutions shot up to 23,000–26,000 annually, sleeping out prosecutions rose less dramatically to around 12,000.[2] The most plausible reason for this contrast is that begging was a more overt nuisance, and the police had less compunction about pouncing on the increased numbers of beggars (a proportion of whom would have been opportunistic fakes) in trade recessions. 'Sleeping out' was a genuine sign of distress. As Sam Weller told Mr Pickwick of the shelterers under Waterloo Bridge, 'You don't see the reg'lar wagrants there. Trust 'em they know better than that . . . it's generally the worn-out, starving houseless creeturs as rools themselves in the dark corners o' them lonesome places.'[3] Common humanity plus a pragmatic regard for the burden on police time and the prison service would have prompted the constabulary to leave harmless destitutes alone; we saw in Chapter 11 how the sleepers in St James's Park were tolerated in the depressed summer of 1887.

The bare prosecution statistics do not tell us a great deal about any changing incidence in begging and sleeping out in society between the 1850s and 1914 (allowing for the increase in population). There was a possible slight proportionate fall in begging but the picture is complicated by the growth of charities in the period and the consequent alternatives to street begging (the only chargeable form under the Vagrancy Act) opening up to the charity hound and begging letter writer. Sleeping out showed no relative fall up to around 1911; the trade improvement coupled with the effects of the new London Night Office (see Chapter 11) may have contributed to the marked drop thereafter. But, as we shall see, even in the inter-War trade depressions, sleeping out prosecutions were to be only a fraction of pre-1914 levels. These figures, moreover, tell us little about the *actual* levels of sleeping out, for police attitudes to prosecution were subject to so many vagaries. Vagrancy as a 'crime' is also partially concealed within statistics of arrests for drunkenness offences.

The actual conviction rate for begging appears to have been somewhat below the general conviction rate achieved by the police though the gap was narrowed as the century wore on; up to 90 per cent of those convicted were male.[4] Sleeping out convictions were well below the average. In the 1870s, whilst the Metropolitan Police was achieving a general conviction rate of around 71 per cent, the rate for sleeping out ranged between 40 and 55 per cent only. For the country as a whole the sleeping out conviction rate only crept above 50 per cent in the 1890s. Again, offenders were overwhelmingly male.

The police experienced considerable problems in enforcing the Act, as these figures suggest. They had to contend with magistrates' well-known tenderness towards vagrants. During the régime of the soft-hearted Lord Mayor, Alderman Wilson, in the 1830s, for example, the City poor law authorities could not even get convictions against vagrants who smashed the relieving officer's windows for refusing to give them tickets to the casual shelter.[5] In fact, the police were then giving up prosecution as the justices were just letting vagrants off, and the City became choked with beggars.[6]

The fundamental quandary was whether the vagrant should be treated as a pauper or a criminal.[7] In Chapter 3 I showed how in the 1830s the London poor law authorities regarded vagrants picked up by the police as a criminal concern, but the magistrates, rather than convict the wretches, used their overriding powers to pass them back to the workhouses. As early as 1846 it was being said that the Vagrancy Act was out of keeping with public sentiment. Sir Edmund Head, the eminent Poor Law Commissioner, told the Select Committee on Metropolitan Asylums that 'one of the evils . . . in the present administration of the vagrancy law, even in the mitigated shape in which it stands now . . . is that magistrates are reluctant to carry out what they consider the harshness of its provisions'.[8] In 1869 the Surrey justices blamed in part the leniency of their brother justices in failing to commit whole batches of vagrants for collective refusal to perform work tasks for the current rise in numbers using the casual wards.[9] The complaint about magistrates continued to the twentieth century. A Whitechapel policeman told the 1906 Vagrancy Committee how, when vagrants were arrested for sleeping out, the JPs invariably discharged them if they promised to go into the workhouse in future, but the promise was subsequently broken.[10] The Committee criticised the lack of uniformity among magistrates: sentences for refusing to perform work tasks or destroying clothes could vary from 3 to 28 days.[11] In 1910 W.H. Dawson, a Yorkshire poor law guardian, stated that an ulterior motive for leniency was to get the vagrant out of the neighbourhood as quickly as possible; magistrates were thereby indirectly encouraging vagrancy.[12]

Experienced vagrants knew how to exploit the technicalities of the law, abetted by the magistrates themselves. Thus, a sleeping out charge could only stick if the prosecution could show that the dependant was 'without visible means of subsistence'. As the 1906 Vagrancy Committee recorded: 'Some magistrates hold that if a man has only a penny in his possession, he is not without means of subsistence; and we are informed that this is the reason that so few persons are charged in London with "sleeping out". Vagrants are said to provide themselves with a penny, so as to be able to sleep out without fear of being taken into custody'.

Police frustrations were enormous. When Lord Palmerston, the Home Secretary, asked Sir Richard Mayne, the Chief Commissioner of the Metropolitan Police in 1853 what instructions had been given to the officers to enforce the Vagrancy Act, it suggests some suspicion that the Act was being disregarded.[13] Between December 1831 and February 1853 the Chief Commissioner had issued 15 reminders to the police of their duties; there were two reminders to be vigilant over street beggars in the space of one month in 1842, and it was repeated again in 1844. However, the Chief Commissioner felt he had to explain the force's problems in a letter to Palmerston in January 1854: 'In many cases parties refuse to appear in support of a charge – they won't take the trouble of doing so, or they consider the beggars deserving objects of charity and choose to give them money – The sentence upon conviction is usually only a few days' imprisonment and the parties resume the trade of begging in the streets.' The figures showed how disheartening attempts at enforcement must have been: in 1852, for example, out of 3,708 prosecutions of vagrants by the 'Met', 1,540 resulted in acquittals.

The Judicial Statistics show that overwhelmingly convicted beggars and sleepers out were sentenced to 14 days or less in jail. Such short sentences were futile, and confirmed vagrants just grew an enormous tail of convictions; child beggars became hardened recidivists very quickly. The Select Committee on Metropolitan Police Offices learned in 1838 of one child beggar named Tomkins who had been imprisoned at least 20 times in the previous three years.[14] The Industrial Schools and Reformatories would at least have dealt with this cancer from the 1850s, but the phenomenon of short-stretch recidivists persisted among adults into this century. Thus in 1905 the Prison Commissioners recorded a Lincolnshire example of a 30-year-old vagrant who had been convicted 23 times in the period 1898–1903, mostly for under 14 days.[15] Lack of central record-keeping by the police made it impossible for them to trace vagrants' past histories; vagrants' peripatetic habits were thus protecting them from longer sentences.

Vagrant-chasing involved a disproportionate drain on the police time. All they experienced for their efforts was a merry-go-round of arrests of the same people, so that, as Sir Richard Mayne told the Select Committee on the Metropolitan Police in 1834, 'the apprehension of beggars and vagrants is ten times more trouble to the police than the other duties of the town.'[16]

The police knew also that they were not endearing themselves to the public by 'picking on' pitiable-seeming beggars who were apparently only trying to keep themselves from the workhouse. In Chapter 3 I described how the non-uniformed constables of the Mendicity Society were more vulnerable to assault by the public than the uniformed Peelers, but well into this century even a Bobby could face open verbal abuse when effecting an arrest. Robert Fabian, the former Scotland Yard detective, tells in his memoirs how in his early career he went to arrest a beggar posing as a blind war veteran in Regent Street. Fabian noticed that his medals did not look correct:

> I arrested him as a fraud. The women were so angry that they nearly lynched me. Waving umbrellas, they shouted: 'Take your hands off him!' 'He's better than the likes of you.' 'Bloody flatfoot!' (and worse . . .).

Fabian's instinct was right, though. The man had been partially blinded when concocting home-made nitro-glycerine for a safe-blowing job.[17]

The police had an innate sense of live-and-let-live. The Metropolitan Police Inspector's Report on West End beggars in 1869 alluded to in Chapter 4 shows that the police themselves distinguished between known 'orderly' and 'deserving' beggars on the one hand and the rogues on the other, and turned a blind eye towards the former. The asperities of the workhouse were too notorious, as Francis Peek told the Lords Select Committee on Poor Relief in 1888; in the recent depression, whilst there had been an increase in begging, he had himself 'seen . . . large bodies of men, mendicants, walking the streets of London accompanied by police, not to do their duty and take them into custody, but to give them their sanction. . . . If the public knew that the guardians were doing their duty and relieving destitution, they would not tolerate this mendicancy and above all, they would not tolerate the police sanctioning it.'[18]

There are numbers of anecdotes about police giving vagrants money from their own pockets to see them to a lodging house, or directing them to some out-of-the-way spot where they could kip down unmolested. There were accepted locales where tramps would be left alone, like 'Itchy Park' in London's East End (a nickname known from Edwardian times at least, to the 1960s[19]), and the warm brickworks of certain provincial cities. However, the police could be officious and even spiteful at times in pouncing on vagrants, perhaps to notch up a more impressive arrest record, or because of new instructions from above to clear the neighbourhood. One tramp told Mary Higgs how a policeman might deliberately jostle a tramp, so he could be arrested for being 'drunk and disorderly'. A tramp's word counted for little in court, and it was politic to plead guilty.[20] Although normally tolerant of 'sleeping out' in Trafalgar Square and the Embankment, the police were compelled to perform cosmetic clearances when numbers built up intolerably in times of depression. In 1886 Howard Goldsmid criticised the meanness of the police who hosed down the seats in Trafalgar Square to make them unuseable and harried down and outs from the Embankment. Embankment swoops were again happening in the depression after the Boer War, and this affronted many people's sense of liberty and fair play. In Parliament the Liberal MPs Horatio Bottomley and Josiah Clement Wedgwood spoke up for the rights of harmless sleepers-out, and in 1910 Bottomley sardonically challenged the Home Secretary: 'does he think there would be any more harm in the poor wretches sleeping on the Embankment than what one frequently sees in this House, that is, Ministers sleeping on the benches?'[21] And one gallant, if cranky, member of the public, a Mr Lebolo Carey, in 1910 wrote a letter to the Chief Commissioner of the Met condemning an incident where a policeman moved on two elderly female down-and-outs from a bench, but left a man alone; his earlier protest had been ignored by the Met and he accused the Chief Commissioner of petty tyranny: 'Go and offer your services, Sir, more fittingly to the Sultan of Morocco or some such type; perhaps they will pay you better!'[22]

The 1906 Vagrancy Committee in fact recommended that sleeping out should not be an offence unless some other public nuisance was thereby caused. As we shall see later, the law was only to be modified in 1935 after a terrible tragedy. The Committee heard evidence against the pointless short sentences of a few days imposed on vagrant offenders. In 1904 of 16,626 persons convicted of begging and 6,219 convicted of sleeping out in England and Wales, 13,831 and 5,198 respectively were jailed for 14 days or less.[23] The prison service had, since 1900, been increasingly concerned about the rising numbers of prisoners 'of the vagrant class', whether for Vagrancy Act offences or other crimes. Thus, of the 12,369 male prisoners and 2,598 female prisoners in English prisons at the end of February 1905, 3,736 of the former and 372 of the latter were 'without fixed abode and with no regular means of subsistence'.[24] In 1904 a sixth of all the male prisoners in Manchester jail were there for vagrancy offences alone. (In fact there was nothing new in this, for the proportions 50 years before seem to have been worse. In 1851 Henry Mayhew reckoned that over half of Britain's prison population were of the tramp class, and Lord Shaftesbury in 1853 put the figure at 70 per cent.[25]

Nonetheless, the trend worried the Prison Commissioners.[26] Prison conditions had been improving since the late 1890s and were now deemed superior to the casual wards: from 1898 the crank and treadwheel had been rapidly phased out. 'Hard labour' for short-term prisoners by 1906 now meant only oakum-picking and sack-stitching; for them stone-breaking was, in practice, extinct. Moreover, though *sentenced* to hard labour, prisoners were subjected to a medical inspection of fitness, and half the vagrants sentenced were excused any labour on medical grounds. What annoyed the Prison Commissioners was that some of the increasing numbers of prisoners sentenced for workhouse disciplinary offences (these had reached over 5,000 in 1901) were found in prison to be medically unfit for the work tasks they had defaulted on in the casual wards. Prison cells were 'larger, better lighted, and better ventilated' than casual ward cells, and the prison diet had been improved since 1899, and now included suet pudding, soup, beans, meat and potatoes at different times of the week, while the casual wards still offered gruel, bread and cheese. Ex-prisoners, moreover, might get help from the Discharged Prisoners Aid Association. Not surprisingly there was a widespread conviction that tramps were deliberately inviting short jail terms as a respite from the casual wards. The time-honoured dodge of getting oneself committed as a free staging lift to one's destination was still flourishing in the early 1900s, it seems.[27] Of all groups of prisoners vagrants were found to be the most 'hopeless', 'lazy' and 'indolent', treating prison as a 'house of rest', according to prison officials.

One instance (among several) was cited from a newspaper cutting before the Vagrancy Committee. Under the headline 'The Attractions of Prison Life', it told of a vagrant, one Ernest Jones, who arrived at the village of Pinchingthorpe in the North Riding and proceeded to throw bricks at the railway station windows. He was arrested and brought before the Bench: 'He confessed his guilt with a weary smile, observing that he did it because he wanted a rest. The magistrates feelingly gratified his desire by ordering a fortnight's imprisonment, and the only regret Jones appeared to feel was that the term was not a longer one.'[28]

The Vagrancy Committee recommended that only nominal sentences be imposed on vagrants, with warnings of a detention colony sentence if the offences were repeated. But in the absence of detention colonies the Home Office instead in 1907 circularised JPs, recommending that jail should not be used as a resort at all unless the offence was worth at least 14 days.[29] The intention was, of course, to eliminate the three day 'holiday' sentences so common in the courts, but there were around the country individual backwoods magistracies where the JPs *were* hard on vagrants. The Home Office Circular was perversely and blimpishly misinterpreted by the Bench at East Langbaurgh in the North Riding in 1910, when they sentenced a man with no previous convictions for 14 days for begging; they used the circular as an occasion to sentence *any* vagrant for at least 14 days. The JPs were taken to task by the Home Office and the sentence was remitted.[30]

The main stronghold of hard-line JPs was Lincolnshire, especially at Grimsby.[31] Lincolnshire had traditionally been prey to vagrancy because of the potato harvesting, and the attraction of Grimsby to tramping sailors. Since the mid-nineteenth century Lincolnshire JPs had steadfastly imprisoned vagrants. In 1903 the JPs of Lindsey Quarter Sessions had even undertaken their own investigation of the Continental detention colonies, and held up the Belgian system as a model. Nevertheless, in the period following the Boer War, Lincolnshire suffered an increase in vagrancy despite its reputation for severity. Vagrant prosecutions had risen from 912 in 1900 to 2,409 in 1904. Instructions to the police were strict: 'If a man goes to a cottage and begs – if he only asks for a cup of water or a cup of tea and bread and butter – and the policeman sees him, he will arrest him for it.'[32] This had still not stopped vagrants firing haystacks or breaking windows to get longer sentences, and in 1912 the Chairman of the Lindsey Sessions complained how the county was 'overrun' with unemployed vagrants seeking a jail sentence.[33] However, John Ostler, a visiting justice to Hull prison, was presenting a different picture to the Home Office in 1907 and 1908. In the jail he found large numbers of genuine hardship cases, many of them offenders, who had been sentenced, chiefly by the Grimsby magistrates. For instance, a 20-year-old youth who had walked all the way from Birmingham to find work and had been sentenced to a month's jail for begging (his first offence); Jack Blake, aged 18, a destitute orphan, found sleeping out in a haystack and jailed for a month, too; and Edward Cooper aged 20 – one month for begging – who had walked from Liverpool to Grimsby to find work at sea.[34]

The Home Office, whilst not approving of the Lincolnshire justices' 'automatic' way with vagrants was unwilling to intervene. This contrasts with its subsequent East Langburgh intervention in

1910, and the Home Secretary's action over the sentencing by the Staffordshire Quarter Sessions of a 66-year-old labourer, Thomas Podmore, to 12 lashes as an 'incorrigible rogue' for begging in 1907.[35]

'Incorrigible rogues' under the Vagrancy Act were recidivist 'rogues and vagabonds', and these alone since the 1824 reform had remained liable to flogging. The Act did not prescribe the form of flogging – whether by birch or cat-o-nine-tails, for instance – nor the maximum number of strokes, but it remained largely a paper provision anyway, for in practice very few were ever convicted as 'incorrigible rogues'. In 1886, for example, there were only 134 such convictions, set against over 14,000 convictions for begging alone.[36] The lack of central records made it impossible to trace vagrants' criminal 'form'. Only in London where the Mendicity Society provided such a service was it possible for the Met to nail 'incorrigible rogues', but they were still a drop in the ocean. In 1905 of the 363 persons in England and Wales prosecuted as incorrigibles 286 were tried in London.[37]

We saw in Chapter 2 how even at the time the 1824 Bill was going through, doubts were expressed about the utility of flogging. Henry Mayhew in 1851 recorded the opinion of young lodging house delinquent types that flogging only hardened the criminal and did not deter him.[38] Between 1889 and 1892 Mr T. Milvain MP, who introduced a succession of bills to extend corporal punishment to a wider range of brutal crimes, proposed in the same measures that flogging of incorrigibles be abolished as inappropriate, but his bills failed;[39] a separate attempt in 1898 also failed.[40]

By 1907, in fact, JPs at Quarter Sessions had lost their powers to order floggings in all but Vagrancy Act cases, and the Podmore case caused an outcry in the press; the Home Secretary stepped in and quashed the flogging.[41] In 1909 Swift Macneil MP introduced a bill to repeal section 4 of the Vagrancy Act in its entirety as a response to the Podmore case.[42] It made no progress, no doubt because it was too sweeping, though senior politicians were all agreed that flogging in such cases could not be countenanced.

In fact corporal punishment was very rarely used after 1900 in Vagrancy Act cases – the numbers so sentenced each year could be counted on the fingers of one hand; two were flogged for sleeping out in 1905, and two for begging in 1913, the last such sentences for those respective offences. Floggings after 1900 were ordered mostly in indecent exposure cases, ranging from 1 to 5 a year up to 1935, and even this was by then considered inappropriate, as the offenders were more in need of psychological help.[43] All remaining judicial flogging was abolished in the Criminal Justice Act of 1948.

18   The First World War and the inter-war Depression

The outbreak of war in 1914 brought a dramatic fall in casual ward usage; on 1 January 1914 there were 7,568 in the country's wards, and exactly four years later the figure was down to 1,091.[1] The departure of millions of men to the war and full employment were the obvious causes. Casual labourers could now find work building military camps and shelters, and there were plenty of odd jobs and food pickings to be had in the neighbourhood of camps, so the statistics may tend to hide the real levels of vagrancy.[2] It is not clear how far vagrants were successful in evading conscription; in 1916 the Recruiting Office did ask boards of guardians for details about able-bodied men in their casual wards, but what response this produced is not revealed in the official papers.[3]

The emptying of the tramp wards brought about wholesale closures around the country; by 1920 284 provincial wards had been shut. London's wards had been sharply reducing even before the war, and the Night Office (see Chapter 11) was doubtless partly responsible. From 17 wards at the end of 1912, it was reduced to 12 by March 1914, and by the mid-1920s was down to just six wards for men and one for women, at Southwark, for a LCC population of 4,500,000.

The official plan was to leave a network of tramp wards at 20-mile intervals, but as demobilisation and the collapse of the post-war boom in 1920 was accompanied by a sharp rise in casual ward use, the hardships to those on tramp caused by the increased distances became punishing (though some wards did reopen).[4] At the end of May 1920 there were 3,188 in the wards; by the end of December 1929 10,217.[5] Registered unemployment then stood at 1,341,000.[6] In 1932, in the depths of the Depression, unemployment shot up to nearly 2,800,000, and casual ward use reached its peak on the night of 21 May 1932 with 16,911 relieved. In Chapter 13 I drew attention to the fact that the correlation between casual ward use and unemployment levels before 1914 was less than conclusive, and that the numbers 'on tramp' formed only a tiny percentage of those out of work. The same applies to the inter-War period.[7] It is true that by 1939 unemployment was half that of 1932, and so was casual ward use,[8] so it is indisputable that trade conditions influenced the levels of use, yet the unemployed overwhelmingly stayed at home or managed to find alternative accommodation in their travels to find work.

The cheap alternatives to the casual ward for the respectable working men, namely the lodging house and 'digs' in a private house with a landlady, were becoming harder to find.[9] Common lodging houses as well as the casual wards had emptied during the war; proprietors went out of business, and did not open again afterwards. The nearly 27,000 registered lodging house beds in the LCC area in 1914 had fallen to 16,875 by 1931.[10] It was the same story in the provinces; Hull had 2,374 beds in 1914 and 1,713 in 1925; Bradford's accommodation fell from 1,797 to 933 in the same period.[11] Landlords were now finding it more profitable to turn their premises into weekly-rental instead of nightly-rental lodging houses, as the common lodging house regulations did not apply, or to convert the house into dingy self-catering bed-sitters at exorbitant rents,[12] for the curtailment of house-building during the War had created an acute housing shortage.[13]

It has been intimated, too, that lodging houses were becoming a less attractive commercial proposition between the wars, owing to the squeeze on profits through rising standards; and official regulation was making proprietors improve their amenities, in London at any rate, where in 1927 only five per cent of registered houses were deemed 'below standard'. In 1933 George Orwell maintained, however, that commercial houses *were* very profitable, as outgoings were so low. It is clear that within the pattern of dwindling beds there was concentration into fewer but larger premises, and that the charitable agencies were providing an increasing proportion of those that were left. A quarter of London's lodging house beds were rented out by philanthropic agencies in 1927, five out of six of these being provided by the Salvation Army alone.[14] (Rowton Hotels, which figure separately, were then providing about 5,000 beds in London.)

Unemployment benefits, army and old-age pensions (as well as the steep decline in alcoholism) now made it possible for a complement of the poor to settle down as 'permanents' in the remaining accommodation, and these were squeezing out the transients, who made less desirable lodgers.[15] Although Mary Higgs wrote feelingly at this period about the shortage of lodging house beds for migrants (and this on the face of it seems plausible), curiously this is not borne out by actual surveys. Regional enquiries conducted by Poor Law Inspectors for the Ministry of Health by 1927 indicated that nationally, on balance, as judged by the levels of vacant beds, 'there is no serious shortage of common lodging houses.' In the LCC, for example, there was an

18 per cent vacancy rate in registered lodging houses in 1926 (though Rowtons *were* fuller than pre-war).[16] Now, we saw in Chapter 11 how few shelterless people there were on London's streets between the wars compared with before 1914, and this would appear to bear out the Ministry's conclusion. So how can we explain the phenomenon of high unemployment and a shrinking lodging house sector with a significant number of unoccupied beds and comparatively low levels of absolute shelterlessness? Possibly the answer lies in the unknown numbers of unlicensed lodging houses in back streets, catering to match-sellers, sandwich-board men and the like.[17] In the bed-sitters there would have been sharing.[18] And overall, as Mary Higgs claimed, there was in reality a hidden vagrancy problem in the 'floating population' of seedy bed-sitter land. To the Ministry of Health, seeking reasons for the noticeable increase in vagrancy between 1925 and 1927, a specious answer seemed to lie in the alleged increased 'attractions' of the casual ward, due to progressive humanisation over the previous 20 years. Detention rules were rarely enforced; stone-breaking was a rarity since tarmac road surfacing was making this obsolete, and the remaining work tasks were, stated a Ministry report, 'a farce now that a given number of hours work has been substituted for a quantitative task. It is very difficult to get a conviction before a magistrate for refusal to work, so long as a man plays about with a chopper or saw for the prescribed period of time'.[19] But in fact the casual wards were attracting less than 3,000 a night more over this period, averaging 7,853 a night in the early part of 1925 and 10,689 in the same period of 1927; and the increased distances between casual wards after the war would have partly offset their internal 'attractions'. It was not, therefore, the casual wards that were drawing custom from the lodging houses.

Free charitable shelters could only offer marginal alleviation; the London Embankment Night Office, however, did yeoman service in directing the homeless to appropriate accommodation and must take much credit for keeping down the flotsam on the streets to negligible levels. In 1935 it was re-named the Welfare Office, and its role was extended to deal with the pressures arising from the immigration into London of unemployed from the distressed areas of the north and Wales. There was improved co-ordination among affiliated agencies to prevent overlapping, and greater attention to minimum acceptable standards of shelter. Thus the Welfare Office began steering its applicants away from the crude 'sit-up' shelters, offered by well-meaning but impecunious philanthropists in crypts and the like. Whilst the Night Office, as its name suggests, was only open at night, the Welfare Office stayed open all day so applicants could be attended to well ahead of the immediate need for a bed. In 1936 the Office dealt with 30,600 applicants (30,000 of them were men); three quarters of them came from outside

Figure 9   *London in the Depression. Down-and-outs sleeping rough in 1930. (Courtesy, BBC Hulton Picture Library.)*

London, and half were under 30 years old. All but a tiny percentage were directed to voluntary agencies, the remnant to the casual wards.[20] Considering that London's common lodging house population was now shrinking to under 10,000, this placement effort was remarkable.

What were the various influences that induced unemployed men to stay put or go on tramp? The National (Unemployment) Insurance Scheme, introduced in 1911, was extended to a wider range of occupations in 1921, but as the Depression took hold unemployment benefit had to be supplemented by the discretionary dole for the long-term unemployed. The growing financial burden of the dole led to a stricter interpretation of the 'not genuinely seeking work' rule under the National Insurance laws.[21] The unemployed were liable to appear before a Court of Referees who judged whether the dole-seeker was a defaulter, in which case his dole would be cut off. Hapless men were reduced to begging for some note from every firm they approached for a job, to 'prove' they had genuinely been seeking work, and they were expected to range far afield. Mary Higgs in 1924[22] claimed that National Insurance reduced the impulse to travel and use the casual wards, since unemployment benefit was drawn from the local Labour Exchanges; however, the Court of Referees put an opposing pressure on men on the dole. As Wal Hannington, a veteran campaigner for the rights of the unemployed, put it: 'Unemployed workers were reduced to the desperate necessity of tramping many miles from their home each day in a fruitless search for work which they knew did not exist, in order to be able to supply evidence of their efforts'.[23] Much 'senseless tramping' flowed from these stringencies, and unemployed miners were particularly hard-hit:

> on the main roads leading from the coalfields to the big
> towns – particularly the Bath road leading from South Wales to
> London – hundreds of men could be seen almost every day,
> footsore and weary, trudging towards London, having left their
> families at the mercy of the boards of guardians.

There they spent a few useless days starving, before dragging themselves home to pass others coming the other way on this sterile journey.

The Wall Street Crash and the deepening economic crisis from 1929 brought further restrictions on the dole through the dreaded means test; the earnings of other members of the family determined a man's eligibility for relief. The Unemployment Assistance Act of 1934, which was intended to rationalise the outlets for dispensing dole money, introduced from 1937 compulsory 'training' of the unemployed in camps that might be a long way from home, and had the facilities and atmosphere of prisoner-of-war camps; these appear to have been the nearest thing to detention colonies Britain ever had (apart from the Borstals). They were branded at the time as quasi-Fascist, and in fact the bulk of graduates just returned to unemployment once their 'training' time was completed.[24]

The means test and the meagreness of the dole probably drove many men onto the roads, for the family friction, and the sense of being a burden to the other breadwinners in the house must have been frequently intolerable.[25] In the north, where there might be low-paid work for wives and daughters in the textile mills, but none for the men, the hurt to men's pride made them leave home,[26] and so the dole, far from keeping men from the casual wards, may have driven many into them.

The government was not convinced that all vagrants' journeys were really necessary, and believed (or wished to believe) that many were shirkers and scroungers. The increase in vagrancy between 1925 and 1927, as indicated by casual ward use, engaged its concern. Trade conditions, and especially the prolonged miners' strike whose start had prompted the brief General Strike of 1926, were the underlying factors,[27] but officialdom saw other causes as well. After all, the estimated numbers of wayfarers in the country then, at 50,000–60,000,[28] were but a tiny percentage of the unemployed; and the apparent logical corollary was that the solid work seekers did not roam, still less use the casual wards. The alleged 'comfort' of the contemporary casual wards; a spirit of restlessness induced in many men by prolonged absence from home in the Great War; the facility afforded to wanderers by car and lorry lifts;[29] and a taste for vagabondage acquired from a prolonged fruitless trudge for work – all these were cited by Ministry of Health Inspectors in 1927 as contributing to the vagrant syndrome.[30]

Estimates of the proportion of true workseekers in the casual wards ranged wildly from 5 to 60 per cent among witnesses before the 1929 Committee on the Relief of the Casual Poor. The Ministry of Health's own survey suggested that just over half were likely workseekers in the provincial wards, the rest being vagabonds. In London the former group was smaller at 44 per cent; this may have been due in part to a perpetuation of the London 'roundsmen' tradition.[31]

Since 1921 the Scottish poor law had become *de jure* responsible for the able-bodied poor, and this included casuals, and it was said by the mid–1930s to have become burdened with a 'miscellaneous parasitical class' of corner boy idlers, poor-house 'ins and outs', the decrepit, ex-prisoners, drunkards and the poorest casual workers like sandwich-board men.[32]

Although unemployment benefit was generally claimable only through local Labour Exchanges, the Vacant Ticket, issued to workers like navvies who generally had to travel to find work, enabled holders to draw benefit at any Labour Exchange. The Vacant Ticket, or a recently-stamped insurance card, was accepted at some casual wards as proof of bona fides as a genuine workseeker, and the holder was given preferential treatment and early discharge. It seemed like the makings of a nationwide wayticket system at last. But even before 1914 abuses were apparent. The national insurance cards themselves became an excuse for begging as cadgers solicited money to buy stamps to bring their cards up to date on the pretext that a trade slump had thrown them out of work. Even in the course of ordinary begging, cadgers found it worthwhile to invest in stamps, as a ploy for softer treatment in the casual wards. Cards were stolen, and there was a black market in them among tramps. The Vacant Tickets were said to be exploited by genuine holders, who used them, when travelling between jobs, to get free hostel treatment in the casual wards. For these reasons some Vagrancy Committees refused to recognise this updated version of the wayticket, and its acceptance by others was in fact based on a misunderstanding of the national insurance machinery, for the cards (as opposed to the Vacant Tickets) were supposed to be retained, in the event of unemployment, by the local Labour Exchanges.[33]

19 Casual ward developments 1918–45

I noted in Chapter 10 how the expansion of Joint Vagrancy Committees after 1918 helped foster a more positive and socially responsible attitude towards vagrants among some local authorities; the sight of so many survivors of trench warfare now reduced to the tramp wards in the post-War depression touched consciences, too. But the central government, which should have taken the lead, signally failed. The Maclean Committee, set up by the Ministry of Reconstruction during the war to look into the future of poor law administration, recommended a whole range of measures relating to the unemployed and vagrant rehabilitation. These included detention colonies for confirmed vagrants with voluntary labour colonies and trade schools for genuine workseekers; more municipal lodging houses to reduce the need for casual wards; and work-finding for vagrants through the Labour Exchanges. But such an emphatic shift towards rehabilitation was beyond any post-war government's will, especially with the overwhelming flood of unemployment to come, and the proposals were ignored.[1] Apart from positively encouraging, and compelling, the formation of more JVCs, the government left the social initiative to the local authorities themselves.

Their response was variable. London was a progressive example. There had been a labour colony for London as a whole at Hollesley Bay since 1905: and there was an industrial workshop at Belmont in Surrey. In 1923 the Metropolitan Asylums Board established the 'Hostel' at Holborn to receive eligible helpables, sent from the casual wards or the Night Office, for rehabilitation away from the demoralising atmosphere of the casual wards; it progressively grew, and in the year ending March 1938 alone it received 2,576.[2] Outside London, for example, Yorkshire Vagrancy Committee pioneered a scheme for permanently resettling (in the main body of the workhouses) aged vagrants 'wandering to their own hurt',[3] and from 1930 the JVC for some of the south-western counties began contributing funds, and sending eligibles, to the 'Young Wayfarers Hostels', a charity scheme to take vagrant youths off the roads.[4] As we have seen, certain JVCs were interested in adopting vagrant children, and some tried to persuade homeless ex-servicemen to settle down permanently in their workhouses.

However, London was unique, certainly before 1929, in co-ordinating voluntary and poor law assistance to the vagrant through its Advisory Committee and Night Office. As the Metropolitan casual wards were separate centres, not workhouse annexes as in the provinces, its staff were full-time specialists with a more professional approach to their jobs. Nonetheless, while providing overall the best physical amenities in the country, London's casual ward officers were found in 1930 to be by-and-large resigned and negative about the chances of ever permanently rehabilitating their clientele;[5] but, remember, those left in London wards tended to be the 'rejects'.

Before examining the casual wards themselves, I will briefly round off the fate of the detention and labour colony idea which was still being mooted between the wars and after wars; indeed a Vagrancy Reform Society was formed to promote it. The nearest Britain ever came to a successful detention colony ideal was the borstal system for delinquent youths from the turn of the century. Great praise was heaped on 'those great havens of hope', as Frank Gray called them in 1931, but the 1929 Committee on Casual Poor Relief dismissed borstal as a model for an adult scheme, as youths were more malleable than adults. Inebriate Reformatories had failed and the Continental experience of detention colonies showed by 1929 that they could not permanently reform inmates, only take them off the streets for a time. The 1929 Committee also believed optimistically that liberalising trends in the conventional prison system (for example, the introduction of educational courses) would lead one day to an approximation to some kind of detention colony regime.[6]

The labour colonies do not seem to have fared well, either. By 1929 Hollesley Bay had ceased to function as such, and was used as a shelter for elderly men and women; while the Salvation Army's Hadleigh Colony after 1918 switched to preparing youngsters for emigration, and the Lingfield Colony, run by the Christian Social Service union, was also by 1930 concentrating on training youths.[7] Experience showed that the farm work they offered was pretty useless to 'townies'; the tramps' wry nickname for the London labour colony – 'Misery Farm'[8] – speaks eloquently of the reality behind the voluntarism.

Although by 1924 some three quarters of the country's poor law Unions were incorporated in JVCs, the latter, for all their good intentions, could not compel individual Unions to spend money or follow the JVC policy line.[9] The sharp rise in the number using the casual wards in the early 1920s, set against the long distances vagrants now had to walk between wards, prompted a Ministry of

Figure 10   *(a) The tramp ward labour yard in 1939. The tramps are lined up and assigned to wood-sawing, chopping, bundling, and so on.*

Health enquiry into provincial casual ward standards in 1924, and it revealed, for all the JVC guidance and encouragement, a lamentable lack of uniformity and some persisting primitive conditions. In only half the wards was a fresh towel supplied to each new arrival; there were insufficient WCs; sleeping facilities varied widely from poor beds down to hammocks and plank beds with rugs for covers. A significant minority, for example a fifth in Hampshire, Hertfordshire and Norfolk, had no heating. Very few imposed full detention and work tasks. The Victorian ethos of minimum outlay and speedy throughput still prevailed.[10]

A Ministry Circular of 1925 reminded Unions of their statutory obligations regarding work tasks, and also prescribed, with an eye to smallpox in particular, that new arrivals should be medically inspected; it also urged that the Unions take positive steps towards vagrant rehabilitation. Oakum-picking had been abolished in prisons by 1924, but was included among the listed worktasks in the 1925 Circular. However, Mary Higgs says it was abolished in 1925,[11] and Mrs Cecil Chesterton claimed credit in 1926 for effecting its abolition through an article exposing its degradation.[12] Stone-breaking and pounding technically remained, though the demand for chippings was falling away. Weeding, pumping, corngrinding and woodchopping constituted the remaining pres-

b) Note that they have to work in their own clothes and doubtless ended up more dishevelled than before.
(Courtesy, BBC Hulton Picture Library.)

cribed tasks, but maximum hours only, not minimum output, were stipulated.

A new smallpox scare in the late 1920s again focused attention on the casual wards. Two fascinating little publications under the title *On the Road*, one covering the south-western counties and the other from Reading to York, were published in 1928 giving graphic first-hand accounts in the form of a diary of rural and small-town casual ward conditions.[13] The resentment felt by ex-servicemen thrown on the scrapheap by the depression is summed up in two pieces of graffiti: one, on Sturminster Newton woodchopping shed, inscribed as 'Lloyd George's Home for Heroes', and the other at Yeovil, a piece of bitter verse:

> The Master has the Meat
> Inmates the Bones
> The Men who fought for Empire
> Hundredweights of Stones.

A wide contrast in standards and treatment was revealed. I can only give a few glimpses. At Pewsey the blankets were collected and folded without fumigation for the new arrivals. At Frome there was no bath or hot water for washing, and the inmates had to

Figure 11   *The exterior of the old Paddington Casual Ward cells from a photo taken in 1938; a grim relic of the past. Behind each grid was an individual stone-breaking cell; the rubble was fed through into the yard outside.*

relieve themselves in a bucket in the dormitory. No heating was laid on, and the men had to wash themselves from a cold water tap in the wall, without soap or towels. 'The only receptacle which was available for washing faces and hands was the bucket which had been used the previous night.' At Devizes the men shared the same bath water.

If a casual asked to see a doctor, the porter or tramp major usually just ignored him and there are only scattered references to medical inspections, despite the current smallpox scare. At Thame it was just a formality: 50–60 men were gone through in five minutes. They kept shirts on, opened at the chest, and the doctor

b) The derelict interior of a forbidding Hackney casual ward cell from a 1935 photo. In the foreground is the dormitory cell; this gives on to the stone-breaking cell beyond. The grid through which the size-graded chips were fed is clearly seen. Note the pipe, which might be for central heating or possibly a drain, running across the floor. (Courtesy, Greater London Record Office.)

had no way of telling if they had been vaccinated or not. As there was no bath, no attendant had had the opportunity to see any suspicious signs of infection.

Despite the 1925 Circular, it was evident that work tasks remained indolent stabs at woodchopping, sawing, weeding and the like, and they were not a physical trial in themselves.

Anger was felt against the uncaring porters in some wards, like the one at Shaftesbury who ignored complaints about the biting wind coming in through a broken dormitory window. Comment was made on the long-term debilitating effect of the poor diet on casuals who were forced to take to the road for months at a time, covering the long distances between the wards. When the writer left Shaftesbury the next stop was at Wareham 26 miles away: 'The prospect of the walk was not tempting, my left hip had developed a sore the size of a shilling through sleeping on hard boards, one of my toes was sore, and another much inflamed.'

However, there were some bright spots. At some wards the attendants were more sympathetic, and this helped compensate for indifferent conditions. Shepton Mallet was exceptionally civilised: a clean, hot bath (in private), clean towels and nightshirts. The sleeping cells were light and airy. The chronicler had facilities to wash his clothes, and the porter provided him with ointment for his sores. At St Albans, the bathing and showering facilities were excellent, and the ward scrupulously clean. A thorough medical examination was laid on: the fully stripped men were examined minutely under a strong light. At Watford, too, the medical inspection was thorough.

All in all, however, a dismal picture is portrayed; cavalier indifference, poor fare, slummy, cold wards and uncomfortable berths, lack of ablutions and medical attention – all were the more general lot of the vagrant in the rural and small-town casual wards of the late 1920s. The picture is confirmed by other writers of the period;[14] Frank Gray MP in his sampling journey, shared a cell with mice at Banbury, and Mary Higgs described one very bad ward in 1928 where the mice scurried over the beds, the lavatories had no seats, the washbasins no plugs and there were two pieces of soap and three towels for 31 men. Whilst the worktasks (where enforced at all) were not oppressive, the mere subjection to this rigmarole rubbed in the inmates' sense of degradation, and they emerged from each ward more physically and mentally crumpled than before.

In Parliament vagrant issues were raised by Frank Gray and Arthur Shepherd, the 'Tramp's MP', and the continuing high levels of vagrancy, coupled with the smallpox outbreak, prompted the setting up of a Departmental Committee on the Relief of the Casual Poor in 1929. It retailed the conditions exemplified above, and worse: how in some wards 'the sleeping accommodation consisted of a shed which would not on a decent farm be considered fit for an animal of any value'. Frank Gray pointed out at this time that whilst lunatic asylums had been 'revolutionised' since 1900, casual wards had been neglected and were still fundamentally Dickensian.[15] This was underscored by the Report: 'One of the General Inspectors of the Ministry of Health told us that in his experience it is easier to get a wireless installation in the workhouse paid for out of the Guardians' own pockets than to get baths or warmth in the casual ward paid for out of the rates.'

The lame excuse offered by offending Unions that better conditions would encourage vagrancy was dismissed by the Committee: slumminess coupled with slackness, it said, was in fact preferred by the habitual tramps to a more clinical but stricter régime,[16] and public confidence in civilised amenities would discourage indiscriminate charity, particularly the giving of car and lorry lifts which aided roving habits. The present casual ward, it felt, was something of an anachronism, for Labour Exchanges (since 1909) and the telephone should make it possible for workseekers to find jobs without trudging the highways, and rail ticket subsidies issued by the Labour Exchanges would enable them to avoid the ward altogether. (Twenty years before the Royal Commission on the poor Law had been saying much the same thing![17]) The London system of co-ordinating public and voluntary agencies should be adopted nationally. Casual ward officers should be full-time professionals with a counselling and welfare role, and the tramp majors should be abolished. The detention rules should be fully enforced (60 per cent of vagrant wards then ignored them altogether) to give time for a casual's case to be fully looked into. In sum, the casual wards should become the hub of a job-finding and rehabilitative system, and to this end their amenities should be improved to create a restorative atmosphere: decent washing facilities; day rooms with reading matter, where men could also smoke; proper beds and private cubicles; an end to compulsory searches for minor valuables; the segregation of young vagrants from the old hands. Diet should be more varied, medical inspections mandatory and routine, and work tasks properly but humanely enforced.

The Report led to the Public Assistance (Casual Poor) Order of 1931: gruel was to be discontinued, and meat and fresh vegetables were to be added to the dietary; the Report's amenities recommendations were prescribed; regular medical checks were to be introduced; stone-breaking and corn-grinding were to be dropped from the work tasks.[18]

During the 1930s there was a start on improvements. In 1933 George Orwell acknowledged recent signs of progress, but these related to the buildings, not rehabilitation and job assistance; but the structural alterations needed in the wards to accommodate, say, day rooms, ensured that this would be a gradual and uneven process. In 1936 some wards still supplied only matting to cover bed springs; day rooms and laundries were not yet standard; 6 pm bedtime and no smoking rules applied in places; and the food, though more varied, was very poor – the tramps' nickname for the dross cocoa that took the place of gruel was 'shell shock'.[19] Tramp majors were still employed – indeed it seems they were still found

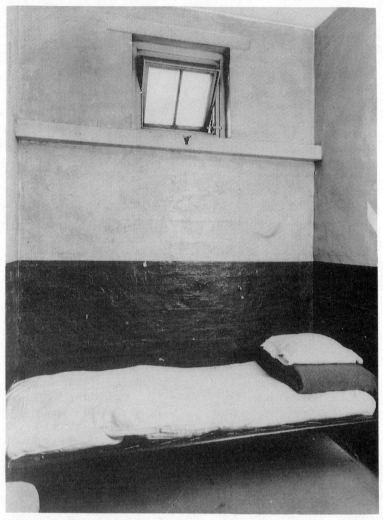

Figure 12   *An improved casual ward cubicle at Wandsworth in 1935, a product of improvements under the London County Council. (Courtesy, Greater London Council.)*

around 1945; St. Albans appears to have had one then,[20] and this curiously was one of the few wards praised by the author of *On the Road* in 1928.

Some rural wards, though, were good. Kettering's reputation stood high, and was honoured with a tongue-in-cheek tribute from *Punch*, parodying 'The Stately Homes of England':

The casual wards of England
Are various in cheer

Some are benevolently run
Others are more severe
But Kettering, oh Kettering
Is good beyond all bettering
And stands without a peer. . . .[21]

The JVC for Berkshire, Buckinghamshire and Oxfordshire was a model of progressiveness, and by 1936 was meeting all the desiderata urged in the 1930 Report.[22]

What of London? There were nine casual wards for men in the LCC in the 1930s, with a total intake of 600–700 a night. There seems to have been a positive approach to rehabilitation, and certainly the physical amenities were now exemplary; from 1937 the dietary included mutton and beef, with gravy and mustard. Each inmate had a cubicle with a decent iron bedstead. The worktask was now primarily woodchopping and bundling, and the traditionally dreary casual ward Sunday, when inmates were confined all day, was lightened with books and magazines.[23]

The outbreak of war in 1939 was again attended by a slump in casual ward use; however, it seems some casuals were evading conscription by slipping from ward to ward.[24] Wards were again closing down: the 371 that existed in 1939 were down to 270 when the new National Assistance Board took them over in 1948 under the post-War welfare state reconstruction; and these were promptly reduced to 134 'Reception Centres' as the nationalised 'spikes' were now called.[25]

20 Some vagrant types and conditions between the wars

We saw in Chapter 16 how few child vagrants there were in England after 1918; not only had they disappeared from the streets, but by this time were also few and far between in casual wards and lodging houses. Around 1930 two per cent at most of the nation's casual ward inmates were children,[1] and the LCC had only two children's beds designated among the 16,700 in its registered lodging houses.[2] The practice of hiring out children to beggars still went on, however, up to the early 1930s at least, for their financial advantage to beggars outweighed the risk of NSPCC discovery.[3]

Moving a little up the age scale we find a different situation. There was much concerned comment between the wars about the apparent increase in vagrancy among youths and young men.[4] Some writers found them only too disturbingly evident in the casual wards and on the highways, and deplored not only the wasted human potential but the dangers of their slide into crime; and we can recall from the last chapter how the 1929–30 Casual Poor Relief Committee specifically recommended their segregation from older casuals.

Commentators were convinced that unemployment, and the drift from distressed areas (notably towards London, as the LCC Welfare Office figures cited in Chapter 18 indicated) was not the only reason; many were the victims of family disruption in the war, which left them restless, or semi-orphaned and unable to get along with new step-fathers. Others, while not originally unemployed, had got bogged down in the dead-end jobs they took on leaving school, and their static wage was now inadequate to pay their way at home, leading to parental grumbling. A minority had mental problems or were social misfits. A director of Feltham Borstal Institution, Middlesex, told the Casual Poor Relief Committee in 1929 how a small minority of the lads in his care who had been on the roads had actually opted for the life.[5] These were the mental 'duds' who knew they were duds, and took to the roads as an adventure, believing in their immature way that the road-wisdom they acquired and the skill at skiving was one thing they could become 'good' at. Most, though, had been driven out by circumstances and hated the experience. He cited some case notes. For instance:

> Flower. Turned from home. Jumped rly coal wagon to Leicester, then walked to Northampton, Wellinboro etc. 2 weeks Hungry, stole, convicted. . . .
> White from Liverpool. Brought up orphanage. Put on Irish farm. Ran away. Lived in streets in Liverpool 3 months . . .
> Burgess. Drunken stepfather. Turned out. Slept rough in brickyard for 2 months . . .

Officialdom, while taking up the contemporary concern about post-adolescent vagrancy, did try to counter exaggeration. Sample surveys of casual ward inmates in 1928 and 1930 showed that less than three per cent were aged 16–21[6], and a Ministry of Health Inspector commented in 1927: 'The young recruits to this class ['mendicancy'], though conspicuous and lamentable, are not so far as numbers go, doing much more than replace the numbers of it who disappear at the other end of the age scale.'[7]

Not all youthful flotsam would have figured as obvious 'mendicants' and casual ward drop-outs. Some drifted into male prostitution. Perverts and procurers, perhaps posing as welfare workers, were on the look-out for new arrivals adrift in London, and offered to guide them to 'boys' hostels', where the corruption began. In the 1930s 'rent boys' (as they are nicknamed today) could be seen hanging about the Mall, Trafalgar Square, the Embankment and Piccadilly, made up and reeking of scent, waiting for pick-ups.[8]

Girls figured far less in the vagrant scene; they were more home-rooted than young fellows, but those who did cut loose were likely to end up in prostitution. Even in the 1930s the pattern of young servant girls, exploited and maltreated by their employers, throwing up their jobs and taking to street-walking still lingered. Modern transport had added a new dimension to their mobility and some became transport caff 'floozies'.[9]

Not surprisingly, in view of mass wartime conscription, a very high proportion (W.A. Gape put it as high as 80 per cent) of post-war tramps were ex-soldiers. Their return to unemployment and the scrap heap, particularly for the disabled, touched the consciences of many, and the thought of worn-out, famished Tommy Atkinses now struggling between the casual wards was very poignant. The *Daily Sketch* in December 1923 reported how a Christmas treat in the north for homeless ex-servicemen was interrupted by a knock at the door:

As the door was opened a man collapsed on the threshold. He was a middle-aged ex-soldier, who had tramped from Ormskirk [about 16 miles away] in quest of a free meal and shelter for the night. He was exhausted from starvation.[10]

Frank Jennings recorded in 1932 how of the 24 men he shared a dormitory with at Kettering Casual Ward 'there were 2 MCs, 4 MMs and one Croix de Guerre'. Their bitterness and sense of rejection sometimes just expressed itself in sour graffiti on casual ward walls, but occasionally frustration boiled over, and deliberate acts of vandalism were committed to get themselves a respite in jail.[11] Some JVCs did try to encourage ex-servicemen to settle down permanently in the main body of the workhouse, but many preferred to remain free.[12] With their war pensions a good many took to the Rowtons, gradually settling into the life and forming close-knit, self-sufficient fellowships, and were still to be found there after 1945, some in their sixties.[13]

Though the sight of bemedalled beggars and buskers was common between the wars, their military pedigrees and destitution were not always genuine; war decorations were freely traded among the vagrant netherworld. There was at least one lodging-house proprietor-impresario in London in the 1920s who organised choirs of bogus 'Ex-Servicemen Songsters' to sing in the gutters,[14] and I have alluded elsewhere in the book to the parallels with the crop of war-crippled beggars that sprang up after Napoleon's defeat; while the British Legion's charitable efforts were open to abuse by ex-service rotten apples who misapplied the aid given them.[15]

The unemployment that underlay much of the vagrancy was a harsh spiritual corrosive. The fear of detention in a casual ward if they stayed in one neighbourhood prodded men on into never-ending tramping; and with the gauntness and seediness came the furtive, hunted look of men fearing to be picked up by the police. George Orwell described an unemployed carpenter, degraded by the 'scum' he had to share casual wards with, who took to sleeping in bathing machines and begging along the south coast, always with an eye out for the police. And Max Cohen, a cabinet maker, who experienced much hardship in the depression, one day encountered someone much worse off than himself in a café in the Strand. The man was an end-of-the-liner: ragged and unkempt, his shoes lined with newspaper and tied with string, and his expression totally beaten. Cohen gave him a cigarette, and he opened up:

'I tramped the country, lookin' for work', he said hoarsely. 'But yer can't get any work – nowhere! I tried – honest. I have been out six years. . . . Boy, never go on the road . . . You'll be driven from one town to 'nother. Y'ave to go to the spike, else you get

locked up. The police is after you all the time. An' they'll nab
yer as soon as they can lay 'ands on yer. Fer nothink at all.
Nothink . . . I slep' out, las' four-five nights. Cold . . . bloody
awful, the cold. Underneath the arches.'[16]

Scots and Irish formed about a ninth each of all the homeless
applicants to the London Welfare Office in the mid-1930s; Irish
vagrants, though noticeable still, especially in Scotland, were only
a tiny fraction of what they had been in the mid-Victorian period.[17]
Though alcoholism had dropped sharply in society since 1914, a
disproportionate number of vagrants were alcoholics, as revealed to
the Casual Poor Relief Committee.[18] London was, it seems,
something of a Mecca for alcoholic down-and-outs, a quarter of
whose casual ward inmates were reckoned to be drunkards in the
early 1930s compared with an eighth in the provinces. Scotland was
still the worst sink of alcoholic vagrancy: methylated spirits ('Red
Biddy'), metal polish, or grisly cocktails of cheap wine, surgical
spirits or eau-de-Cologne with the meths held sway, and the
practice of drinking coal-gassed milk, later to spread to London's
Skid Row, originated north of the border.[19]
Some tramps were the colourful 'Knight of the Road' types – the
nomadic eccentrics with their belongings stuffed into a kerchief and
slung over their shoulders on a stick, or suspended from a string
round their middles, fully equipped for self-sufficiency with
utensils, mugs, plates and a 'drum' or can for brewing up. These
shaggy, grizzled roadsters with their layers of waistcoats and
overcoats and their newspaper supply for extra insulation fitted
most closely the 'romantic' notion of a tramp. They either stuck to
a particular locality, where they were well-known and tolerated as
'characters', or were 'shuttlers' who peregrinated up and down the
same highway for years at a time, or just aimless ramblers with
purely random, transitory destinations. Lady Oxford once asked
such a tramp what decided his direction: 'I always turns me back
on the wind ma'am', he replied.[20] The West Country was a
popular winter destination because of its mild climate, and though
often solitary, they might team up for a time with other tramps,
and even make camps together. There were even class distinctions
among tramps. The 'gentleman tramps' (W.A. Gape met one
known as the 'Devonshire Duke') with their affected airs and
graces, talking of lawyers and over-due legacies really did exist.
The skilful, successful tramp who could always cadge enough for a
decent lodging house was a 'top cock' and he looked down on the
'croker', the dustbin scavenger; a 'croker' was slang for 4d, and
referred to the cheap lodging house prices these tatterdemalions
could just afford.[21] These roadsters were dubbed with colourful
nicknames; W.H. Davies met up in his time, with among others,
the 'Talking Fish', 'Dodger', 'Punch', 'Red-Nosed Scotty' and

'Monkey Sam'. Apart from the pseudo 'gentlemen', there were occasionally men of genuine education who had for various reasons sunk to a vagrant life. Hippo Neville refers to the 'Cheltenham Doctor', a struck-off medical man who lived by treating other tramps' ailments and those of cottagers whose doors he knocked at in the West Country. And Frank Jennings found among the casual ward dossers some decayed gentility – like the concert artist ruined by drink, and the baronet who had lost his wealth in financial disasters.[22]

What was the physical condition of the inter-war tramp? Malnutrition and alcoholism took their toll, but Dr E.O. Lewis's survey of casual ward users for the 1930 Casual Poor Relief Committee found that tramps were on the whole well-attired, remarkably free of consumption and relatively clean: 'As one indication . . . we may state that very few of the bodies of these casuals had any flea bites'.[23] Scottish tramps, who did not have access to casual ward baths and fumigation facilities, as existed in England, were said to be dirtier and more verminous.[24] Dr Lewis did find that older tramps had circulatory problems, and that bronchitis was the commonest single complaint. Other writers leave us a far worse impression of the tramps' condition. Casual ward bath-water was not always salubrious, as we have seen, and quite a number of tramps avoided the baths for other reasons: they wrapped themselves in paper for the winter, and became greasy and smelly, but thought that a layer of dirt helped shield them from infection.[25] George Orwell refers to the doss-house derelicts who were coughing all night or enuretic and had to get up repeatedly to relieve themselves. When stripped for medical inspection they presented a repellent sight: 'Flat feet, pot bellies, hollow chests, sagging muscles – every kind of physical rottenness was there. Nearly everyone was undernourished and some clearly diseased; two men were wearing trusses . . .' A veteran Irish tramp of his acquaintance had eczema, bronchitis, dyspepsia, back pain, urethritis, varicose veins, bunions and flat feet. It was probably only the rock-bottom alcoholics and the mentally sick tramps who were unutterably filthy; most knew they had to keep a minimum standard of cleanliness to be acceptable to the lodging houses and the Salvation Army; and who would give money to a tramp whose stench kept them at a distance?

21 Begging and charity between the wars

Any discouragement to street hand-outs that might have been expected from the extension of National Insurance from 1921 was negated by the appeals of the war disabled, mass unemployment, the persisting stigma of the poor law and the new bogey, the means test. Begging was still very much part of street life, but prosecution statistics are of an entirely different order from before the war. Whereas between 1900 and 1914 begging prosecutions (in England and Wales) averaged between 16,000 to over 25,000 a year (depending on trade conditions), there was a dramatic drop, as one would have expected, during the war, and in 1920, the last boom year, the figure was 3,634. But even as the depression set in the figures did not correspond with the growing mass misery as they would have done before 1914. Thus in 1929 there were 4,265 prosecutions, and in 1934 4,760. As unemployment fell in the later 1930s prosecutions did fall away somewhat – there were 3,390 in 1938.[1] However, when we look at actual *convictions* the picture becomes even more puzzling. Up to the very early 1930s the conviction rate hovered around 60 per cent, the same as in the late nineteenth century, and rather below the police's general conviction rate; but after 1931 it suddenly jumps to well over 90 per cent. The effect is that in 1931, at the worst of the Depression there were 2,432 convictions, fewer than the 3,213 in 1938 when unemployment was falling to half the levels of 1931–2.

I can find no obvious answer to all this. Was there really far less begging than before the war? The only comparable fall that could have a possible bearing was in alcohol consumption (see Chapter 12); was there a correlation, then, between beer and begging? Or were police easing up on prosecutions compared with before 1914 whilst begging remained actually at earlier levels? Why should the police have had such a remarkably improved conviction rate after 1931? And why, despite an apparent greater readiness to convict, were JPs in the 1930s sending a far smaller proportion of those convicted straight to jail than a generation earlier? In the 1890s upwards of 80 per cent of convicted beggars went to jail with no option of a fine; in the 1930s it was around 40 per cent.

Post-war conditions inspired novel begging dodges. The national insurance cards, unemployment and real or fake war disability, all provided opportunities for creative liars. 'Shellbacks' (bogus deep-sea fishermen) could now heighten the pathos of their land-bound predicament with stories of wartime sinkings,[2] invalid war poets sold their doggerel to the public, having bought the words from some seedy scribbler;[3] the sporting of some purchased war decorations in any begging venture was sure to pluck the public's heartstrings. But in all other respects the dodges were continuations of those practised before the war.[4]

Of course, much of the apparent pathos was genuine. Nigel Gray cites an instance of an unemployed miner and a foundryman singing in Piccadilly Circus who were soaked through and had been living on scraps from hotel dustbins and Berwick Street market, so they could send a pittance to their families back home. Similar stories could be repeated many times over of mouth organists and spoon players in the gutters of London's smart shopping centres who had lost the dignity of labour in the distressed areas.

Pedlars and street entertainers persisted as before 1914. Barrel-organ grinders could gross 7/6d to 10 shillings a day, especially from a good pitch outside a pub, though the organ's daily hire charge (the renters-out in the 1920s were still largely Italian or of Italian extraction) would take up to five shillings of this.[5] 'Screeving' (which appears by 1930 to mean pavement artistry rather than begging letter writing)[6] had its tribulations; rain could ruin the work, fingers and backs got sore, and there was the danger of 'spoilers' who stood round to make trouble and drive potential custom away unless the screever treated them. For the hard-up casual worker there might be jobs going as an 'angel' (sandwich-board man), or as a 'kidder' or 'nobber' – the former a street-seller's stooge and the latter a money collector for a street entertainer.

Indiscriminate street alms-giving remained widespread. In Scotland, it seems, this remained so common it made the Vagrancy Act virtually a dead letter.[7] As in Victorian times the Trafalgar Square area was a focal point of public largesse. W.J. Smart recorded in 1938:

> I have seen dozens of women in Trafalgar Square at the dead of night crowding round hampers of clothing being distributed free, trying on blouses and skirts and coats in full view of the public.[8]

Long queues at Admiralty Arch waited for free hand-outs of tea and sandwiches, with no questions asked. (The 'Silver Lady' mobile soup kitchen, familiar in contemporary times, was already going the rounds then.[9]) Smart goes on: '. . . sometimes taxis appeared on the Embankment throwing out clothes of all kinds to all and sundry without even stopping to ask if the recipient wanted them' (and this in spite of the Night Office). Policemen sometimes gave down-and-outs money from their own pockets,[10] and perhaps the most quixotic givers were the 'Penny Parson' in the south of England, who stood by the roadside giving pennies to passing tramps, and the 'Pie Parson' in the Midlands, who likewise doled out mince pies at Christmas.[11] Skilful begging could still bring in plump rewards. Frank Gray reckoned in 1931 that a beggar with children could earn over £3 in a good week (a working man's wage then was around £2 a week). And John Worby, posing as an unemployed man with a (non-existent) pregnant wife, claiming he had walked all the way from Manchester, netted 25 shillings from just three donors in a West End street. There was meanness, too, however. People might turn aside in scorn at a shabby beggar, perhaps suppressing an uneasy 'there but for the grace of God go I' feeling; tramps could be the butts of young louts;[12] and Laurie Lee found staid English gents most tight-fisted towards buskers. Women, it seems, were more easily touched. Factory girls were generous, and prostitutes could be open-handed towards some gutter-shuffler more degraded than themselves.[13]

Those casual wards which discharged tramps on Sundays unwittingly aided begging, for dischargees had the begging excuse before Sunday promenaders and churchgoers that they could find no work that day; Dorset CVC began clamping down on Sunday discharges for this reason in 1927;[14] and the Yorkshire JVC stopped the Christmas day distribution of old clothes (donated by charity) to casuals, as scroungers were making a Christmas bee-line for the Yorkshire wards.[15]

Organised charities in the form of shelters and labour homes continued as pre-1914. Providence Row Night Refuge and the *Morning Post* shelter still functioned in the 1930s, for example, and the Church Army's Labour Tents had, since the war, been transferred to permanent premises, renamed as the 'King George Work-Aid Home'.[16] On one night in February 1934 London charities were sheltering nearly 2,500 persons (about four times the number in the casual wards). Over 500 of these were in the crude 'sit-ups',[17] commonly crypts, warehouses and other improvised cover where the shelterers slept on chairs, benches or mattresses on the floor. They slept in their own clothes and had no washing facilities. As we have seen, the new LCC Welfare Office began steering applicants away from them on hygiene grounds and because, whilst well-meaning, they did nothing to rehabilitate the down-and-out. But the Victorian and Edwardian charge that they actually encouraged vagrancy no longer seemed to apply, thanks to efforts at screening applicants. The most famous of these, incidentally, in the crypt of St Martin-in-the-Fields, originated during the First World war as an overnight shelter for soldiers adrift on leave in London.[18]

Much charitable effort was, however, being directed towards rehabilitation as well. Because of the concern about youthful vagrancy, charities were established specifically to receive young drifters and set them on the path to employment, and they formed links with official bodies, like casual wards, to receive recommended eligibles.[19] The Central Association for Young Wayfarers, the Young Wayfarers' Hostels, and the Wayfarers'. Benevolent Association are examples, and Frank Gray MP was instrumental in converting an old workhouse into a youth hostel. I have mentioned the work of the Salvation Army and the Christian Social Service Union in this regard in Chapter 19. A similar effort for a wider vagrant age range, prompted by concern at the rising levels of unemployment, was undertaken by the Franciscan Anglican monks, Brother Douglas and Brother Giles at Flowers Farm, Batcombe, near Cerne Abbas from 1921. Tramps were taken in directly off the highway, and received a caring though spartan ministration. The emphasis was on restoring their morale and hope; in return for the care they worked in the centre's market garden. By the early 1930s Franciscan Homes had branched out into several counties, and other philanthropic agencies had copied the idea.[20]

Some of the charity was still tinged with religious condescension. Hot gospel was poured down the vagrants' throats along with the hot soup, and recipients were expected to be humbly grateful. George Orwell describes one incident he witnessed at a church near King's Cross, where tramp recipients were obliged to attend a service, segregated in a balcony from the regular congregation below. The tramps got their own back by chatting, smoking and laughing throughout the service to the discomfiture of the minister.

22 Vagrants, crime and the Vagrancy Act 1935

The traditional ambivalence towards the tramp carried through into the 1930s. He might be an object of pity, perhaps, but underlying fear of the figure of tramp-ogre could quickly rise to the surface and was stirred by the increase in vagrancy in the 1920s. Newspapers carried charged headlines like 'Theft by Tramps', 'Artful Tramps' (caught sleeping in drying sheds at Liverpool), 'Pestered with Beggars', and 'Inhuman Conduct' by a tramp at Eastbourne who burned a servant girl to death with methylated spirits at the door of a house.[1]

It is not surprising that tramps should have a grudge against society when they felt thrown on the scrapheap after fighting for king and country, and when they were branded with a criminal record for committing minor thefts out of sheer desperation. While casual ward conditions continued to be worse than those in jail, the latter could even become a welcome rest to hungry men, and was worth breaking a workhouse window for. Mary Higgs in 1924 quoted a sardonic ballad of Reading jail inscribed on one of its cell walls:

> Thousands there are who scarce can tell
> Where they may lay their head.
> But I've a warm and well-aired bed,
> A bath, good books and bed.
>
> While they are fed on workhouse fare
> And grudged their scanty meal
> Three times a day my meals I get
> Sufficient, wholesome good.
>
> Then to the British public 'Health'!
> Who all our cares relieve
> And while they treat us as they do
> They'll never want for thieves.[2]

171

The Magistrates Association urged in 1923 that casual ward conditions be brought up to the standards of jails, to reduce the temptation to petty crime,[3] and the Governor of Exeter jail recommended before the 1930 Casual Poor Relief Committee that more constructive tasks be given in the wards to reduce the number of offences provoked by frustration and anger.[4]

Quite apart from such crimes of protest, there was, of course, a delinquent sub-culture among tramps; but this involved begging dodges and petty theft, and tramps were rarely violent. George Orwell made the point that in most casual wards just a handful of porters was all that was needed to supervise a ward full of vagrants, for they were mostly harmless and docile. But should serious crime break out in neighbourhoods where tramps were abroad, they were the first suspects.[5]

This prejudice indirectly led in 1933, in the case of a vagrant, one John Thomas Parker, to a tragedy which highlighted the predicament of those forced to sleep out and led to a reform of the Vagrancy Act in 1935. First, I will give some background about sleeping out between the wars. As in the case of begging, prosecutions for sleeping out, after a wartime drop, remained at only a fraction of pre-war levels. Thus the period 1910–14 saw an average of 8,594 prosecutions a year. During 1920–24 they averaged 2,607 a year and continued to fall. Even in the depths of the Depression the numbers were still falling: in 1929 1,910 were prosecuted; in 1931 1,612. The offenders were overwhelmingly male. The conviction rate, up to the very early 1930s, was very low, around 33–40 per cent, following the historic pattern, and, not surprisingly, the chances of being sent to jail upon conviction were lower overall than in begging cases.[6] All the puzzlement I expressed in the last chapter in comparing pre- and post-war levels of prosecution apply here. Some magistrates were giving the 'visible means of subsistence' rule the most indulgent interpretation to let vagrants with a few coppers in their pockets off the hook, but there was nothing new in this. The Vagrancy Act also excused defendants who could give a good account of themselves, and the plea of job-hunting might be good enough for many JPs, when unemployment was measured by the million.[7] The trend by 1934, moreover, shows a remarkable parallel with that for begging; prosecutions in that year, at 1,164, were lower than in 1931, but convictions, at 973, had jumped to over 90 per cent. Nevertheless the proportion of those convicted in 1934 who were actually jailed without option of a fine was much lower than in earlier years; for in 1931 over three-fifths were so jailed, but in 1934 only a quarter.

For the shelterless vagrant night-time meant hanging about the all-night coffee stalls, hoping perhaps for a free cuppa and crust paid for by some other customer,[8] and then wandering off for a kip on the Embankment or under Charing Cross Bridge. It was the inability of the London Night Office to cope with this reviving use of the Embankment that led to its expansion into the Welfare Office in 1935, as we have seen. The scenes of misery were not dissimilar to those observed by the Salvation Army in the 1890s; 'suicide bridge' there speaks for itself.[9] Usually the police turned a blind eye to sleeping out at accepted sites, but occasionally they mounted swoops to clear the Embankment when they felt numbers were building up, and struggling 'sleepers out' were seized; ironically, if you sat on a bench but remained awake the police would leave you alone.[10] The 1930 Casual Poor Relief Committee spoke of 'the benevolence of the police' in handling the vagrancy problem, but little of the vagrants' own point of view was heard before the Committee.

'Sleeping out' and the law were thrown into sharp focus in 1933. John Thomas Parker, an unemployed war veteran, was on the tramp in the Midlands in the summer of that year, looking for work.[11] He had a history of minor charges for gambling and drunkenness but had never been imprisoned. He was picked up by the police in Warwickshire after being found sleeping in a steamroller, and was taken before the Bench at Coleshill, eight miles from Birmingham, where he received 14 days' jail. Parker was the unfortunate victim of two sets of circumstances. Firstly, there had been a spate of housebreakings in Warwickshire recently; the police put vagrants high on their list of suspects, and he had been caught up coincidentally in this sweep. Secondly, the JPs at Coleshill, in contrast with the more compassionate Justices in Birmingham, were hard on vagrants and, it seems, his war record never came up at the hearing. He was removed to Winson Green Prison on 31 May, and proved to be an unruly prisoner. It was to be claimed subsequently that he suffered from claustrophobia (a psychological disturbance not unknown among ex-soldiers), and his unruliness was exacerbated by his sense of injustice. His claustrophobia was denied, or at any rate undetected by the prison doctor. He was given three days' solitary confinement, and while being escorted struggling to the punishment cell, he allegedly (by the prison warders' account) threw himself down a flight of stairs, knocking his head at the bottom. The officers carried him into the cell, but observing after 15 minutes that he had lost consciousness, summoned the doctor, who pronounced him dead (2 June).

A prisoner, Walter Batty, who happened to be at the bottom of the stairs, claimed in a later statement that while he saw Parker fall, he did not see his head 'bump'; this implied that the fatal blow was struck otherwise – throwing suspicion on the warders. The Home Office, however, discounted Batty's evidence as he was a shifty, unreliable character, and at the inquest no less an eminence than the celebrated forensic pathologist, Sir Bernard Spilsbury, bore out the warders' version of how the blow was struck, and the verdict was 'accidental death'. Parker's death had, however, aroused a storm of indignation among ex-servicemen's associations, and the case was taken up in Parliament by two Conservative MPs with distinguished military careers, Brigadier-General Edward Louis Spears and Colonel J. Baldwin Webb. A whole range of political and social opinion, from the Howard League to high Tories, were out for a change in the Vagrancy Act to curb the hounding of sleepers-out. The government response, however, was to point to the rarity of sleeping-out charges, and the fewness of actual jail sentences (only 330 in 1931); while a Home Office inquiry into police policy regarding sleepers indicated to its satisfaction that they would not be arrested unless they were suspicious characters or were 'found in circumstances likely to cause danger or nuisance to the community'. The chief of the Midlands force at Wolverhampton exemplified this with model guidelines to his men: only habitual vagrants should be arrested; respectable itinerants should be offered shelter and food at a police station where necessary.[12] In short, while Parker's death was a tragedy, they saw no reason to amend the Vagrancy Act as it was enforced in practice.

Spears was unhappy about other aspects of the business, and he plied the immovable Home Office with his doubts. There were some questionable features about the warders' evidence, he reckoned, but they had not been cross-examined at the inquest, as Parker's relatives could not afford a lawyer. Spears was outraged at the final indignity heaped on Parker – his dissection for anatomy students: '. . . it is past belief that in this country this should have been the end of a man whose one crime was that he slept a night in the open'.[13]

In March 1935 Spears introduced a private member's bill to modify the Vagrancy Act. His accompanying speech resonated with a call for justice and freedom that transcended party leanings: 'There never was a more blatant example of one law for the rich and another for the poor', for if you had money in your pocket and chose to sleep out as a "health giving" pursuit, the law would not touch you: but if you are poor, so poor that you have not the price of a night's lodging in your pocket, you are a criminal if you sleep out and . . . are liable to be sent to jail'.[14] (Intriguingly his words parallel almost exactly the castigations of the rag-bag 1824 Act by H.G. Codd just 100 years before quoted at the end of Chapter 2.) Spears' bill passed without opposition. The Vagrancy Act of 1935[15] abolishes the simple offence of 'sleeping out'; the defendant is liable only if he 'persistently' wanders about, or fails to go, after being directed, to a 'reasonably accessible place of shelter', or if in sleeping out he causes damage to property or is a public health danger or nuisance in some other way.

The Act had an immediate impact. The 973 convictions of 1934 dropped to 335 in 1936, and only 75 were jailed without option of a fine. This remained roughly the order of statistics up to the war.[16]

23 Britain 1945–70: the roofless, the rootless and the Welfare State

The post-war Labour government was committed to the vision of the famous wartime Beveridge Report – full employment coupled with a specialised and differentiated range of welfare services to replace the conglomerate poor law.[1] The ethos now was to identify the causes of need in each case and to take remedial action before the rot set in too deeply; the poor law ethos had been to alleviate the symptom, destitution, with minimal demand on the public purse.

It was through the National Assistance Act of 1948 that the Welfare State impinged upon the vagrant and the homeless. The new National Assistance Board took over the casual wards as state institutions, to be known, under Part 2 of the Act, as Reception Centres. But whereas the casual wards had taken in any wayfarer, the RCs were charged with taking in persons of an 'unsettled way of life' – the habitual tramps – only. Positive efforts were intended to readjust them to a regular life style: to teach them to hold down a job and live in a fixed abode. Associated re-establishment and rehabilitation centres were established for retraining programmes.

Vagrants, though outside the National Insurance scheme, now became entitled to welfare payments, the discretionary National Assistance benefit which replaced the poor law and the pre-war Unemployment Assistance Board payments. With a basic subsistence in his pocket, the availability of rehabilitation programmes, and the successful achievement of full employment after 1945 the vagrant had lost his excuse to beg. Begging never completely disappeared, but it was reduced to sidling requests for coppers for a cup of tea or bus fare in the West End, at railway stations and in a few beggars' haunts like Cambridge and Brighton. The tramping workseeker would also be a thing of the past, with full employment and a full job-hunting service provided by the Labour Exchanges.

In the optimistic days of early post-war Britain it was expected that once the immediate housing shortages caused by war damage had been made good,[2] a permanent home would be available to all workers. It was anticipated, though, that there would always be a residue of persons temporarily distressed through fire, flood and so forth for whom emergency shelter must be provided. Part 3 of the 1948 Act obliged local authorities to establish hostels for persons 'in urgent need', and it was envisaged that such accommodation would only have to be temporary. Local authorities moreover only assumed responsibility for those with dependent children. The able-bodied single homeless would have to fend for themselves.

At first it looked as though the good intention would be achieved, and vagrancy would wither away. The LCC homeless-ness survey of February 1949 found only six persons sleeping out in central London, and regular homelessness censuses were discon-tinued thereafter.[3] The LCC credited the availability of social security payments to vagrants and their ability to afford lodging house and hostel beds for the transformation. The numbers of vagrants in the reception centres fell away, too, and the NAB was able to shut down more and more. From 134 centres in 1948[4] the figure was reduced to 43 by 1960,[5] and just 17 by 1971.[6] In 1965 just 1,200 persons a night were using the RCs throughout the country.[7] Vagrants obtain their benefit through DHSS (formerly NAB) offices. Officials there liaise with Labour Exchanges to check the applicants' willingness to seek work; they would also advise them on available lodging house and hostel accommodation, but would refer them to a RC instead if they were considered habituals. The 1948 Act continued the poor law principle of making applicants liable to prosecution for persistently and wilfully failing to maintain themselves, but scroungers could dodge this by moving to parts of the country where job-prospects were poor.[8] To reduce the chances of misappropriation, lodging allowances would be payable directly (now by Giro) to the landlord, but clothing allowances could well go on drink instead. A low level 'black economy' developed in which dodgers would claim the DHSS allowances whilst taking on informally-paid casual jobs as market porters and washers-up in restaurants. In London the special DHSS offices for drunks and misfits require a hard-boiled staff to deal with claimants, whose tempers can quickly flare up in frustration. The BBC TV journalist, Tony Wilkinson, who in 1980 went undercover as the vagrant 'Tony Crabbe' for the *Nationwide* programme, witnessed a fight break out at the down-and-outs DHSS office in the East End; and when one man in a queue fell asleep and slumped to the ground, his followers just stepped over him as they moved up the line.[9] An employment exchange in London specialises in offering casual jobs to down-and-outs. Queues form there during the night, some sleeping in cardboard boxes, and when the doors open in the morning there is a scramble.[10]

Any hope that 'Part 3' accommodation needs would dwindle were shattered by 1960. The local authority hostels (some of them former workhouses), though intended to provide emergency accommodation, were in fact from the late 1950s taking in increasing numbers of *long-term* homeless families (to be precise, the mothers and children; husbands had to look after themselves outside). Despite full employment and increasing general affluence, there were disturbing signs of increasing homelessness. The number of persons in LCC 'Part 3'-type accommodation fell to its minimum at about 1,500 in 1957, once the war losses had been made good, but thereafter began rising, and in 1965 stood at 5,750 and was rising still.[11] London's problems were the acutest in the country. In 1968 Inner London (the old LCC area) with six per cent of the population of England and Wales, had 37.5 per cent of the country's 'accepted' homeless in 'Part 3' hostels. All the official figures exclude those technically not accepted as homeless, for instance those families sharing with relatives (whatever the overcrowding), and those who have made themselves homeless by default, for instance by walking out in family rows. This let-out provided local authorities with considerable scope for turning away applicants from their increasingly overburdened 'Part 3' services.

The causes of this increasing problem in the booming sixties were complex and outside the scope of this book, but were connected with inner-city redevelopments in which houses were demolished and office blocks and new roads took their place, the failure to match job creation with house creation (most particularly in the London region), and the 'baby boom' of the 1960s.[12] The decay of the inner cities was an evident fact of life by the mid-1960s. Other sociological developments aggravated the problem: whilst Greater London's population was declining in the 1960s the actual number of independent households seeking separate accommodation increased. This was because households were splitting up and getting smaller through, for example, the tendency for children to leave home earlier and set up for themselves, and because of an increase in divorce and in the number of unmarried mothers.[13]

The 'Part 3' hostels belied the intentions of 1948, for they became an isolated perpetuation of the old Dickensian, deterrent poor law. Not only were husbands excluded but the mothers were expected to have found accommodation in three months, or else they were evicted, too, and their children taken into care. As far as the local authorities were concerned the accommodation was (in principle) temporary and as they wanted the inmates out as soon as possible, conditions must be kept more unpleasant than in any private rented accommodation.[14]

The journalist and playwright Jeremy Sandford visited 'Part 3' hostels, including Newington Lodge, in Southwark in London, to gather material. In an article in 1961 he revealed how three or more families were crammed into one room, containing up to 13 beds, and how 65 people had to share two toilets. Dysentery was rife, and new arrivals had to have their backsides swabbed. In the afternoons the inmates were turned out into the streets, regardless of weather, as they were supposed to be looking for accommodation. They went in dread of the bullying officers and were reluctant to complain.[15] In 1962 Mary Cecil, who had been separated from her husband, described her own experiences at Newington Lodge in another article.[16] A barely furnished cubicle was allotted to her and her children; the mattresses were an inch deep, and the pillows so hard they 'might have been filled with sand'. The staff were brusque, peremptory and unfeeling. The inmates had to clean the place, and the food was unappetising – 'grey porridge and greasy kippers' for breakfast. During the day they all had to congregate in the day room, mothers sitting while their children milled about: 'The room was as desolate as everywhere else; some broken and bashed-about chairs, a rickety table, no radio, telly or tinny piano, not even a proper window. It was like a communal cell, a painting by Hogarth.'

Sandford's television play *Cathy Come Home*, first screened in 1966, had a dramatic impact in alerting the public to the squalor of 'Part 3' hostels. The story figured the progressive descent of a fictional homeless couple, Reg and Cathy Ward, till they are split up when Cathy has to enter 'Cambermere Lodge' with her children. As the three month deadline approaches, she leaves rather than see her children taken into care, and the play ends when she and her children are found sleeping in a railway station, and the latter are removed by police and welfare officers against her anguished protests.

Cathy led to the formation of the housing campaign movement 'Shelter', but while conditions in 'Part 3' hostels did improve in the late 1960s,[17] the numbers of homeless increased, for the 12,400 persons in 'Part 3' nationally in 1966 had risen to 20,000 in 1972;[18] the swamped local authorities began turning in desperation to bed and breakfast hotels.

By the mid-1960s the worsening situation was also evincing itself in an increase among those sleeping rough. Fundamental to the problem was the long-term change in housing patterns. The chances of finding a bed-sitter to rent were dwindling rapidly. In 1914 90 per cent of homes were rented from private landlords; in 1950 this was down to 44 per cent and by 1971 to 14 per cent.[19] Owner-occupation had grown, and so had local authority rented housing, but the latter has catered for families, not single person households, and it is this social category that has grown so rapidly in modern times and which to the present day is least catered for and in the direst predicament. Whereas in 1931, seven in every hundred lived alone, by 1971 it was one in five: the greatest increase was among the young[20] owing to the dispersion of families in modern times. Major factors in the decline of the private rented

sector has been the demolition of the Victorian villas (suitable for
sub-letting), rent control and tenant protection laws, and the
greater profitability of converting the villa stock into leasehold
flats. Hand-in-hand with this shrinkage has been the decline of that
traditional resort of the down but not entirely out, the common
lodging house. Inner-city redevelopment and comparative low
profitability are the causes. Liverpool, for example, had 5,895
registered beds in 1930 and 695 in 1971. Manchester had 2,427
beds in 1950 and 906 in 1970.[21] In 1965 the 34,600 beds in the
whole country were only a little more than the number that
London alone had ninety years before;[22] these fell by nearly 6,600
over the next seven years[23] and the decline continues.[24] Private
commercial lodging houses offered well below half of all beds by
1965 and municipal hostels about a sixth, but voluntary organisations were now dominating the scene more and more, with the
Salvation Army still the largest of these. Although, as we shall see
later in the book, specialist voluntary agencies for the young, the
alcoholics, females and so forth have entered the scene increasingly
since the 1960s and have established new hostels to replace the
crowded old lodging houses and the larger barrack-like Salvation
Army institutions, the modern preference for small, intimate
hostels with higher standards of amenity has made it impossible to
make up the bed-loss.

Cathy Come Home should be set against the campaign launched in
the early 1960s by concerned charities like Christian Action and
the Simon Community to awaken the public to the problem of
homelessness. A rally in Trafalgar Square in 1964 was attended by
ecclesiastical eminences like Donald Soper, Mervyn Stockwood and
the Archbishop of Westminster.[25] The media latched on to make it
a fashionable issue, while a spate of pamphlets and books in the
middle and later 1960s focused attention on society's casualties and
derelicts.[26]

The LCC was sufficiently alerted to the problem in 1963 to
conduct the first homelessness surveys since 1949, and found over
120 people sleeping rough in central London, while the National
Assistance Board undertook a national survey in 1965[27] and found
just under 1,000 sleeping rough in the whole UK, over a quarter of
whom were in London alone. These official counts were certainly
underestimates, for the searchers did not (and could not) know the
secret places where down-and-outs were adept at concealing
themselves.[28]

How many single homeless were there in the country, whether
sleeping rough, or in some kind of shelter? The single homeless
have not to date been the concern of any public authority, so there
are no official estimates; in any case, much real homelessness
would be concealed by youngsters' sharing 'crash pads', squatting,
and living in the remaining lodging houses and shelters. But

different unofficial estimates put it conservatively at 50,000 around 1970 in Britain as a whole and 12,000 in London alone: this included those in lodging houses, reception centres, prisons and psychiatric institutions, as well as those sleeping rough.[29] It was symptomatic of the growing crisis that the Embankment Welfare Office was shut in 1969 because Westminster Council (which had taken over from the disbanded LCC in 1965 all the placement responsibilities) could no longer cope with the increasing number of applicants.[30]

It was also evident by the early 1960s that the reception centres were not succeeding in their intended objective, for while they were then claiming a high rate of job-finding at a time of full employment, their ex-clients were not holding them down for long, as the small numbers of vagrants then finding their way to RCs were the residue – the mentally disordered, the alcoholics, the inadequates and the workshy.[31] In fact, the location of many RCs well away from convenient centres of population and jobs, for example Stormy Down, 25 miles from Cardiff, indicates that their real purpose was now to segregate the inmates from society. The routine continued much from the earlier casual wards – the showering and inspection for vermin on entry, the dressing in nightshirts and the compulsory light worktask (usually cleaning the place) – but there was no power of detention once the task was completed, and the diet was fortified to rebuild the vagrants' stamina. The arrivals were interviewed, and advice was given on job-finding. Job-hunters could be excused work tasks and once in employment they could stay until private digs were found for them. Many however came to look on the RC as a permanent 'home', spending their social security pocket money on meths and rough cider. The atmosphere of many RCs was very bleak. Robin Page at Brighton 'Spike' in 1970 found bunk beds in a dormitory with cold, bare concrete floors; the dining hall likewise had a bare concrete floor, and the lights were shadeless. But the most notorious 'Spike' – and by far the biggest in the country – was the one at Camberwell in South London. It was originally built as a workhouse in 1878, a gaunt, three-storeyed structure with 900 beds in the early 1970s, and which even before the war was considered fit for closure.[32]

When Tony Wilkinson visited Camberwell in late 1980 he found the dormitory blocks like grim warehouses; there were 150 in his own dormitory, which was lit by one red light bulb. Meals were eaten, workhouse-like, at long institutional tables, and the staff were cold, brusque and aloof. Many of the inmates there seemed mentally disordered – babbling schizophrenics and the like.[33] He summed up his experience later as 'a sojourn in a mental hospital with no doctors, it was a warehouse for misfits, a storage space'.[34] Robin Page at Camberwell in 1973 was revolted at the physical specimens he saw in the shower: 'a collection of pot-bellies, sore-covered legs (sometimes caused by louse bites) and flabby muscles'. Tony Wilkinson leaves us with an even more ghastly description of the physical grotesques he saw there: '. . . a whole collection of trolls, wizards, big bad uncles, sprites and ogres. Many were the faces of church gargoyles, sunken noses, bulging eyes, faces with sheep's hair and eagle's beaks, faces pitted with burns, or erupting buboes . . .'

Although not all 'Spikes' were as depressing as Camberwell,[35] all had to come to terms with the fact that a high proportion of their inmates would never be able to face the outside world, or at least never find jobs.

24 Homelessness and the official response 1970–85

From 1973 the world recession brought a steady rise in unemployment in Britain to over 1,300,000 by 1979, and with the advent of a Conservative government that year devoted to public spending cuts, unemployment spiralled (causally, coincidentally, or both) to over 3,000,000 by the mid-1980s.[1] Public housing investment programmes have been severely hit, and the homelessness problem has got drastically worse.[2] This is primarily a Metropolitan crisis, for the south-east has been least affected by the depression, so the drift of young job-seekers to a region of sky-high rents and property prices has aggravated an already parlous situation.[3] Greater London in the early 1970s, even before the recession, had about half the country's persons in temporary accommodation,[4] and in 1971 some London boroughs, with their 'Part 3' hostels filled up, began installing homeless families in private hotels, paying the nightly charge for bed and breakfast.[5] This began spreading to the provinces and then mushroomed since, so that by mid-1986 local authorities in Britain were said to be placing some 12,000 families a year in bed and breakfast accommodation[6] ('b-and-b' as I shall refer to it). The costs are staggering. In 1984 b-and-b's in the south-east charged on average over £156 a week for a couple with two children.[7] If the family are unemployed and on supplementary benefit from the DHSS, the rent costs are shared between the local authority and the DHSS, but 95 per cent of those living in b-and-b's (whether employed or not) have found their own way there, independently of the local authorities, and where these are on supplementary benefit, too, the DHSS has this extra bill. The costs to the DHSS of b-and-b started getting out of hand in the 1980s – from £52,000,000 in 1979 to £380,000,000 in 1984,[8] a reflection of the increasing numbers resorting to them, growing unemployment and rising rents on a sellers' market. B-and-b's have in fact filled the place of the old common lodging houses,[9] but at least the lodging houses had the merit of cheapness. The pressure on local authorities to accommodate homeless families was intensified by the 1977 Housing

(Homeless Persons) Act. This well-intentioned measure was subsequently starved by the lack of public funds to make it work. It compelled local authorities to find accommodation *other* than 'Part 3' shelter, through their housing department, for certain 'priority' groups – families with children (including one-parent families), and certain categories of the single homeless like the mentally and physically handicapped, the aged, and the 'vulnerable' (the plight of homeless youths at risk from sexual exploitation was meant here, in the wake of the 1975 *Johnny Go Home* revelations, as we shall see later in the book). Local authorities now became responsible for the eligible categories who were newly arrived in their area or had just dumped themselves on them, and there was much resentment at the scope for queue-jumping in the housing waiting lists presented by the Act. It widened the range of homeless the authorities now had to 'accept', so the figures for official homeless before and after 1977 are not comparable. Thus the figure of a 700 per cent increase in 'accepted' homelessness in the GLC area between 1970 and 1985,[10] whilst revealing a truly shocking rise, is distorted by this factor. But the number of homeless households accepted by local authorities as 'priority' cases under the Act has risen from nearly 75,000 in 1981 to 85,000 in 1983.[11] Since the money is not there to find them all permanent council accommodation, the Acts's effects have been to enrich the proprietors of seedy hotels.

The policy of the Conservative government under Margaret Thatcher since taking office in 1979 has been to look to voluntary organisations to offer shelter (with public subsidies) for special groups like the young and alcoholics, and to housing associations[12] to fill the gap caused by the decline in the private rented sector. A proper discussion of the subject is outside the scope of this book but it should be pointed out that modern hostels, offering individual rooms and civilised amenities in small, intimate units, cannot offer the same bed density as the older 'barracks' they are replacing; as, for instance, the Salvation Army closes the latter in favour of the former, so on balance they are losing accommodation. Moreover, official reliance on voluntary initiative can give local authorities an excuse to do nothing themselves,[13] and voluntary organisations like the Cyrenians and St Mungo's are too small to make a real impact on a vast social problem. The government's espousal of voluntarism has led it to plan the closure of the Reception Centres (renamed Re-settlement Units in 1980), and disperse the down-and-outs into small, therapeutic hostels. In 1985 Camberwell 'Spike' was shut, but the government-assisted 'Camberwell Replacement Scheme', a collection of small hostels run by voluntary organisations and housing associations to take its place, has been just a one-off, and the government is not providing sufficient funds for a comprehensive nationwide 'care in the community' programme.[14] To knowledgeable observers the closures appear to be a money-saving move by the government, and one has remarked that the plans 'have been ill-thought out and that broad policies for single homeless people are chaotic and getting worse'.[15]

This 'chaos' was also reflected in the government's new DHSS board and lodging regulations announced in 1984, an emergency response to the runaway expenditures on b-and-b assistance already described. The increasing numbers of youthful recipients attracted the government's concern (among under-25s they rose from 23,000 to 37,000 in the two years to the end of 1984), and the image of youthful 'Costa del Dole' lotus eaters became firmly imprinted in the government's mind, from allegations that south coast seaside guest houses were advertising in northern newspapers for custom among the unemployed and even offering to pay the rail fares, such were the profits to be made from DHSS-financed rents.[16] The government was also suspicious that some claimants were defrauding the DHSS with false claims for rents paid.[17]

The regulations announced in December 1984 applied to those under 26: the maximum DHSS board and lodging allowance was to be reduced, and the period for which it was to be paid was to be limited to periods ranging from two to eight weeks in any DHSS district. Thereafter the claimant must move to another district to re-qualify. The object was keep youngsters 'on the move' looking for work. They did include exemptions, for example for the physically or mentally ill, those with children, and those with difficult circumstances at home that prevented their return, but the regulations aroused a storm of protest. They suffered technical legal reverses in their implementation, but enforced they were.[18] Opponents claimed that youngsters were not leaving home on a whim, as the government seemed to assume. Roland Boyes MP said in December 1984[19] that the crisis of the growing numbers of young homeless 'is not the result of a rapid growth in the attraction of young people to the so-called bright lights of large cities. In many instances they have been forced to leave home because of the breakdown of relationships with parents. It is no coincidence that that has arisen at a time of record unemployment.' With one in three marriages breaking down in divorce in the 1980s coupled with the inevitable family friction when unemployed children languish at home, the young homeless are so often fugitives from domestic disintegration, and they are at the mercy of officials' interpretation of the exceptions to the regulations. The new board and lodging allowance maxima have been attacked as below the prevailing levels of rents demanded in the area that youngsters are most drawn to in the search for work and that they will be forced into worse and more crowded b-and-b rooms. To critics they smack of a return in modern form to the old harassing approach to vagrants: as Michael Meacher MP put it, the government was 'reviving the practice of parish relief of the Elizabethan poor law era whereby the poor were hounded from parish to parish until they were eventually forced to return to their parish of origin.'[20]

Finally, one other response to homelessness, and a makeshift expedient at that, has been an official tolerance towards 'squatting' in short-life empty property by recognised squatters' groups. The squatting campaign was a side-effect of *Cathy Come Home* in the late 1960s; squatters felt their action was justified by the large volume of condemned but still serviceable property acquired by local authorities and left empty for long periods prior to demolition. After early struggles to evict squatters, some local authorities relented. The 1977 Criminal Law Act made squatting a criminal offence and not just a civil trespass (this was set against the background of squatting in private premises by 'hippie' groups; displaced owners could now call in the police and avoid the rigmarole of a civil court order). But at the same time, responsible squatter placement groups were now securing the co-operation of local authorities in sheltering young people in patch-repaired condemned properties.[21]

25 From lodging house to bed and breakfast hotel: the story to date

The worst lodging houses in the post-War period had changed little since George Orwell's day. Merfyn Turner in 1960 found one in the Midlands, for example, 'where three hundred men lied in indescribably poor conditions', and was 'reminiscent of Newgate and the debtors' prisons, and second rate public urinals'. Lodging houses had long ceased to be the bawdy establishments of Victorian England, but were often highly unsatisfactory from a sanitary standpoint. The inmates included the aged, the mentally incapable and the alcoholic. Tim Cook found similar conditions in 1975, and cited one field researcher's description of the degradation within: 'epileptics having fits surrounded by applauding men, obsessional behaviour (an hour to cut a sausage), men continually scratching themselves, men eating scraps from the floor and from other men's plates'.[1]

Some, Turner found, had developed a positive liking for the life, its freedom and companionship. But any blithe notion of the "'appy dosser' must be dispelled by more recent surveys that have shown that hostel-dwellers are deeply unhappy with their enforced communalism, and yearn for privacy and the luxury of having a key to their own room.[2] One sympathetic observer refutes a prejudice that residents are largely social security scroungers, since those with no fixed abode receive lower benefits and find it hard to register on doctors' panels.[3]

Most of the remaining lodging houses and hostels in the early 1970s were in buildings built before 1914, and crude night shelters of the crypt, railway arch and disused factory type exist to the present time. The same criticisms of them as expressed before the war still apply today, and in 1985 the Campaign for the Homeless and Rootless described them as 'the worst and most deplorable element in the ragbag of "housing" provided for single homeless people'.[4] But they persist because there continues to be a need for them. The closures due to urban redevelopment have hit all types of shelter; thus in 1972 a large Rowton Hotel, Butterwick House in Hammersmith, was closed in such a scheme with a loss of 750 beds. The local authority only provided enough substitute buildings for 100 beds and left it to charities to run them.[5] In 1968 the Salvation Army had four hostels and 461 beds in Birmingham, but after the great city centre redevelopment project, it was down to one hostel and 187 beds by 1978.[6]

Contemporary journalistic forays into the world of the down-and-out show just how abysmal the remaining cheap hotels and hostels are. The *Sunday Times* in 1978 described the Highgate Hotel in Birmingham, where 65p then bought a seven by five foot cubicle for the night. In this depressing five storey pile there were only nine baths for the 450 inmates. The WCs lacked doors and seats, and no toilet paper was provided. The corridors were dark and cavernous. Bedsheets were discoloured, and a 25p fine was imposed for bedwetting. The residents were largely alcoholics, mental hospital discharges and old age pensioners trying to cling to their independence.[7]

Jeremy Sandford recorded in 1972 his visit to a Glasgow doss-house where most men were eating with their fingers, as they could not afford the 3d hire charge for utensils; while London's Bruce House, though municipally owned, had over the previous 20 years degenerated to a dump, he found. A notice on the wall cautioned: 'Prevention of Consumption. Do not spit'. A man was cooking up a disgusting-smelling stew from rotten vegetables on a hot plate: 'Another man, one of whose feet has been securely wrapped in a polythene bag tied with string round his ankle is trying to grill bacon in the top of a tin that formerly held Snowcem. The pigeons go where they want through the smokey atmosphere, picking up titbits.'[8] More recently Tony Wilkinson, whose excursion was prompted by the rapid rise in unemployment after 1979 (there were an estimated 51,000 living in hostels or lodging houses in Britain in 1981[9]), found similar conditions at Bruce House in 1980: a bed then cost £1.65p a night, the price, he said, of 'danger, squalor and neglect' in this huge barrack, despite refurbishment.[10] Winos were sitting in the huge TV chamber passing bottles around; aggressive drunks were picking fights. Litter was piled high, chairs were upturned and heaps of fouled bedding lay in the corridor (though the bedsheets in the small sleeping cubicles were on the whole clean, if worn). None of the WCs had toilet paper and their floors ran with urine. What shocked him particularly was that the fire doors were bolted. The authorities, he reckoned, were more concerned with security than the lives of the inmates, for as we shall see later in this chapter, hostels and lodging houses present a considerable fire risk.

The fact is that Westminster Council, which ran Bruce House, was deliberately letting the place run down, for it wished to redevelop the site. Its 700 beds in 1973 were down to 400 by the end of 1985, and the Council was waiting for a commercial developer to buy it up for a nominal sum, on condition that the scheme included provision for a new shelter – but offering only 100 beds.[11]

In his tour through London's dosserland Wilkinson found the prevalence of alcoholics – and he felt himself physically at risk on at least one occasion from unpredictable and aggressive winos. One commercial shelter – a collection of huts under a railway arch, a bit like a prisoner-of-war camp – specifically excluded drunks. Desperate overcrowding was another of his experiences; at a cheap Bayswater hotel he paid £4 a night to share a room 20 feet by 15 with four other men.

Rowton Houses followed the same pattern. From the 1950s the Rowton organisation decided to upgrade itself into the field of higher-class commercial hotels, and neglected the upkeep of its working men's establishments.[12] Already by 1963 they were described as a little lower in the scale than Bruce House.[13] Rowton's six hotels in London in 1960 were down to three by the early 1980s,[14] and when Rowton's announced in 1982 its plan to close down all its remaining working men's accommodation and evict the inmates, it provoked a crisis. By then conditions at Rowton's were at least as bad as those just described for the Highgate Hotel and Bruce House. At Arlington House in Camden there was a ratio of one bath to 62 residents; the WCs were all in the basement of the five-storey block. The ventilation was poor and the tiny seven foot by five foot sleeping cubicles were unbearably hot in summer. At Tower House (Tower Hamlets) conditions were even worse. Ceiling and wall plaster was coming away; the toilets were flooded with urine; the sheets were not changed between lettings; and in 1983 the lodgers there had 100 times the national rate of TB. Rowton's were also in the habit of locking fire doors, and in 1982 three Tower House residents who dared complain to the fire brigade were evicted. The clientele appears to have gone downhill as well since before the war; many of the apparently unemployed at Arlington in 1982 were thought to be in the 'black economy' but claiming social security. However, Sandy Craig in 1984 did find still the shabby-genteel type of resident, like the retired clerk who was always neatly attired and groomed.[15]

The London boroughs in which the Rowton's were situated now faced a dilemma. Their closure would mean that the boroughs would have several thousand new down-and-outs on their streets. They decided to buy up the hotels instead, and Camden faced the biggest bill with Arlington House which cost it £1,400,000 in 1983. But it had a white elephant on its hands, for the costs of renovation and of finding accommodation for the inmates displaced by the reduced bed-densities were to prove staggering, and the government failed to help out.

I noted in Chapter 24 how official circles look to voluntary agencies and housing associations, both duly subsidised from public funds, to fill the gap in supply for the needs of the homeless as the old lodging houses and barrack-shelters dwindle. Space does not permit a full treatment of the development of voluntary hostels, but they began to multiply from the early 1960s and a clearing house to place applicants in appropriate centres, the National Association of Voluntary Hostels, was formed in 1961.[16] The hostels aim to cater to special needs, like drug addicts, alcoholics and the young, for example, and the welfare workers often live in and share their clients' (or 'patients') life-style in the centres to forge a bond. The Simon Community, founded by a former probation officer, Anton Wallich-Clifford in 1963, was a pioneer in this approach, and developed offshoots like 'Simonlight' (for meths drinkers) and 'Simonscene' (for drug addicts). St Mungo's broke away from 'Simon' in 1969 and continued Simon's original soup run.

The Anglican Franciscans were still running their rescue centre at Cerne Abbas in Dorset in the 1960s as in the 1920s, and a religious venture at Pilsden in the same county performs today a similar function.[17] In Lancashire the *Morning Star* hostels for vagrant alcoholics got off the ground as a Catholic venture with help from local businessmen in 1963. Christian Action, a religious social outreach organisation, originally founded in 1940, was, by the 1960s, particularly concerning itself with homelessness and began running hostels. It helped focus attention on the needs of vagrant women, who, as they only form a very small percentage of all vagrants, have often been overlooked.[18] The Salvation Army has also contributed to the care of vagrant women at its Hopetown Hostel in Whitechapel,[19] while Centrepoint in London's Soho gives emergency shelter to the homeless young. These few examples only skim the subject. The trend in hostel care towards intimacy and the recognition that more civilised amenities for inmates, such as individual rooms, are essential to the rehabilitation process, means that beds cannot be offered on the mass scale of the old barrack dormitories. Thus the newer hostels cannot meet the demand for shelter, intensified in the mid-1980s by unemployment and the shrinkage of the private rented sector.[20]

The Campaign for the Homeless and Rootless, formed in 1973 as a research and advisory body for concerned charities, has as its cardinal campaigning principle that shelter for the homeless should be a public authority not a voluntary agency responsibility as the latter do not have the resources to cope with the sheer scale of the problem. It was estimated that in 1983 around 12,000 slept rough each night in London each night.[21]

The Salvation Army also reflects the change of approach in vagrant care. Since the war, and up to 1980, commentators have continued to criticise the impersonality of Salvation Army care.

Expressions like 'warehouse' and 'Dickensian fortress-like building' have been used to describe its enormous dormitory barracks, and the therapeutic sterility of such shelter has also been criticised.[22] At least (according to Tony Wilkinson) the Salvation Army did not seem to ram religion down the throats of its clients as it did in pre-war days. The human wreckage that found its way to the Sally Ann – the battered alcoholics, the enuretics, the verminous, the bronchitics and consumptives, needed long-term upliftment. From 1981, therefore, the Salvation Army embarked on a plan to close the great 'warehouses' and replace them with networks of 'cluster flats';[23] these are more expensive and space-consuming bed for bed, however, and must mean a contraction in the bed-places that the Salvation Army will have to offer.

Philanthropic work for the homeless takes other forms as well. 'Crisis at Christmas' was formed in 1974 to raise funds and distribute blankets and food to the down-and-outs, and prick the public's conscience in the season of good cheer and bad weather; soup runs still go the rounds of the known dossers' haunts, like Charing Cross Bridge. Day centres like the ones at Lambeth and St Martin-in-the-Fields, London, and St Anne's Day Centre, Leeds (which is also a detoxification centre for alcoholic vagrants), offer down-and-outs counselling and a chance to wash and tidy themselves.[24] The 'Silver Lady' soup van and old-style soup-and-sermon religious missions, like the London Embankment Mission, still operate. Nothing has changed basically since the 1930s.[25]

Cheap bed and breakfast hotels were originally a cut above the common lodging houses to those who could afford them. Thomas Callaghan[26] resorted to a b-and-b in north London around 1945 as a respite from lodging house squalor. At least you might get a room to yourself, but conditions could be very seedy. Callaghan's host rarely changed the sheets, and uneaten food was reheated and served up again the next day.

I noted in Chapter 24 how b-and-b's have, in more recent times, come into increasing prominence to give emergency shelter to the homeless, and how the sellers' market had given profiteers (and indeed racketeers) rich pickings.

The scandals connected with b-and-b hotels were becoming known as early as 1974, when Shelter exposed the crowding, lack of privacy, inadequacy of WCs and baths, exclusion of lodgers during the day when they had to walk the streets, and exorbitant rents.[27] 'Breakfasts' were sometimes nominal – a packet of Corn-flakes and a bottle of milk left outside the door. One Earls Court hotel was described in 1983: for £30 a week a single lodger endured irregular or non-existent hot water, grimy windows, threadbare and dusty carpets and a bed that was not made up for him. A girl told the investigator about the breakfasts: 'Sometimes they have run out of bread, so there's no toast. Sometimes the milkman hasn't arrived, so there's no tea.'[28] Many unattached young people coming from the depressed provinces to London to find work end up in such places, and single girls are vulnerable to sexual propositioning from managers; and tenants are sometimes warned unpleasantly not to complain about conditions.[29]

From time to time scandals and tragedies centred on b-and-b's have received press exposure. In 1982 Iffley Road Oxford received unenviable publicity after wholesale police arrests there in connection with alleged frauds on the DHSS by b-and-b lodgers. The 'Nanford Guest House' there with 75 beds brought the proprietor an estimated potential income of £3,000 a week. The place was crowded out and filled with the noises of babies, cassettes, television and 'drunks from other rooms'. An eye witness said that 'a middle-aged alcoholic can expect a room with three others and a caterer's baked bean can as a po.' At another Iffley Road b-and-b 11 adults and 6 babies occupied 6 bedrooms.[30]

But probably the most long-running scandal surrounded 'Princes Lodge' at 747 Commercial Road, Stepney.[31] This former seamen's hostel was reopened as a b-and-b hotel in 1980 by a company called 'Namecourt'. They advertised in the press as follows:

Couples and Children
Single Parents and Children
Couples or Two Friends Sharing
NO MONEY?
WE CAN HELP!
Own room, free cooking facilities/heating/constant
hot water etc. . . .

The reality was very different. Horror stories began filtering through to the press. The overcrowding was desperate: though designed for 90 persons, it held anything from 200 to 500; glue sniffing, prostitution and fights were rife; few of the ovens in the kitchen worked; people had to eat their breakfasts on the floor; whole families were squeezed into single pokey rooms; mice ran over the babies' cots. It was a serious fire hazard; 40 firemen were needed to tackle a blaze there in June 1980. A *Sunday Times* investigation in 1981[32] found the place teeming with children of many nationalities; toilets were filthy and some not working: 'Last Wednesday an asphalt roof outside a first-floor bathroom was covered with raw sewage from a blocked soil waste where the access plate had been removed.' The *East London Advertiser* in October 1982 told how a man, his wife and three children lived in a room 11 feet by 16 for £63.90 a week. There was no table to eat their spartan breakfasts at. The man said: 'Day and night there are fights going on, women drunk or on drugs run around the landing naked and openly having sex in front of young children.' People generally were too scared to complain, but neighbours were writing to the press, and local teachers noted the disturbed behaviour of 'Princes Lodge' children. A Thames TV crew that went down to do a feature on the place was assaulted. Although some London boroughs stopped sending their homeless there, Namecourt just advertised more distantly for private custom and in 1982 was said to be making anything from £200,000 to £500,000 a year from the place.

A campaign group was started to press Tower Hamlets borough to impose a compulsory purchase order. The great problem for local authorities under stress like Tower Hamlets is that they have to turn a blind eye to many abuses and breaches of the law in the worst b-and-b's, such is the pressure of homelessness and the shortage of accommodation.

In March 1984 John Pilger in the *Daily Mirror* published a graphic exposé of Princes Lodge.[33] A family with six children paid nearly £197 a week for two rooms (the children slept in the larger one, which was 6 feet by 15, in shifts). Of the 16 toilets for 500 people, not one was in a suitable condition: '. . . no hot water in bathrooms, no drinking water, no radiators working, blocked basins, overloaded electrical points, defective lighting, broken bottles on the main staircase . . .' – the litany went on. Publicity forced Tower Hamlets to move: first a Control Order to take over, effectively, the management of the place, and then moves to buy it.

Of course, many b-and-b's, whilst more scrupulously managed, are still very expensive and out to make exorbitant profit: the 'Costa del Dole' opportunism was mentioned in the last chapter.[34] 'Houses in Multiple Occupation' (HMOs) is the generic term for all sublet premises. In 1983 it was reckoned that 85 per cent of the country's HMOs were below a satisfactory standard, and the most lethally objectionable feature of this is the fire risk.[35] Exposed, frayed and overloaded wiring in crowded b-and-b's and bed-sitters, inflammable bedding near heaters and stoves, lack of fire extinguishers, and negligence by (perhaps drunken) lodgers, all conspire to make such places incendiary piles. In 1977 there were 172 fire deaths in HMOs, and the trend was rising despite a provision in the Housing Act 1980 compelling local authorities to enforce fire regulations; in 1982 there were 279 deaths.[36] In 1978 at Clacton nine people died in a fire at a hostel for ex-psychiatric patients.[37] In 1979 the Grove Hotel, Leeds, went up in flames, and despite its 'disgusting state of disrepair' with leaking roof and broken flooring it had still been passed as 'satisfactory' by Leeds Council – again, an instance of a hard-pressed authority winking at abuses; two people died in that fire.[38] An outbreak of fire in a Camden b-and-b in 1984 that asphyxiated an Asian woman and her two young children revealed the following circumstances: 'When it started, no alarm rang. It had been switched off. The fire extinguishers were empty. The fire exits were blocked. It was night time but the stairs were in darkness because there were no bulbs in the light sockets.' And in the deceased woman's cramped room, the cooker was next to the bed.[39]

Non-commercial hostels have proved just as bad. In 1980 when the Missionaries of Charity Hostel in Kilburn, London, went up in flames, 10 people died.[40] Tony Wilkinson's shock at the padlocked fire doors at Bruce House in 1980 has been mentioned; the inmates were blatantly ignoring regulations by smoking in their cubicles in close proximity to toxically inflammable foam mattresses.[41] But it was the fire that engulfed three connected HMOs in Clanricarde Gardens, Notting Hill, in 1981, killing eight people and making 100 homeless,[42] that really prompted campaign action. HMO reform campaign groups, under the auspices of the Campaign for the Homeless and Rootless, were formed around the country, to expose conditions locally and shame local authorities into action. The movement was behind the Houses in Multiple Occupation Bill in December 1982, to consolidate and strengthen existing relevant housing laws to compel local authorities to act. However, the government had reservations about its 'practicability and cost' and the Bill failed; a diluted version was introduced again in the House of Lords in 1986.[43]

26 'Horizontal meffers' and other contemporary vagrant types

The colourful, eccentric tramp character, as depicted by tramp-authors like W.H. Davies and Jim Phelan, is a rarity.[1] The vast majority of tramps are miserable wretches with personality and psychiatric disorders, or the plain unemployed and homeless.

Alcoholic vagrancy has taken on a sharper significance, since alcoholism, from its low point between the wars, has re-emerged as a growing social problem since the 1950s. The level of drunkenness convictions in the United Kingdom in the early 1980s was around four times the level of the late 1940s.[2] In 1968 nearly two-fifths of Camberwell 'Spike' intake were found to have a drink problem[3] and a GLC Survey of down-and-outs in central London in 1984 showed that 30 per cent were on the bottle, too.[4] Robin Page, in his visit to a Salvation Army shelter in 1973, saw many of these alcoholic wrecks, the victims of drunken flare-ups: 'Many . . . had black eyes, bent and broken noses and scars above the eyes and on the cheeks showing what could happen at the slightest provoca-tion . . . a red-faced man had a bottle of cheap wine which he was proudly showing to a sickly-looking and prematurely-grey friend, and soon they retired to the toilets, to return afterwards, swaying and happy.' Tony Wilkinson in 1980 at the Tower Bridge Hotel found the place full of alcoholics and felt a sense of danger from the volatile and potentially violent tempers of aggressive drunkards. In the sleeping quarters, the 'smell of sweat was now mixed with the stench of vomit. . . . Oh on the far wall I saw spatterings of what looked like half-digested food, and I almost turned to walk out.'

Among the alcoholic vagrants there is a distinct scale of descent – from rough cider and cheap wine at the top, down to meths. The 'Skid Row' dregs will take anything that offers temporary oblivion, including surgical spirits, paint stripper and boot-polish sandwiches.[5] In the 1960s a spate of publications – un-intentionally lurid and nauseating – gave the public an insight into the revolting squalor of the world of the meths men.[6] Before the war they hung out, it seems, under railway arches,[7] and after the war they moved into the bomb sites ('ramps') of the East End of

194

London, to 'skipper' among the derelict buildings ('derries'). There they lived on dustbin garbage and rotten vegetables from Spitalfields Market and were known to kill stray cats on bomb sites for food. The jakies (meths drinkers) would do casual market jobs to raise money for drink, and some also bought drugs, like heroin or pep pills, dealing with pedlars who operated sometimes in public lavatories. Their lifestyle and ingestions led to progressive physical breakdown – incontinence, liver destruction, the loss of sight, and the sense of taste and touch; some had suffered the amputation of toes or even entire limbs from frostbite. They were riddled with TB and vermin, their clothing was fouled with their own urine and excrement, they suffered from exposure and rarely survived beyond 50. According to Sally Trench (a girl from an affluent background seized with an urge to live among the jakies to try and help them in the 1960s), during the exceptionally bitter winter of 1963 the police were picking six bodies a week off the bomb sites. Geoffrey Fletcher was conducted to a 'skipper', a ruinous house: 'Unshaven men slept in their filth. The whole place was coal black from carbon deposits, the rats scuttled away from the torchlight and on the remains of a bed a man slept, his companions on the floor'. In the next room was a bed 'heaving with vermin' on which a meths man and woman slept in the nude. The glassless windows were shielded with a tarpaulin and the floor 'covered with rotten vegetables, bits of rag, broken glass and piles of human excreta'. The whole place reeked of 'vermin and human and animal piss beyond redemption'.

Meths men are gregarious; they like to drink in 'schools' sitting round a fire on the bomb sites, passing the bottles around. They pool the proceeds of their begging and scavenging, and familiarly label each other with sordidly descriptive nick-names like 'T.B. Rose', 'No Toes' and 'Itchy Bill'. Their female meths-drinking companions are sluttish hangers-on who offer their insalubrious sexual favours to all and sundry in return for meths. Some are broken-down prostitutes, reduced to a minimal fee for their service, hence their nickname 'Woodbiners'. Not infrequently meths drinkers have been killed by falling in the fire – sometimes accidentally, through fuddlement, but sometimes also, it has been observed, in an act of seeming wilful self-destruction.

Charitable effort for vagrant alcoholics has been varied, including amateurishly run shelters in church premises, Salvation Army hostels with attempted rehabilitation, the *Morning Star* hostels in the north-west of England,[8] 'Simonlight', and Rathcoole House in South London. The last was founded in 1966 as a response to the nuisance in Southwark caused by the high concentrations of vagrant alcoholics in the neighbourhood of Camberwell Spike. These 'horizontal meffers' were stretched out on park benches or begging from passers-by, and caused much concern on account of the (believed) potential threat to local children.[9]

The proven futility and failure of sending drunken vagrant offenders to short terms in jail with transitory efforts at rehabilitation led to a token change in official policy from 1967. The 1967 Criminal Justice Act empowered the courts to send drunken offenders to projected rehabilitative centres instead of jail, if they volunteered to go, but so few centres were built that the Act was a dead letter. In 1972, in the wake of the Home Office Report on 'Habitual Drunken Offenders', the new Criminal Justice Act empowered the police to conduct drunken offenders to detoxification centres directly and avoid a trial, if they volunteered to go. But the government grew disillusioned with the cost-effectiveness of the detoxification centres, and only one, at Leeds, had been left open.[10] However, from 1973 the government began allocating funds to voluntary organisations to help all kinds of alcoholics, and so gave a boost to this kind of venture; the Federation of Alcoholic Rehabilitation Establishments was formed (now called Alcohol Concern), and by 1986 there were 98 such centres in England and Wales.[11]

Scots and Irish have continued to form a conspicuous minority among England's down-and-outs, and Scotland, with its historically higher rate of alcoholism, has furnished a disproportionate number of Skid Row types.[12]

Female vagrants formed only about one in twenty of all down-and-outs, at any rate into the early 1970s, though I am told that they now form a bigger proportion, an untoward side effect of women's liberation as women become more footloose.[13] Many are mentally ill or alcoholic; others have tragic backgrounds that have scarred them psychologically, for example broken homes and marriages, experience of sexual abuse as children, or unmarried motherhood.[14] On the whole they have more personality disorders than their male counterparts; Honor Marshall in 1971 referred to the 'Carrier Bag Syndrome' (that is, their characteristic habit of carrying their junk around with them in carrier bags), and the pathetic sight of these derelicts huddled 'in railway waiting rooms, derelict houses, all-night launderettes, even telephone kiosks'. Such a woman was the half-dotty 'Edna the Inebriate Woman', the subject of the television play written by Jeremy Sandford in 1971 to draw attention to their plight.

The mentally ill, and those with histories of psychiatric treatment, also form a very high percentage of male down-and-outs. The National Assistance Board's survey of the single homeless in 1965[15] found that a quarter of Reception Centre inmates were mentally ill. Tony Wilkinson at Camberwell Spike in 1980 found the place full of psychological oddities:

One of them began shouting at the others, telling them that they should be in the army, berating them for cowardice. Another was making what appeared to be a political speech . . . but none of the words made sense. My neighbour . . . asked me if I had heard of the world revolution that started in the Britannia public house. 'It's what they call an Allah revolution,' he said. 'They're children about that big, and they get children, and they don't need a drink or smoke. Everyone was caught unawares.'[16]

Estimates in the mid-1980s of the proportion with a history of mental illness among those actually sleeping in the streets ranges from 17 to 40 per cent.[17] Psychiatric hospitals had always housed substantial numbers of homeless, but in the 1950s, with the development of new drugs, the trend started of discharging patients into the community and stabilising them with medication. The success of this policy depended firstly on the availability of sheltered homes and half-way houses run by public authorities to make 'community care' in place of hospital institutionalisation a reality, and secondly on some means of guaranteeing that these mentally fragile dischargees would be self-regulated enough to take the drugs routinely as prescribed. Since 1960 governments have officially encouraged community care and the reduction of the psychiatric hospital populations, but by 1970 this policy was already in trouble. Community care facilities were inadequate: doctors were discharging patients too early; certain drugs had only a temporary effect; and the hospitals were now finding the same mental cases they had discharged returning to their portals in rapidly increasing numbers. As one critic put it: 'the open-door policy was transmuted into a revolving door policy.'[18] Those who did find their way back to the hospitals 'would join the army of vagrants and would elbow each other off the park benches or lengthen the queues outside the doss-houses. Others would embarrass the courts and prisons where their crimes – usually petty and purposeless, unless interpreted as a plea for care and protection – have landed them.'

The decline in the number of psychiatric beds since 1960 has made the situation more difficult, and current official enthusiasm for closing psychiatric wards and relying on community care is seen, as in the case of the projected closure of Resettlement Units, as a thinly disguised money-saving move by the government; for community care is under-funded, and the proportion of helpless mental cases now on the streets is tangible evidence of this. The 1977 Housing (Homeless Persons) Act was supposed to make the mentally ill one of the priority groups that local authorities are obliged to house, but they have failed in this duty.[19]

The increase in homelessness among young people has been a noticeable and worrying phenomenon since the late 1960s. In the 1960s youthful vagrancy was probably more associated in people's minds with the beatnik and 'hippie' drop-out and drugs culture, their aimless lives centred on the cafés in the Trafalgar Square and Charing Cross area, punctuated by spells of 'conning' (begging with phoney hard-luck stories). At night they would throng the pavement outside Boots' all-night chemists in Piccadilly waiting to pick up the next day's drug prescription after midnight.[20] Brighton was the south coast Mecca for this sub-culture. Young people slept under beached boats, or occasionally in Brighton Reception Centre, and begged in the streets or on the pier.[21] Girls who joined this scene soon became prostitutes to ensure a supply of drugs. Michael Deakin and John Willis tell, for instance, of 'Annie', who ran away from her step-mother at 12, and at 13 was already street wise in London – begging, haunting cafés and sleeping all night on Circle Line trains. Among her experiences she lived with a drug pusher as his distributor in a filthy 'squat' in Paddington, was raped by a drug addict, and slept with a wino in return for supplies of Mandrax. She was caught uttering a forged prescription and was entrusted by the courts to a voluntary commune-cum-welfare centre to help stabilise her.[22] This pattern of youngsters migrating to London from the provinces and ending up as drifters, dossing in seedy 'pads' in Notting Hill, Paddington and elsewhere, was becoming more apparent in the early 1970s, when this young rootless population in London was estimated at up to 5,000.[23] The connection between unemployment and homelessness was even more marked among young blacks, whose unemployment rate even in 1971 was double that for white youths of the same age; worse housing conditions on the whole among blacks, and culture clashes with their immigrant parents were driving a disproportionately large number of black youths away from home.[24]

In a House of Lords debate on the young homeless in 1973 the Bishop of Southwark related how he made midnight tours of his diocese, to see the down-and-outs: 'I wanted to see what actually happened to some of these young people who were sleeping rough out on the riverside and in disused and battered buildings. . . . I saw too much. I saw [the police] hurrying these youngsters on between midnight and three o'clock in the morning.'[25]

In 1967 the Simon Community's 'Simonscene' shelter opened its doors to young drug addicts. In 1969 Centrepoint, an overnight shelter for youngsters, was opened in Soho, but even by 1976 it could only offer 25 beds, and the Church Army hostel for the young at Walmer House only had 31 beds.[26] Other agencies both in London and the provinces (like 'Project Spark' in Leeds and 'the Boot' in Birmingham[27]) sprouted from the early 1970s to help homeless youths, while advice centres like 'Girls Alone in London' and 'After Six' tried to find lodgings for newcomers to the capital, to safeguard them from the procurers, who scouted around the railway and coach termini for potential sex and drugs fodder.[28]

The numbers of under-25s seeking accommodation in London

grew steadily in the 1970s against a background of rising unemployment. Thus, Centrepoint in 1977 received 6,500 applications, and by 1980 these had grown to 13,500;[29] and over the year up to early 1981 the Providence Row Night Shelter in London's East End reported a 16 per cent increase in the numbers of under-25s seeking assistance.[30] 'Jock' Stallard MP complained in the Commons in 1981 that it was all very well for the government to tell the unemployed to move to find jobs; but in London they could not afford the accommodation, even if they found work.[31]

Local authorities do have power under the 1967 Housing Act to build municipal lodging houses, but they have not bothered. It is these, plus more DHSS hostels, and not reliance on voluntary organisations that should be the real approach to alleviating the problem of the young homeless, according to critics like CHAR. The misery of youngsters who are victims of this public neglect is exemplified by the case of a 19-year-old from Leeds who had come to London to further his aspirations to become an artist. When asked by John Pilger of the *Daily Mirror* in 1984 where he had slept recently, he replied: 'Bruce House Monday, Waterloo Station Tuesday, Victoria Station Wednesday', and the previous night he had just walked the Embankment till he reached a tea and coffee kiosk, by which time it was daylight.[32]

Apart from the workseekers there has been the perennial problem of young runaways. In 1985 an estimated 30,000 children ran away from home in Britain. For many, admittedly, it is just a premature attempt to fly the nest and they soon return home voluntarily. But for others it is a desperate escape from intolerable home circumstances, such as drunken or quarrelling parents or sexual abuse.[33] For others still there is the lure of the bright lights of the big city and a reluctance to return to the confining dullness of a provincial town. These youngsters soon find that the streets are not paved with gold, and some drift into the tawdry fringe society centring on the West End amusement arcades. These in the 1970s gained notoriety as venues for homosexual pick-ups, and the temptation for these hungry youngsters to slide into male prostitution as 'rent boys' or 'dilly boys' sometimes becomes irresistible. The television documentary *Johnny Go Home* in 1975 brought such moral dangers dramatically to the public attention when it highlighted the villainies of one Roger Gleaves the self-styled 'Bishop of Medway'; his pose as the prelate and welfare worker of the bogus 'Old Catholic Church' served as a cover for his nest of perversions. Gleaves had a history of sexual perversion and a criminal record, but through lack of liaison between the Home Office (which knew his background) and local authorities and the DHSS (which did not), Gleaves was able to set up charity hostels for homeless youths in five London boroughs. These readily offered him short-life premises owing to their own acute housing problems, while the DHSS paid the rents for the unemployed lodgers in this registered charity.

Gleaves toured the railway termini in uniform with a disarming openness that hoodwinked the railway police, picking up newly-arrived 'lost' youngsters on behalf of his pseudo-charity, and taking them back to his hostels. Once in his grip there, the youths were captives in a reign of brutality and homosexual assaults executed by Gleaves' vicious and similarly perverted 'wardens'. Gleaves also made a tidy income as a job-finder, hiring out his lodgers as casual labour, whilst corrupted youths worked as rent boys from his premises. The whole operation had echoes of the bawdy 'kidkens', or youths' lodging houses run by the real-life Fagins of Dickens' day. Gleaves' career came to an end in 1975 when he was arrested for complicity in the murder of a former lodger who was believed to know the whereabouts of a warden who had run off with some DHSS cheques. *Johnny Go Home* caused a stir in Parliament, but while a DHSS departmental study group subsequently recommended improvements in public hostel provision for the young, at the end of the day the government was unready to provide the extra funds needed at a time of economic stringency.[34] Whilst the documentary fostered an image of wholesale moral danger to youngsters on the loose in London, David Brandon, an authority on homelessness, did subsequently emphasise that this was exaggerated, for most youths manage to fend for themselves in 'squats' or 'crash pads' without falling prey to procurers.[35]

The vulnerability of homeless youths to more lethal dangers was, however, shockingly brought to light much more recently with the conviction in 1983 of the mass murderer, Dennis Nilsen. Nilsen, a lonely homosexual, had, from 1978, taken to picking up homeless drifters in London's gay bars. He took them back to his flats, first in Cricklewood and then Muswell Hill, where he murdered them. He dissected and disposed of the bodies in various ways, and was finally uncovered when a Dyno-rod engineer, called in by other flat-dwellers to unblock a drain in the Muswell Hill premises, found lumps of human flesh. Nilsen confessed to 15 murders. As a sample of his victims, there was 15-year-old Martyn Duffy from Liverpool. He was restless and mentally unstable, with homosexual leanings. He drifted to London and slept in a railway station, where Nilsen found and befriended him. Another victim was Malcolm Barlow, aged about 24; he was mentally retarded and lived as a male prostitute with no fixed abode. Nilsen met him by accident in the street, dazed by the side-effects of drugs he took for epilepsy.[36]

The Nilsen case was seized on by campaigning groups like CHAR to highlight the potential dangers to homeless youngsters; this made the announcement of the government's new board and lodging regulations for the under-26's just over a year later appear all the more insensitive.

27 'Lazy lewd loiterers':[1] the Vagrancy Act to date and the inglorious history of 'Sus'

The increase in homelessness and 'sleeping rough', and the campaigning and publicity that drew attention to it from the mid-1960s prompted the Home Secretary, Reginald Maudling to appoint a departmental committee under a civil servant, A.J.E. Brennan, to look into the workings of the Vagrancy Act in 1971.[2] Although this book is concerned primarily with the begging and 'wandering abroad' provisions, I shall devote space here to the history of 'sus' or 'frequenting', as the furore over it in the late 1970s again brought the whole of the Vagrancy Act into question. There were to be two House of Commons Home Affairs Committee investigations into the vagrancy laws some years after Brennan in 1979–81, the first dealing specifically with 'Sus', and the second with other vagrancy offences.[3]

Begging prosecutions are only a fraction of their pre-war levels. This perhaps reflects a decline of begging as people are less willing to give 'indiscriminate alms' in the Welfare State. Tony Wilkinson records that prior to his undercover excursions into the world of the down-and-out he had 'felt little sympathy with beggars who approached me in the street. The State was meant to have protected me from such people.' Begging, compared with before the war, has diminished in scale and variety,[4] though the increasing numbers of tourists have provided a favourite contemporary quarry, with the railway termini as one type of honey-pot for winos. The *Star* in April 1986 referred to these 'rheumy-eyed derelicts' who pounce on tourists at railway stations, as forcible luggage carriers: 'Then with a hostile look in the eye, they hold out grubby, semi-mittened hands for generous remuneration. This they get.'[5] Some door-step peddling also verges on begging. The 'Moonies' religious cult sells flowers door to door for claimed religious enterprises, and mass unemployment has brought an increase in youthful pedlars, a few of whom at least appear to be trading on public sympathy for the young unemployed by offering to sell smallware at exorbitant prices and wave home-made identification cards as a substitute for a proper pedlar's certificate.[6]

Whereas in the later 1930s there were on average over 3,500 begging prosecutions a year in England and Wales, after the war these fell to 700–900 a year, and in 1968 under 500.[7] The rise in unemployment, which was gradual but steady in the 1970s, appears to have been paralleled by a rise in begging prosecutions, which fluctuated around the 900–1,300 a year mark in that decade; but the escalation in unemployment since 1979 shows no proportionate rise in prosecutions. Thus, as in the inter-war period, there is no clear correlation between begging and trade cycles; in 1982 there were 1,232 prosecutions but in 1984 they were down to 658. Conviction rates are around 95 per cent, and the same percentage of defendants is male. Prison (without option of a fine) has been used less and less. This punishment was applied to under a fifth of those convicted in 1968, falling to just over a twelfth in 1982, and in 1984 no one was jailed.

The Committees fully accepted that simple begging, where it was not persistent or accompanied by threats, was often a symptom of a social problem like alcoholism or inadequacy, and there was a good case for removing it from the criminal law. However, this would create an anomaly, for it would then be legal for someone to beg on the doorstep on his own behalf quite freely, whilst genuine charity collectors are subject to licensing and police permits. The feeling was that the law should be left as it is, since in practice it is rarely used and the penalties are unoppressive.

'Sleeping out' prosecutions have followed an interesting pattern since 1945. The 1935 Vagrancy Act, as we saw in Chapter 22, limited its application, with an immediate impact on prosecution levels. However, from 1945 to the mid-1950s numbers more than doubled to around 1,000 prosecutions a year on average, falling back to an average of around 700 a year until the mid-1960s. It is almost as though at a time of full employment and growing affluence the authorities felt that there was less excuse for 'sleeping out' and were readier to prosecute, for after 1965, as the homelessness issue came more to the fore and was getting worse, prosecution levels were falling and by 1972 stood at 373.[8] The progressive closure of Reception Centres from 1948 meant there were fewer 'reasonably accessible' places of shelter to which the police could direct vagrants as a prerequisite of any grounds for prosecution under the 1935 Act; this must have affected prosecution levels. Also, there were now alternative ways of dealing with sleepers-out. Those who were mentally ill could be removed by the police directly to a 'place of safety' under the 1959 Mental Health Act, while others would be hidden in the criminal statistics as drunken offenders or as damagers to property under the 1971 Criminal Damage Act. The Brennan Committee saw sleeping out even more than begging as a social rather than a criminal problem, and felt it should only be considered a real crime where it causes a public nuisance, for instance where it involves blocking a staircase or occupying a bus shelter; or where a vagrant, though doing no damage, refuses to leave private premises when told to do so.

In fact the 1935 Act has fallen into virtual disuse in the depressed 1980s. In 1980 there were 276 'sleeping out' prosecutions, and in 1984 just 40.[9] As for begging, the defendants are overwhelmingly male and conviction rates are extremely high, but imprisonment, which, since 1945, has only been used in a small minority of cases as a punishment, has virtually disappeared in the 1980s. Convicted sleepers-out can expect a fine, suspended sentence, probation or a conditional discharge in nearly all cases.

To groups such as the National Association of Probation Officers, CHAR and the National Council for Civil Liberties the mere retention of these laws on the statute book is an affront to the homeless and helpless; their abolition would not create gaps in the law, they claim, as specific related crimes are fully covered by other laws; for instance to beg with menaces is covered by the Theft Act and Public Order Act.[10] However, both Brennan and the Home Affairs Committee believed on balance that as the law was scarcely applied for these two offences it was better to leave well alone, as it was still a potentially useful standby for the police on occasions.[11]

The story of 'sus' (otherwise 'frequenting') is more overcast. Section 4 of the Vagrancy Act provided that 'every suspected person or reputed thief frequenting any . . . street, highway . . . or place of public resort [etc] with an intent to commit felony' shall be deemed a 'rogue and vagabond' and liable to up to three months in jail. The object was to enable police, at a time when policing and detection were rudimentary and the crime wave serious, to take preventive action against people they knew to be bad characters simply from their hanging about in certain places and even though no specific crime was provable. The police's hand was strengthened by the Prevention of Crime Act 1871[12] which made it clear that known bad character was sufficient for a conviction even though the defendant had made no overt attempt to commit a supposed crime, and the Penal Servitude Act 1891[13] added the well-known phrase 'loitering with intent' to the policeman's charge sheet. In sum, if you were a known bad lot in a particular place, the police were empowered to read your mental intent to commit a crime from the mere fact of 'frequenting' or 'loitering' there. The law created a presumption of guilt, contrary to the general principle in criminal law; and in order to establish that the defendant was of the class of 'suspect persons' the police were allowed to adduce evidence of previous convictions in the proceedings. Again, this is barred elsewhere in criminal law, as it would tend to prejudice the court against the defendant; previous convictions can only be adduced *after* conviction, when the judge has to consider the severity of punishment.[14] 'Frequenting', in fact, was far less common a charge than begging or sleeping out prior to 1914. Thus in 1878 there were 2,237 'frequenting' charges as against 14,247 for begging and 6,307 for 'wandering abroad'.[15] And the police's conviction rate in the magistrates' courts for frequenting was no higher than their general conviction rate, despite the loaded element of near-presumption of guilt. Prosections up to 1939 never appeared to rise above 3,000 a year,[16] and the figures for the 1970s were of the same order.[17] Certainly some judges between the wars were outspoken against 'frequenting' as an infringement of civil liberty.[18] Lord Justice Scott in 1937 said that the historically recognisable substratum of unemployed riff-raff – 'rogues and vagabonds' and 'sturdy beggars' who were formerly a menace to public order, and for whom the 'frequenting' charge was intended – no longer existed in the twentieth century. Social legislation, such as public assistance and National Insurance, had abolished this class, and the 'frequenting' charge was an anachronism: 'To retain such laws seems to me inconsistent with our national sense of personal liberty or our respect for the rule of law.'[19]

It was said that in the pre-war depression 'frequenting' bore heavily on unemployed men whose shabbiness made them suspect to the police, and 'some critics of the law declared it to be unsafe for an unemployed man to cross a car park'.[20] It was suspected of being used by the police to haul in potentially 'dangerous' unemployed at a period of hunger marches and mass demonstrations. The National Council for Civil Liberties condemned it in 1934 as an easy way for ambitious policemen to improve their record by getting innocent people convicted.[21] The *News of the World* in 1935 carried a headline, 'Law that Menaces the Innocent', reporting the belief that the 'frequenting' law was in line for change as an aftermath of the 1935 Vagrancy Act.[22] Some magistrates had been complaining about the law, and a recent case was cited of a man arrested by the police for 'loitering' in front of a house. The man claimed he was a gardener by trade and was just taking a professional interest in the house's garden. The magistrate adjourned the hearing to check him out, found he was indeed a gardener (as the police should have discovered) and dismissed the case.

The police were conscious of the public disquiet, and the Annual Report of the Metropolitan Police Commissioner in 1935 defended 'frequenting' on the grounds that it was a most useful tool for pre-empting crime.[23] In February 1936 the Home Secretary, Sir John Simon, was urged in Parliament to caution the police against using 'frequenting' to 'stigmatise' the destitute, and the high rate of acquittals by sceptical magistrates was referred to, to suggest that a review of police powers of arrest was needed. Simon, however, defended the police and merely echoed their view of the law's usefulness as a deterrent to crime.[24] No review of the law was forthcoming then or at any time into the 1970s, despite sporadic grumblings.[25] The Brennan Report in 1974, while suggesting some technical modifications to the law, broadly repeated the opinion of Sir John Simon in 1936 about its value to the police. A strong point in its favour, to the police and Brennan, was that it supplemented limitations in law of criminal attempt. Thus, where some youths were seen trying the doorways of a succession of shops, and a suspicious character was seen following a woman with shopping bags and trying to get close to them, these acts were not far developed enough to amount to an 'attempt' to commit a crime; however, the police could nip in in good time on a 'sus' charge to prevent a serious shock to the victim, say by an attempted bag-snatch.[26]

The Metropolitan Police were, however, sufficiently aware of disquiet to restrict the right to make 'sus' arrests to senior officers from 1977, following a police working party's recommendation,[27] but the subject was about to take on a new and potentially explosive dimension. For years, negro youths in London's immigrant areas, like Brixton and Notting Hill, had been complaining about police harassment in the streets. They were being stopped, questioned and arrested over street crimes for no good reason – or even on wholly trumped-up charges, they alleged. 'Sus' proper and 'stop and search' (generically lumped with 'Sus') were the instruments of this alleged racial harassment. (Stop and search under the Metropolican Police Act of 1839, gives London police the right to stop and search anyone they believe to be in the possession of stolen property.) Social investigations of the connections between race, crime and arrests in the late 1970s showed that blacks were 15 times more likely to be arrested for 'sus' than whites, and that the Metropolitan Police were responsible for over half the arrests in the country, with Merseyside trailing second.[28] Between 1977 and 1979 a 'Scrap Sus' campaign was concerted by black activists and liberal sympathisers. The whole argument about police 'prejudice' and 'harassment' takes us beyond the proper bounds of this book, but a number of points should be made. The disproportion in arrests of non-whites applied to negro youths but certainly not to Asians, for it was among the former that the type of crimes, namely mugging and street snatches, that 'sus' was being used to anticipate, were disproportionately prevalent. The negro youths' habit of loitering on corners and their higher rate of unemployment and worse housing conditions drove them to idle away time resentfully in the streets, and any knot of black teenagers was an immediate target of suspicion by police, beset as they were by the soaring levels of street crime in inner city immigrant areas. Against the Met, it was argued that in other parts of the country with high black concentrations, like Birmingham, the police found little need to use 'Sus' to preserve order. Crime levels had multiplied since the 1930s, yet 'Sus' arrests had remained fairly constant in that time, indicating that it was *relatively* of less and less use in policing. The fact therefore that blacks seemed to figure as its particular target in modern times carried alleged overtones of racism. The Met for its part insisted that 'Sus' was being used as an emotive symbol of racial discrimination out of all proportion to its true significance. In 1979, for example, 947 negroes were arrested for 'Sus' in the 'Met' area (roughly 40 per cent of all 'Sus' arrests there) but up to 300,000 criminal offences of all types had been committed in London that year.[29] The ferment generated by the 'Scrap Sus' campaign prompted the Liberal peer, Lord Avebury, in 1978 to introduce a bill in the Lords to remove the whole 'frequenting' clause from the Vagrancy Act.[30] Lord Gifford, a supporter of the Bill, found the criminalising of the act of loitering objectionable:

> All sorts of people loiter because they have nowhere to go. Badly housed people loiter in public places because they do not like staying inside. Children after school loiter; teenagers loiter; window shoppers loiter; people waiting for buses and taxis loiter. Yet there is something dirty about the word 'loiter'. No doubt it was originally used to describe people considered to be the riff-raff of society in the nineteenth century, and all too easily it can now be used to describe those who are thought to be riff-raff by the enforcers of the law.

The Labour government could not support the bill, as 'Sus' appeared to fill a gap in the unsatisfactory law of criminal attempt, which had been recently vitiated with anomaly by a judicially formulated 'impossibility' rule: if you manifestly attempt to steal something, say by putting your hand in someone else's pocket, no crime has been attempted if what you are after is not there; the crime is 'impossible', and so, by lawyer's logic, is the 'attempt' also! The government was awaiting the outcome of a Law Commission report on the law of attempt, before reconsidering 'Sus'; Avebury's bill failed, as did an identical bill introduced by John Fraser MP in the Commons in June 1979.[31] The House of Commons Home Affairs Committee now turned its attention to the subject and in April 1980 published its own report on 'Race Relations and the "Sus" Law'.[32] Its recommendation that 'Sus' be abolished shows a radical change of political mood since the Brennan Report six years before, now that the racial dimension had entered the debate. Its abolition, it claimed, would not leave a gap in the law, for not only would Stop and Search remain, but also the 1967 Criminal Law Act provision that empowered police to arrest people they have 'reasonable cause' to believe to be about to commit an offence (though the courts here can only bind over for good behaviour, not fine or imprison).[33] ' "Sus" ', said the report, 'has acquired a symbolic significance out of all proportion to its incidence as a criminal charge' and stood as a 'symbol of the frayed relationships between the police and young blacks'. Indeed, this fraying ripped open completely when, in April 1980 the destructive riot in the largely immigrant St Paul's district of Bristol (following a police raid on a black club known for drug peddling) gave the 'Sus' issue a new urgency. In June the Law Commission's report on Criminal Attempt was published, and the new Conservative government (which had taken the same view as the previous Labour government) now had no excuse to leave 'Sus' as it was.[34] In December 1980 the Criminal Attempts Bill was introduced: it abolished 'Sus' under the Vagrancy Act, but strengthened and clarified the attempt law, for example by abolishing the 'impossibility' rule. The abolition of 'Sus' was thus already in the pipeline (it became law in August 1981) when further black riots, starting in Brixton, erupted in the spring and summer of 1981.[35] Moreover, the use of 'Sus' by the police had shown a distinct fall comparing 1980 with the later 1970s,[36] which seems to bear out the police view that its harassment of the blacks was more bugaboo than reality.[37]

With 'Sus' keeping the whole Vagrancy Act on the grill, 'Jock' Stallard MP, an inveterate campaigner for the homeless, and himself the product of the migration of unemployed Scots to the south in the 1930s, thought the time ripe in February 1981 for a bill to abolish its begging and sleeping out provisions.[38] The bill got nowhere, but once 'Sus' was safely into dispatch, the Commons Home Affairs Committee turned its attention to other Vagrancy Act offences in April,[39] and, as we have seen, concluded that it was better to let dying dogs sleep.

'Trampoloquia': a select glossary of tramp cant

Period classifications:

(A) Regency to early Victorian
(B) Mid-Victorian
(C) Late Victorian
(D) Edwardian to First World War
(E) Inter-war
(F) Post-1945

Classifications relate to the period discovered in my researches and do not preclude the possibility of usage before or after the period indicated. Interested readers should also consult Eric Partridge's *Dictionary of the Underworld*.

Abraham Man: beggar feigning insanity (Tudor times to B); veteran tramp (E)
Alleluyah Stew: Salvation Army soup (D)
Angels: sandwich-board men (E)

Back Door Cant: wheedling patter at the tradesman's entrance (B)
Beak: magistrate (B–F)
Becoming dead to a place: becoming too well known in a place (B/C)
Bender's Mixture: cigarettes made up from dog-ends (E)
The Bible: a pedlar's stock of merchandise (C–E)
A bit of this: temporary shacking up with a woman (E)
Blanket Stiffs: those tramps who never go into the casual wards (E)
Blob (= Blab): a hard-luck story (B)
A Bloody Toff: a man who gives alms (E)
Blue Billy: methylated spirits (E)
Bone: good (good pickings) (B)
Boss: any stranger who seems likely to respond sympathetically to a beggar (E)
Bottled Bellyache: cheap beer (E)
Bottler: collector for a street performer (D–F)
Brief: pedlar's licence (D)

208

Briefs: fake testimonials (A/B)

Broad: girl of easy virtue (E)

Brum (= Birmingham): counterfeit coin (B)

Brummagem Jewellery: cheap imitation jewellery made in Birmingham and sold by pedlars (D)

Bugging: assaulting, setting upon (F)

Bull: policeman (E)

Bum: charity scrounger (E/F). From the Americanism for a local layabout (derived from the German *Bummler*, a loafer)

Busking: seeking employment as an entertainer in a drinking parlour; or selling obscene songs (B); street entertaining (F)

A Call: a house where a tramp always can get something (E/F)

Carver: one who cheats his partner (E/F)

Castle: a wealthy house (E/F)

Cat's Meat: oddments of meat collected by tramps (E)

Chanting (Chaunting): street singing (A–E)

Char: tea (E/F)

Charity Hounds: those who professionally scrounge off charities (D)

Chat: a louse (*Chatty* = verminous) (E)

Chavies: children (B/C)

Chin Straps: pieces of bacon scrounged by tramps (E)

Chokey: jail (D)

Chuck: food (D/E)

Clem: starving (C–E)

Clobber: clothes (C–F)

Clod: a penny (rhyming slang from 'clodhopper', a copper coin (E/F)

Clodhopper: a street dancer (E)

Cock (or Top Cock): beggar who is master of his line (E/F)

Coffin: doss house bed comprising a box with a tarpaulin covering (E)

COINS: (B/C): *thonicks* = half pence; *kenuck* or *saltee* = one penny; *duce* = tuppence; *thrummer* = threepence; *groat* = fourpence; *sprat* = sixpence; *deaner* or *midget* = 1 shilling

COINS: (E): *deaner* or *hog* or *sinker* = shilling; *tosheroon* = half a crown; *sprowsie* = sixpence; *croker* = fourpence

To Con: to beg with a false story (F)

Conjurors: people who make a living in any way, honest or crooked (E)

A Cooper: a casual ward to be avoided (E)

Coopered: ruined, spoilt, played-out (as a beggar's dodge) (B/C)

Cove: a fellow (A/B)

Crash Pad: emergency doss in a friend's room (F)

Crib: house (as visited by a beggar) (B); for example, *Suck Crib* = beer house (B/C)

Crocus: quack doctor (B/C)

Croker: (see COINS (E)): bottom-grade tramp who can only afford a fourpenny lodging house (E/F)
Cross-Coves: beggars who indulge in theft as the opportunity arises (A/B)
Cross-eyed: pretending to be blind (A/B)
Crows: look-outs who protect beggars' pitches (E)
Crummy: verminous (E)
Cuckoo Tramps: resident workhouse inmates who leave in the spring and return later in the year (E)

Deaner (see also COINS): a shilling; also a miser (E/F)
Delicates: bogus lists of benefactors to some distressed beggar (A/B)
Derrick: casual ward (E)
Derries: derelict houses used as skippers (F)
Dick: plain clothes man (E)
Dilly Boy: young male prostitute (short for 'Piccadilly') (F)
Ditched: to have got into trouble (E)
Dollcie: opulent (D/E)
Doner: tramp's 'wife' or female companion (B)
Door Thumpers: outright beggars (E)
Doss: a place to sleep (B–F)
Dosser: one who sleeps in lodging houses or cheap hotels
Downrighters: blatant, undisguised beggars (to cadge 'on the downright') (D)
Downy Earwig: a sympathetic parson (E)
Dozey: feeble-minded, or a soft touch for charity (B)
Drag: name of a street (B/C)
Drop: money given to a beggar
Drum: tramp's billy can (E/F) (*Drumming up station* = place where there is enough wood for a fire to 'drum up')
Drum: house or lodging (B) (*Flash drum* = brothel)
Duck: miscellaneous scraps from butchers, cooked up (D)
Duckett: hawker's licence (B/C)
Duds: clothes (apparently finery) (B)
Dumps: buttons (B/C)

Fake: to cheat (B/C)
Fakement: any bogus document; a notice carried by a beggar proclaiming the spurious cause of his predicament (B)
Fawney Man: seller of fake jewellery (B–E)
Feather: a bed (D/E)
Flat: a dupe, or mug (A) (See *Flatty*)
Flattie: a policeman (E); also, a townsman (E/F)
Flatty: one who does not understand tramp argot (B/C)
Flummuxed (or *Flummut*): dangerous (to a beggar) (B/C)
Fly: someone who is crafty and understands tramps' argot (B/C)

Front the Gaff: call on a house by the main entrance (E/F)
Funkum: lavender or other perfume sold in packets by pedlars (E)

Gad: to go about (B/C)
Gag: begging ploy or hard-luck story (*Gagger:* exponent of such) (B–E)
Gag-maker: writer of fake documents (B)
Gammy: bad, unfavourable, dubious (A 'gammy house' = one not safe for a beggar to call at; a 'gammy moniker' = forged signature; 'gammy stuff' = quack medicine) (B)
Gee (or Jee): a cheapjack's stooge who stimulates business by pretending to buy something (E)
Gegors: professional beggars (B/C)
Gentleman of the Road: euphemism for a tramp (E/F)
Ghost Story: tramp's 'story' (C–E)
Gloak: tell the tale (E)
Glock: half-wit (B/C)
Gorm: chewing tobacco (E)
Grafts: petty thieves' dodges to make money (E)
Griddler (or *Grizzler*): street singer (A) (A–E)
Grubbikens: workhouses where little or no worktask is demanded for food given to casuals (a *grub ken* – see *ken*) (B)
Gulling a Choker: deceiving a clergyman (B/C)

Half-sharps: mental defectives (B)
Hard-up: tobacco (B); cigarettes made up from dog-ends (E)
Haystack Queens: derelict prostitutes (F)
High Flyer: a 'genteel' beggar; a sophisticated beggar (B/C)
Hobo (American): a migratory workseeker (D–F)

The Itch: scabies (B–D)

Jack: a stranger (E)
Jake: methylated spirits: *Jakies* = meths drinkers (from jake or jack = crude spirits) (E/F)
Jerry stealing: stealing a watch (B/C)
Johnny: a policeman (E)

Ken (Short for *Kennel*): a house or establishment (from Tudor times to D). Thus, *Boozing Ken* = tavern; *Nethersken* = lodging house (see *Grubbikens*). '*Padding Ken*' or *Paddincan*, also a lodging house, (used to E/F)
Kerbstone twist: old chews of tobacco (D)
Kidding: acting as a pedlar's stooge, by pretending to buy articles, to stimulate others (E)
Kife: a bed (B/C)

Kip: a night's lodging (E/F)
Knocked: taken by the police (E)

Land Sailor: beggar pretending to be a sailor en route to another port (A)
Land Squatters: those with particular begging territories (E)
Lays: beggars' dodges (A–D)
Lighthouse: tramp who knows police (E)
Line of Guff: tramp's story or patter (E/F)
A Linen: newspaper (E/F)
Lump: 'Spike' or casual ward (E)
Lurk: beggar's dodge or performance (A–C)

Mark: a beggar's quarry (D); a soft touch for a beggar (E)
Milestone Inspector (or *Unemployed Milestone Inspector*): facetious euphemism for a tramp (E)
Misery Farm: LCC farm and trades colony for vagrants (E)
Moniker: name, signature (B)
Mott: a woman (A/B) (Also in the form *morte* in Tudor times)
Moucher: itinerants and wandering beggars (B–E)
Muggers: tramp pedlar who sold earthenware (particularly, it seems, in the Scottish borders) (A–C)
Mumper: itinerant and beggar (especially in the West Country) (pre-nineteenth century to F); *Mumpers' inns* = low lodging houses (A)
Mush Faker: itinerant umbrella mender (*Mush* = short for mushroom) (B)

Nark: deputy's informer and toady in common lodging house (D)
Needies: travellers or beggars (B–D)
Needy Mizzler: dosser who *bilks* or decamps from a lodging house without paying (B)
Nethers: lodging money (B/C)
Nobber (Nobbler): collector for street entertainer or pavement artist (E)

An Old Mare: a woman who gives a moral lecture when refusing a beggar (E)
An Old Soldier: a charity hunter and scrounger (C)
On me Uppers: dead broke (E)
On the Cross: anything stolen (B/C)
'On the downright' (see *Downrighters*): begging door to door (A/B); plain begging (B/C)
'On the Fly': begging on the highway (A/B)
'OPS' ('Other People's Stumps'): dog-ends (D)
Overlapping: begging from different charities which are unwittingly duplicating their aid (B)

Overseer Hunters: cadgers who went the rounds of the parishes seeking soft or unwitting overseers of the poor to beg parish casual relief from (A)

Pack: house of a poor man (B/C)
Pad: to go about. Hence, to *pad the hoof* = to walk the highway; *padding ken* or *padding crib* = travellers' lodging house (B–F for this meaning of 'pad'; *paddincan* as variant of *padding ken*, used E/F)
Pad: a beggar's station. Thus, to *stand pad* = to keep to a pitch (B)
Patterer: pedlar with slick line of sales talk (B)
Pawnee (Parni): water (Romany derivation) (C–E)
Peg: any place where a free meal can be obtained (e.g., Salvation Army) (D)
Penny Sit-Up: shelter with no bed, just a floor space to rest in or bench and table to sleep at (D)
Peter: tramp's sack (E/F)
Pharaoh Flights: fleas (B)
Picking a poke: stealing a purse (B/C)
Pickups: cigar stumps (sold to other tramps) (B)
Pitch the Crack: to break off from some dodge and clear off (B)
Pitching the Fork: begging (E)
Plant: hiding place (E/F)
Poke-out: food given at the door (E)
Poll: prostitute; *To be polled up*: to be living with a prostitute (B)
Postmen: tramps who hitch rides in vehicles (E/F)
Praters: hymn-singing 'griddlers', or pseudo-evangelising tramp 'parsons' collecting money for supposed religious work (B/C)
Pricks: pins (D/E)
PRISON SENTENCES (B/C): *carriage drag* = 7 days; *a moon* = 1 month; *a drag* = 3 months; *half stretch* = 6 months; *a stretch* = 1 year
Pulling up: stopping people to beg (E)
Punk and Plaster: bread and margarine (E)
Punting: begging (D)

Quod (in Quod): in jail (B)

Racket: a begging dodge (B)
Raising the Wind: raising money (A/B)
Rakes: combs (D)
Ramp: bomb site or any demolition site (F)
Rasher Waggon: frying pan (B/C)
The Rats: delirium tremens (D)
Red Biddy: methylated spirits (E) (Possibly Scottish only)
Rent Boy: young male prostitute (F)

Ribby, or *'on the Ribs'*: totally broke (E)

A Right Old Bastard: man who refuses to give to a beggar (E)

The Robert and the Dee: the policeman and the detective (C)

Rooty: bread (E)

Sally Ann: Salvation Army (F and earlier)

Scaldrum Dodge: fake wounds and skin afflictions (B)

Scoff: food (C)

Scotchmen: body vermin (B)

Scran: victuals; casual ward bread (B–E)

Scranning: begging (B/C)

The Scratch: Scabies (the *Itch*) (B)

Screever: professional writer of begging letters (B–D); beggar who sits with his begging appeal chalked on the pavement (A/B); pavement artist (B–E)

Scrumpy: rough cider; the 'tramp's cocktail' of half jake and half cider (E/F)

A Set-down: a square meal (E)

Shackle(s): soup (D/E); to *shackle-up* = to cook in the pot (E)

Shake-down: rough or improvised bed (B–E)

Shallow cove: pitiable, near naked beggar (*Shallow Mott* = female counterpart) (A–C)

Sham: a gentleman; *Pure sham* = gentryfolk (E/F)

Sharps: needles (D/E)

She's Alright: a willing woman (E)

Shellback: beggar whose tale is that he is a landbound deep sea fisherman (E/F)

Shellshock: workhouse cocoa (E)

Ship: the tale (E/F)

Shivering Jemmie: same as *shallow cove* (q.v.) (B/C)

Shovels: spoons (B/C)

A Show-Out: a handsign by which tramps recognise each other (E/F)

Shuttle Folk: tramps who pad habitually up and down the same highway (E/F)

Sit-Up: see *Penny Sit-Up* (E)

Skid Row: derelict world of jakies and other sump vagrants (F)

Skilly: gruel (B–E)

Skimish: booze; *Skimished* = drunk (D/E)

Skipper: barn, shed, etc., for shelter (Tudor times to F); *Skipperer* = one who so shelters

Slags: police term of contempt for society's drop-outs and marginals (F)

A Slang: a hawker's licence (E)

Slop: a policeman or detective (E)

Slum: fake document (B)

Slummers: religious evangelists who visit the lodging houses (E)

Smoke: London (E)

Snells: pedlars' nick-nacks (B); needles (C)
Snide: counterfeit money (B/C)
Sniffs: scissors (D)
Snips: scissors (D/E)
Snout: tobacco (E/F)
Soft Tommies: soft touches for charity (B)
Song and Dance: a begging story (E)
Sons of Rest: tramps' euphemised description of themselves (E/F)
Spike: casual ward: after 1948 the Reception Centres (D–F)
Spiv: one who lives by his wits; wide boy or black marketeer (E/F)
    (possible acronym: 'suspect person itinerant vagrant' – Hansard,
    House of Lords, 30/11/1978, Baroness Phillips, Col. 1410 et seq.)
Split: a detective (E)
Splitting the Toby: arranging the next day's journey (E/F)
Steamer: a mug, simpleton (E/F)
Stiff: a phoney begging letter (B)
Stiff: hawker's licence (B/C)
Stirabin (Staripen): prison (B/C) (Romany derivation)
Stove-up: clothes that have been fumigated (E)
Stretchers: laces (D/E)
Sucker: tramp's victim (E)
Super: dosser who earns money by hailing cabs outside theatres (C)
    (Short for 'supernumerary', a theatre casual or extra.)
Sus: suspect person frequenting public places under s.4 of 1824
    Vagrancy Act – the charge (F)
Swag Sellers: pedlars (E); *swag shop* = pedlars' wholesaler (E)

Tail: prostitute (B/C)
Tap: to beg; *tapper* = beggar (E); *Coming on tappers* = begging (F)
Tatter: dealer in rags (B); also as *'tattler'* = dealer in second-hand
    clothes, scrap metal dealer or horse trader (E)
Doing a Tear-up: tearing up of clothes by tramps in casual ward, to
    obtain a fresh set from the workhouse (B)
Tight: towns that do not give much (E)
Timber merchant: match seller (E)
Toby: the highway; *On the Toby* = tramping (also as *Toe-be*) (A–E)
    (In eighteenth century, *Tobyman* = highwayman)
Toe-rags: strips of cloth wound round toes by tramps to stop them
    chafing against the shoes (B–E)
Toke: bread (B)
Tomato Can Tramps: those who curl up anywhere (E)
Tommy: food (D/E)
Top Cock: see *Cock*
Totter: dustbin scavenger (E)
Translators: repairers of second hand clothes and shoes, who re-sell
    them to vagrants and dossers (A/B)
Tumbling: dole-giving (B)

Twopenny Hangover: doss house where inmates slept leaning over a stretched-out rope which was dropped in the morning (E)

Vial: provincial town; *Gammy Vial* = town where police pounce on pedlars (B) (See *Gammy*) (*Vile* as town dates from Tudor times)

Weary Willies: those for whom any kind of work is 'too much' (D)
Whale and Whitewash: fish and sauce (E)
Wheeler: tramp who makes a point of travelling from casual ward to casual ward (E)
Woodbiners: decayed prostitutes who hang about with *jakies*; their price has sunk to a cigarette (F)
Working: spinning a yarn to a prospective victim (E/F); *working the Noble* = acting as an ashamed beggar with a respectable appearance and a tale of economic come-down (B/C)

Young Mug: itinerant workseeker of any age (E/F)

Select bibliography and abbreviations

Sources most specific to particular chapters may be found within those individual chapter references. Hansard references are to the Commons, unless otherwise stated. All PP Volume references are in Arabic numerals.

Percy Alden and Edward E. Hayward, *The Unemployable and the Unemployed* (1909)
Stanley Alderson, *Britain in the Sixties*, 'Housing' (1962)
Amyatt Amyatt (also known as Amyatt Brown?), *On the Repression of Vagrancy and Indiscriminate Alms-giving* (1878)
Peter Archard, *Vagrancy, Alcoholism and Social Control* (1979)
Ron Bailey (a) *The Squatters* (1973)
          (b) *The Homeless and the Empty Houses* (1977)
T. Barwick Lloyd Baker, paper on Vagrants and Tramps, Manchester Statistical Society (1869)
Henrietta Octavia Barnett, *Canon Barnett, His Life, Work and Friends* (1921 ed.)
John R. Battley, *The Monasticism of the Casual Poor* (1940)
Thomas Beames, *The Rookeries of London* (1852)
John A. Bentley *The Submerged Tenth* (1933)
G.F.A. Best, *Shaftesbury* (1964)
Edward Bishop, *Blood and Fire* (1964)
W.G. Boase, Report to the Poor Law Board on Vagrancy, P 1847–8, Vol. 53, p. 253 et seq.
Charles Booth, *Life and Labour of the People of London* (1892)
William Booth (a) *In Darkest England and the Way Out* (1890)
          (b) *The Vagrant and the Unemployable* (1904)
David Brandon (a) *The Treadmill* (1969) (pub. by Christian Action)
          (b) *Homeless* (1974)
          (c) *The Survivors* (1980)
Bryan Breed, *The Man Outside* (1966)
George Atkins Brine, *The King of the Beggars* (1883)
Gill Burke, *Housing and Social Justice* (1981)
James Dawson Burn, *Autobiography of a Beggar Boy* (1882 edition)
Richard Burn, *Justice of the Peace* (1830 and 1869 editions)
John Burnett, *A Social History of Housing* (1978)
Thomas Callaghan, *Tramp's Chronicle* (1983)
CHAR, Campaign for the Homeless and Rootless
Wilson and Victor Carlile, *The Continental Outcast* (1905)
Mary Carpenter (a) *Reformatory Schools* (1851)
          (b) *Juvenile Delinquents* (1853)
Sir William Chance, *Vagrancy* (c. 1906)
Kellow Chesney, *The Victorian Underworld* (1970)

217

Mrs Cecil Chesterton (a) *In Darkest London* (1926)
                       (b) *Women of the London Underworld* (1938)
Christian Action, *Dossers' Charter* (1970)
John J. Clarke, *Public Assistance and Unemployment Assistance* (1937 edition)
H.G. Codd, *Report to the Poor Law Commission on Vagrancy*, PP 1834, Vol. 38, Appendix E, p. 227 et seq.
David Cohen and Ben Greenwood, *The Buskers* (1981)
Max Cohen, *I Was One of the Unemployed* (1945)
Richard Collier, *The General Next to God* (1968)
Patrick Colquhoun (a) *The State of Indigence and the Situation of the Casual Poor* (1799)
                  (b) *A Treatise on Indigence* (1806)
                  (c) *Account of a Meat and Soup Charity established in the Metropolis in the Year 1797*
Confessions of an Old Almsgiver (1871), J. Hornsby Wright
Tim Cook et al. (a) *Vagrancy: Some New Perspectives* (1979)
                (b) *Vagrant Alcoholics* (1975)
COS, Charity Organisation Society
Sandy Craig et al., *Down and Out* (1984)
Denis Crane, *A Vicarious Vagabond* (1910)
C.W. Craven, *A Night in the Workhouse* (1887)
CVC, County Vagrancy Committee
Philip Danvers, *On the Means of Eradicating or Suppressing Mendicancy* (1842)
W.H. Davies (a) *Beggars* (1909)
           (b) *Autobiography of a Super Tramp* (1908)
           (c) *The Adventures of Johnny Walker, Tramp* (1926)
           (d) *The True Traveller* (1912)
Dorothy Davis, *A History of Shopping* (1966)
Dr Graham Davis, 'Image and Reality in a Victorian Provincial City. A Working Class Area of Bath 1830–1900', unpublished Ph.D. thesis, University of Bath, 1981
William Harbutt Dawson, *The Vagrancy Problem* (1910)
Michael Deakin and John Willis, *Johnny Go Home* (1976)
Clare Demuth, *'Sus': A Report on the Vagrancy Act 1824* (1978)
J. Denvir, *The Irish in Britain* (1892)
DHSS, Department of Health and Social Security
DC, Departmental Committee
DC on Habitual Offenders, Vagrants, etc. (Scotland), PP 1895, Vol. 37
DC on Vag. 1906, Inter-Dept. Comm. on Vagrancy, PP 1906, Vol. 103
DC on Relief of the Casual Poor (Cmd 3640), PP 1929–30, Vol. 17
DC on Vagrancy in Scotland, PP 1935–6, Vol. 14
Charles Dickens (a) *Household Words* 22/5/1852, 'Departed Beggars'
               (b) *All the Year Round* 16/6/1860, p. 230, 'The Uncommercial Traveller'
               (c) *Household Words* 18/5/1850, 'The Begging Letter Writer'
Andrew Doyle, Report on Casual Wards to the Poor Law Board, PP 1866, Vol. 35
Alex. Dunlop, *A Treatise on the Law of Scotland Relative to the Poor* (1825)
George Zachary Edwards, *A Vicar as Vagrant* (1910)
Paul Edwards and James Walvin, *Black Personalities in the Era of the Slave Trade* (1983)
Pierce Egan, *Life in London* (1821)
An Exposure of the Various Impositions Daily Practised by Vagrants of Every Description (1840 or later) (Anon.)
FARE, Federation of Alcoholic Rehabilitation Establishments (now 'Alcohol Concern')
Henry Fielding, *A Proposal for Making Effectual Provision for the Poor* (1753)
Geoffrey Fletcher, *Down Among the Meths Men* (1966)
Josiah Flynt, *Tramping with Tramps* (1899)
Lionel Fox, *The English Prison and Borstal System* (1952)

John Edward Francis, 'Dick and Jef' (1939) (St Martin-in-the-Fields crypt)
Thor Fredur, *Sketches from Shady Places* (1879)
Albert Fried and Richard Elman, *Charles Booth's London* (1969)
W.A. Gape, *Half a Million Tramps* (1936)
Enid Gauldie, *Cruel Habitations* (1974)
Howard Goldsmid, *Jotting of a Dosser* (1886)
Teresa Grafton, 'No more Time?' (The 'Boot' Night Shelter) (1979)
Frank Gray, *The Tramp* (1931)
Nigel Gray, *The Worst of Times* (1985)
GLC, Greater London Council
James Greenwood, *Pall Mall Gazette* 1866: reprint, 'A Night in the Workhouse'
James Greenwood, *The Wilds of London* (1874)
John Greve et al. (a) *Homelessness in London* (1971)
                  (b) *Investigation into Homelessness in London* (1985)
Arthur Griffiths, *Chronicles of Newgate* (1884)
William A. Guy, *Vagrancy: its Nature, Causes and Cure* (National Assoc. for the
    Promotion of Social Science, Sessional Proceedings, 1870–71)
Sydney Hallifax, *Annals of a Doss House* (1900)
J.E. Handley (a) *The Irish in Scotland 1798–1845* (1943)
             (b) *The Irish in Modern Scotland* (1947)
E. Hanmore, *The Curse of the Embankment and the Cure* (1935)
Wal Hannington (a) *Unemployment Struggles 1919–1936* (1977 ed.)
               (b) *A Short History of the Unemployed*
               (c) *Ten Lean Years* (1940)
Thomas Harman, *A Caveat or Warning for Common Cursetors, Vulgarly called Vagabonds*
    (1573)
David Harris, *A Plea for Industrial Brigades as Adjuncts to Ragged Schools* (1873)
José Harris, *Unemployment and Politics (1886–1914)*
Mary Higgs (a) *Where Shall She Live?* (1910)
           (b) *Down and Out* (1924)
           (c) *Glimpses into the Abyss* (1906)
           (d) (with Edward Hayward) *Comfortable Quarters* (1912)
           (e) *Three Nights in a Women's Lodging House* (1905)
           (f) *Where Shall He Live?* (1931)
           (g) Casuals and their Casual Treatment (1928)
Mary Kingsland Higgs, *Mary Higgs of Oldham (1854–1937)* (1954)
Alsager H. Hill (a) *Our Unemployed* (1868)
                (b) *Vagrancy: the Relation of Country Districts to Great Towns* (1881)
Janet Hitchman, *They Carried the Sword* (1966) (story of Dr Barnardo's Homes)
Eric Hobsbawm, *Labouring Men* (1964)
Edwin Hodder, *Life and Work of the Seventh Earl of Shaftesbury* (1892 edition)
James Hole, *The Housing of the Working Classes* (1866)
Ralph Holinshed, *Chronicles* (1586: 1807 edition)
John Hollingshead, *Ragged London* (1861)
Thomas Holmes, *London's Underworld* (1913)
Home Affairs Committee of House of Commons
    2nd Report: Race Relations and the 'Sus' Law (HC 559) (1980–81)
    4th Report: Race Relations and the 'Sus' Law (HC 744) (1980–81)
    3rd Report: Vagrancy Offences (1980–81)
Home Office Working Party on Vagrancy and Street Offences (1974) (Brennan
    Report)
J. Hornsby Wright, see *Confessions of an Old Almsgiver*
John Camden Hotten, *The Slang Dictionary* (1874)
'Housemaster of Windlestone Hall', *Just a Tramp* (1938)
HMOs, Houses in Multiple Occupation
Howard Association (see also H. Tallack), Vagrancy and Mendicancy Report
    (1882)

Humanitarian League (Joseph Collinson), *Flogging and the Vagrancy Act* (*c.* 1908)
David Hume, *Commentaries on the Laws of Scotland.* Vol. 1 (1819)
Brian Inglis, *Poverty and the Industrial Revolution* (1971)
John Ivatts, *Homelessness and Legislation: A Study of the Effects of the 1977 Act* (1984)
John Archer Jackson, *The Irish in Britain* (1963)
Randle Jackson, Report to the Surrey Magistrates on the increase in Crime 1828 (*The Pamphleteer*, Vol. 29)
Frank Jennings (a) *Tramping with Tramps* (1932)
              (b) *In London's Shadows* (1926)
JVC, Joint Vagrancy Committee
Gareth Stedman Jones, *Outcast London* (1971)
Edmund Kelly (a) *The Unemployables* (1907)
              (b) *The Elimination of the Tramp*
Bart Kennedy, *London in Shadow* (1902)
Charles Lamb, *A Complaint of the Decay of Beggars in the Metropolis*
John Law, *In Darkest London* (1891)
John Leach (and John Wing), *Helping Destitute Men* (1980)
Laurie Lee, *As I Walked Out One Summer Morning* (1971 edition)
George Cornewall Lewis, *Inquiry into Irish Poor*, PP 1836, Vol. 34, Appendix G, p. 427 et seq.
H. Llewellin-Smith, see *New Survey*, Vol. 3, Chapt. on 'The Homeless Poor'
Jack London, *The People of the Abyss* (1902)
LBA, London Boroughs Association
LCC, London County Council
LCC, *London's Homeless* (1937)
Norman Longmate, *The Workhouse* (1974)
Donald Low, *Thieves' Kitchen: the Regency Underworld* (1982)
William Golden Lumley, *The Minutes of the Poor Law Board for the Repression of Vagrancy* (1848)
Honor Marshall, *Twilight London* (1971)
Chris Massie, *Confessions of a Vagabond* (1931)
Henry Mayhew, *London Labour and the London Poor* ('LL & LP') (4 Vols. 1851–61)
Mayhew (Quennell), 'Mayhew's London'; selections from LL & LP by Peter Quennell (1969)
Henry Mayhew and John Binny, *The Criminal Prisons of London* (1862)
R. Menzies-Ferguson, *The Vagrant: What to do with Him* (1911)
W.A. Miles *Poverty, Mendicity and Crime* (1839)
MIND, National Association of Mental Health
W.T. Moncrieff, *Tom and Jerry* (stage version) (1828)
Charles Loch Mowat, *The Charity Organisation Society 1869–1913* (1961)
Alan Murie, *Housing Inequality and Deprivation* (1983)
NAB, National Assistance Board
NAB, Report on Homeless Single Persons, 1966
NAVH, National Association of Voluntary Hostels
NCCL, National Council for Civil Liberties
William Beaver Neale, *Juvenile Delinquency in Manchester* (1840)
Hippo Neville, *Sneak Thief on the Road* (1935)
New Survey of London Life and Labour 1932–34
William Newton, *Secrets of Tramp Life Revealed* (1886)
Sir George Nicholls, *A History of the Scotch Poor Law* (1856)
R.M. Noordin, *Through a Workhouse Window* (1929)
Philip O'Connor, *Britain in the Sixties: Vagrancy* (1963)
OPCS, Office of Population Censuses and Surveys
On the Road (a) *Casual Wards in Some S.W. Counties*, reprinted from the *Western Gazette*, Jan-May 1928
            (b) *From Reading to York*, Feb-March 1928
George Orwell, *Down and Out in London and Paris* (1933)

G.W. Oxley, *Poor Relief in England and Wales 1601–1834* (1974)
Robin Page, *Down Among the Dossers* (1973)
PP, Parliamentary Papers
Eric Partridge, *Dictionary of the Underworld*
Alexander Paterson, *Across the Bridges* (1912)
Geoffrey Pearson, *Hooligan* (1983)
Francis Peek (a) *The Workless, the Thriftless and the Worthless* (1892 edition, reprint
          from two articles in the *Contemporary Review*, 1888)
          (b) *Social Wreckage* (1888)
Jim Phelan (a) *We Follow the Roads* (1949)
          (b) *Wagon Wheels* (1951)
          (c) *Tramping the Toby* (1955)
Neil Philip and Victor Neuberg (editors), *Charles Dickens: A December Vision: His
Social Journalism* (1986)
Leon Radzinowicz *A History of the Criminal Law* (1956)
RC, Reception Centre
Arthur Redford, *Labour Migration in England 1800–1850* (1964 edition)
Hugh Redwood, *God in the Slums* (1930)
Stuart J. Reid, *Sir Richard Tangye 1833–1906*
Report to the Board of Trade, On Agencies and Methods for Dealing with the
Unemployed, PP 1893–4, Vol. 82
Report on Swiss Methods of Dealing with Vagrants (Preston-Thomas), PP 1904,
Vol. 82
RSU, Resettlement Unit
C.J. Ribton-Turner, *A History of Vagrants and Vagrancy* (1887)
Madeline Rooff, *A Hundred Years of Family Welfare* (the COS) (1969)
Michael Rose, *The English Poor Law 1780–1930* (1971)
Millicent Rose, *The East End of London*
Edgar Rowan, *Wilson Carlile and the Church Army* (1928 edition)
B. Seebohm Rowntree, *Poverty: a Study in Town Life* (1902)
RC, Royal Commission
RC on the County Constabulary, PP 1839, Vol. 19
RC on the Feeble Minded, PP 1908, Vol. 39
RCPL 1834, Royal Commission on the Poor Laws 1834
RCPL 1909, Royal Commission on the Poor Laws 1909 (Cd. 4499)
RC on Reformatories and Industrial Schools, PP 1884, Vol. 45
Raphael Samuel, *East End Underworld: Chapters in the Life of Arthur Harding* (1981)
Jeremy Sandford (a) *Cathy Come Home* (1976 edition)
          (b) *Down and Out in Britain* (1972)
Karl de Schweinitz, *England's Road to Social Security* (1943)
George Seaver and Coleman Jennings (editors), *Tales of Brother Douglas* (1960)
SC, Select Committee
SC on Mendicity in the Metropolis: PP 1814/5, Vol. 3; PP 1816, Vol. 5
SC on the Law relating to Vagrants: PP 1821, Vol. 4
SC on Irish and Scots Vagrants: PP 1828, Vol. 4
SC on Irish Vagrants: PP 1833, Vol. 16
SC on Metropolitan Police: PP 1834, Vol. 16
SC on Metropolitan Police Offices: PP 1837–8, Vol. 15
SC on Metropolitan District Asylums: PP 1846, Vol. 7
SC on Law of Settlement: PP 1847, Vol. 11
SC on Criminal and Destitute Juveniles: PP 1852, Vol. 7
SC on the Removal of Scottish and Irish Paupers: PP 1854, Vol. 17; PP 1854–5,
Vol. 13
SC on the Irremovable Poor: PP 1857–8, Vol. 13; PP 1859, Vol. 7; PP 1860,
Vol. 17
SC on Poor Relief: PP 1864, Vol. 9
SC on Poor Removals in the UK, especially to Ireland: PP 1878–9, Vol. 12

SC (Lords) on Poor Relief: PP 1888, Vol. 15
SHAC, Shelter Housing Aid Centre
Michael Sheridan, *Rowton Houses 1892–1954*
George R. Sims (a) *The Mysteries of Modern London* (1906)
           (b) *Living London* (3 vols) (1906)
           (c) *How the Poor Live* (1883)
W.J. Smart (a) *Christ and the Homeless Poor* (1938)
         (b) *Christ and the Thames Embankment* (1935)
George Smeeton, *Doings in London* (1840 edition; 1st edition *c.* 1826)
John Thomas Smith, *Vagabondiana* (1817) (in later editions – 1883 for example –
    republished as *Mendicant Wanderers through the Streets of London*)
J.H. Stallard, *The Female Vagrant and her Lodging* (1866)
Joseph Stamper, *Less Than the Dust* (1931)
John Stewart, *Of No Fixed Abode* (1975)
F.S. Stuart, *Vagabond* (1937)
Survey of Casual Wards Outside London, PP 1924, Vol. 19, p. 525 (Cmd 2267)
Howard Tallack (see also Howard Association), *The Problem of Diminishing Prevalent
    Destitution and Temptations to Crime* (1869) (Reprint from *Friends Quarterly Examiner*)
Sir Richard Tangye, *Some Peculiar Beggars* (reprint from *Chambers's Journal*
    1/1/1897)
Phyllis Thompson, *Within a Yard of Hell*
J. Thomson and Adolphe Smith, *Street Life in London* (1877)
J.J. Tobias (a) *Crime and Industrial Society in the Nineteenth Century* (1972)
        (b) *Nineteenth Century Crime* (1972)
Sally Trench, *Bury Me in my Boots* (1968)
Merfyn Turner, *Forgotten Men* (1960) (National Council of Social Service)
E.J. Urwick (editor), *Studies of Boy Life in Our Cities* (1904)
E. Vivian, *On Vagrancy* (1868)
Rachel Vorspan, 'Vagrancy and the New Poor Law in late Victorian and
    Edwardian England', *English Historical Review*, Vol. 92, Jan. 1977, p. 59 et seq.
Thomas Walker, *The Original* (5th edition 1875)
Anton Wallich-Clifford, *No Fixed Abode* (1974)
William Watson (a) *Vagrancy in Scotland: its Causes and Cures* (1880)
              (b) *Pauperism, Vagrancy, Crime and Industrial Education in Aberdeenshire
                    1840–75*
              (c) *Can Juvenile Vagrancy be Prevented?* (1850)
              (d) *Chapters on Ragged and Industrial Schools* (1872)
Sidney and Beatrice Webb, *History of Local Government*, Vols. on the Poor Law, viz.
    'The Old Poor Law' and 'The New Poor Law' (1927)
Arnold White, *The Destitute Alien in Great Britain* (1892)
Jerry White, *Rothschild Buildings 1887–1920* (1980)
Tony Wilkinson, *Down and Out* (1981)
A.E. Williams, *Barnardo of Stepney* (1966)
John Dove Wilson, *Memorandum on Scottish Vagrancy Law to 1895*, DC on Habitual
    Offenders, etc., PP 1895, Vol. 37 Appendix 21, Part 2
A. Wohl, *The Eternal Slum*
C. Woodham Smith, *The Great Hunger: Ireland 1845–9* (1968 edition)
John Worby (a) *The Other Half: The Autobiography of a Spiv* (1937)
        (b) *Spiv's Progress* (1939)
Thomas Wright ('The Riverside Visitor'), *The Pinch of Poverty* (1892)
Norman Wymer, *Father of Nobody's Children* (Dr Barnardo) (1954)
Everard Wyrall, *The Spike* (1909)

Notes and references

Chapter 1

1 For its effects see A. Redford/C. Woodham-Smith/PP 1856, Vol. 29, p. 189 et seq. (Irish Census).
2 Redford.
3 Lewis.
4 Codd.
5 Watson (a) and (b).
6 Randle Jackson.
7 R. Holinshed.
8 H. Fielding.
9 Colquhoun (b).
10 Oxley; Rose (a) Inglis.
11 Randle Jackson, citing official stats.
12 Radzinowicz (Vol. 1 for a discussion of this subject).
13 17 Geo. II Ch. 5. For a résumé of Vagrancy Acts to 1821 see SC on Vagrancy Laws, PP 1821, Vol. 4, p. 9 et seq. 17 Geo. II Ch. 5 [1744] was the single most salient Act.
14 32 Geo. III Ch. 45.
15 Richard Burn.
16 SC on Mendicity in the Metropolis 1815–16. This contains details about the enquiry of 1803 and its background.
17 Lewis; and Nassau Senior's Report on Irish Poor Law, PP 1837, Vol. 51, p. 5 et seq.
18 Hansard 5/2/1838, Col. 784, debate on Irish Poor Law Bill. Remarks of MPs Hindley and O'Connell.
19 Lewis.
20 See Handley (a), Lewis, Redford, Denvir, J.A. Jackson and Wohl – for Irish immigration, its contribution and English and Scottish attitudes.
21 Handley (a) and SC on Scottish and Irish Removals 1854–5, ev. of John Trevor of Chester at Q3446 et seq.
22 Boase; and see SC on Scot. and Irish Removals 1854–5, ev. of Joseph Ellison at Q890.
23 S. & B. Webb (*The Old Poor Law*).
24 Hansard 14/3/1821, Sir George Chetwynd, debate on a SC into the Vagrancy Law.
25 See Colquhoun (b).
26 Colquhoun (a) and (b).
27 59 Geo. III Ch.12.

Chapter 2

1   Hansard 24/5/1821, 1st Reading.
2   Chetwynd edited the 1830 edition of 'Richard Burn', the JPs' Bible.
3   Hansard 14/3/1821.
4   See bibliography.
5   SC 1821, ev. of William Adkins.
6   Chetwynd, Hansard 24/5/1821.
7   For abuses see also RCPL 1834, Vol. 38, Appendix E. Reports of Commissioners Codd, Henderson and Pringle.
8   Cited in Ribton-Turner.
9   James Dawson Burn.
10   See RCPL 1834, Vol. 28 Part 2, Capt. Chapman's Report; SC on Irish and Scots. Vags. 1828; SC on Irish Vags. 1833.
11   Hansard 12/3/1822, debate on Bill, 1822 Act (3 Geo. IV Ch. 40). And see DC on Vag. 1906, Historical Introduction.
12   Hansard 4/2/1824, Mr Littleton MP's defence of Chetwynd's Act.
13   PP 1824, Vol. 19, p. 257 et seq.: Return of Commitments and Costs of Maintaining and Passing Vagrants.
14   5 Geo. IV Ch. 83.
15   Debate, Hansard 3/6/1824. Peel himself favoured the retention of flogging.
16   Section 20 of the Act needs to be considered here. It provides that all convicted rogues and vagabonds can be removed, as quasi-paupers, to their places of legal settlement. But Ireland never had a parish settlement principle, even after its Poor Law Act of 1838 – so that convicted Irish vagrants could presumably never be removed to Ireland under this clause; but Scotland did have a traditional settlement law – so it seems that convicted Scots vagrants were removable as 'paupers' under this clause. But would this have Sturges Bourne or English Poor Law Removal procedure?
17   21/6/1824, 5 Geo. IV Ch. 85. In my own narrative I use the spelling 'jail' for preference. 'Gaol' I draw from quoted sources, where so spelt.
18   By the Prevention of Crimes Act 1871.
19   DC on Vagrancy 1906; Historical Introduction.
20   See note 10 for references.
21   See SC on Vags. 1821, ev. of William Lee, and SC on Scots. and Irish Vags 1828, and SC on Irish Vagrants 1833 for comparative figures for various counties.
22   RCPL 1834, Vol. 38, Appendix E, Inspector Henderson's Report.
23   1833 Act (3/4 Will.IV Ch. 40). Further temp. Acts in 1837, 1840, 1844. The 1845 Act (8/9 Vict. Ch. 117).
24   Hansard, 2nd Reading of 1837 renewal Bill, Robert Palmer MP.
25   See Woodham-Smith, Handley (a) and (b), Denvir, and Redford – for the impact, both short- and long-term, of the famine on Irish immigration here.
26   Censuses 1841 and 1851.
27   See SC on Irish and Scots. Removals PP 1854, Appendix 6, p. 570, for Scottish figures.
28   See SC on Irish and Scots. Removals PP 1854–5, ev. of Andrew Doyle at Q2362–3; SC on Law of Settlement and Poor Removal Act 1847, Vol. 11, ev. of Richard Hall Q6678 et seq.
29   PP 1860, Vol. 58, nos. of Irish returned home from England; PP 1854, Vol. 55, no. of persons removed to Ireland 1849–54; Hansard 21/7/1875 (Mark Stewart MP).
30   Redford.
31   SC on Law of Settlement 1847, Q4370–9.
32   Handley (b).
33   Handley (b).

34 Handley (b).
35 RCPL 1834, Vol. 37, p. 190.
36 Correspondence cited in RCPL 1834, Vol. 28 (Part 1). Capt. Pringle's Report.
37 Codd.

Chapter 3

1 RCPL 1834, Vol. 38, Appendix E, G. Henderson's Report from Lancashire.
2 Dr Graham Davis.
3 H.G. Codd (see bibliog.).
4 SC on Vagrancy 1821: ev. of William Dickinson.
5 SC on Vagrancy 1821: ev. of W.H. Bodkin, 101st Annual Report of the Society for Suppression of Mendicity (1918).
6 Mayhew, LL & LP, Vol. 4, p. 400 et seq.; DC on Vagrancy 1906, ev. of Sir Eric Buchanan at Q11,059. Annual Reports of the Society.
7 Hansard 14/3/1821, Mr Harbord MP. Debate to appoint Sel. Com. on Vagrancy.
8 SC on Met. Police Offices, PP 1837–8, ev. of T. Lepard Smith at Q1014.
9 83rd Ann. Report (for 1900) of the Society.
10 1900 Annual Report; DC on Vag. 1906.
11 Ann. Report of Society 1869.
12 *Athenaeum* 26/8/1848, p868–9; statistics on mendicancy by J.P. Boileau.
13 Source as for note 11.
14 The play was inspired by Pierce Egan's celebrated *Life in London* 1821. The following is Moncrieff's own addition.
15 Act 2 Scene 6.
16 Boase.
17 Mayhew, LL & LP, Vol. 4, p. 400 et seq.
18 SC on Vagrancy 1821, ev. of H. Bodkin.
19 SC on Mendicity 1815–16, ev. of William Hale.
20 Report on London and Berkshire to the P–L Commissioners 1833. Reprint in British Library at CT 364(4). For magistrates' bias towards vagrants' version, see Lumley and SC on Met. Asylums 1846, ev. of Samuel Miller at Q5507–5514.
21 For the following account see SC on Metropol. Asylums 1846, ev. of George Cornewall Lewis at Q1 et seq. and ev. of Sir Richard Mayne at Q1587; case histories and correspondence P. 506 et seq. 8th Ann. Report of P–L Commission, PP 1842, Vol. 19. 5th Ann. Report of the P–L Commission, PP 1839, Vol. 20, p. 51 Appendix A, no. 7.
22 8th Ann. Report P–L Commission.
23 Danvers.
24 See 5th, 6th and 7th Ann. Reports of the P–L Commission; Lumley; ev. of George Cornewall Lewis before SC on Metrop. District Asylums 1846 for the history of the Orders to 1842 (at Q1 et seq.).
25 See 3rd Ann. Report P–L Commission, PP 1837, Vol. 31, for Hatfield system.
26 Lewis as in ref. 25, and 7th Ann. Report of P–L Comm., PP 1841, Vol. 21, p. 175.
27 8th Ann. Report of P–L Comm. (see ref. 22).
28 5/6 Vict. Ch. 57, Re-enacted in 1847.

Chapter 4

1 The Prince of Wales, later George IV, is said to have visited a beggars' dive on a slumming jaunt. [George Smeeton – see bibliog.]
2 Paul Edwards and James Walvin.

3   Act 2 Scene 6.
4   British Library. Under 'Songs' at C. 116 i(163).
5   Known in later editions as 'Mendicant Wanderers through the streets of London'.
6   Mayhew LL & LP, Vol. 4, p. 432.
7   Lamb.
8   Charles Dickens (a).
9   Mayhew, LL & LP, Vol. 3, p. 315.
10 Tallack (a).
11 Howard Association; Vagrancy and Mendicancy Report 1883.
12 See Smeeton, and John Thomas Smith.
13 SC on Mendicity 1815–16, ev. of Joseph Butterworth; see also R. Chambers, *Book of Days* for other Regency period examples.
14 SC on Mendicity, PP 1814–15, ev. of John Smith.
15 Brine.
16 *An Exposure . . .*
17 W.H. Davies (a).
18 See Harman for a Tudor glossary.
19 Basic sources: Chesney; Smith; Smeeton; Mayhew (LL & LP) Vol. 4 (p. 393 et seq.) and Vol. 1 (p. 414–18); Newton; Ribton-Turner; *An Exposure . . .* (1840); Brine; Walker.
20 PP 1870, Vol. 36: Annual Report of the Commissioner of Met. Police for 1869, Appendix E.
21 83rd Ann. Report of Mendicity Society (1900).
22 Sims (b).
23 LL & LP, Vol. 4, p. 412.
24 Charles Dickens (b).
25 *Confessions of an Old Almsgiver.*
26 Sources, see ref. 21.
27 Thomas Holmes and Frank Jennings (b).
28 Samuel.
29 Edwards and Walvin; Smith; Cohen and Greenwood.
30 Edwards and Walvin (ref. 29) citing James Grant's *London*.
31 Dickens (a).
32 Mayhew, LL & LP, Vol. 4 (p. 424).
33 See ref. 21.
34 Vagrancy and Mendicancy Report 1882.
35 DC on Vagrancy 1906, Report para. 191 (p. 52).
36 See Brine; also Ribton-Turner for letters from Brine.
37 Mayhew, LL & LP, Vol. 1, p. 247, Hotten; W.H. Davies (a); J. Phelan (a).
38 Cited C.J. Ribton-Turner.
39 SC on Mendicity 1815–16.
40 Hansard (Lords) 5/7/1853, debate on Juvenile Mendicancy and Vagrancy Bill.
41 Dickens (c).
42 See LL & LP, Vol. 4 (pp. 403–12) and (pp. 441–6).
43 Tangye.
44 A famous actor who died in 1811 [see Dict. Nat. Biog.].
45 DC on Vag. 1906, ev. of Sir Eric Buchanan at Q11,059 et seq.
46 83rd Ann. Report of Mendicity Society (for 1900).
47 Ribton-Turner was the COS Secretary. See Ribton-Turner p. 664–6.
48 George Sims (b) (Vol. 3, p. 151 et seq.). See also Holmes.
49 See ref. 46 at Q11,163.
50 See Jennings (a) and Worby (a).

Chapter 5

1 Cited from official source in Griffiths, Vol. 2.
2 SC on Vagrancy 1821: letter from Mr Barrow of Kendal Vagrant Office.
3 Mayhew, LL & LP, Vol. 1 (p. 420).
4 See Hodder, Hansard 6/6/1848: call for a govt.-aided emigration scheme for Ragged School children.
5 Cited in Colquhoun (b).
6 See Tallack (a); and Ribton-Turner p. 659, newspaper extract 15/2/1886.
7 SC on Mendicity 1815–16, ev. of Sampson Stevenson.
8 SC on Mendicity 1815–16, ev. of Thomas Finnigan.
9 Hansard (Lords) 5/7/1853: Shaftesbury on Juvenile Mendicancy Bill.
10 Samuel.
11 Mayhew, LL & LP, Vol. 1 (p. 417).
12 Series ran from 27/12/1870 to 2/2/1871. See articles of 26/1/1871 and 2/2/1871.
13 Hansard 24/7/1849.
14 Barnardo.
15 Mayhew (Quennell, p. 383).
16 For the Shoe-Black Society see: Hodder; SC on Crime and Destitute Juveniles 1852, ev. of John Macgregor; Thomson and Smith; Mayhew, LL & LP, Vol. 4 (p. 439); Barnett.
17 Shoe-blacks were not the only waifs to be considered by philanthropy for model hostel accommodation. There was a hostel scheme for newsvendors, too. (See G.F.A. Best.)
18 Harris.
19 See Urwick for the later history of the Shoe-Black Society.
20 See RCPL 1834, Vol. 28, Part II, Chapman's Report (Exeter House of Correction); see RCPL 1834, Vol. 38, Appendix E, Codd's Report; Letter from F. Smythies of Colchester.
21 Millicent Rose.
22 Hugh Douglas, *Burke and Hare* (1974).
23 Chadwick's Report on Britain's Sanitary Condition 1842: H. of L. PP 1842, Vols. 26–28.
24 See White; PRO H.O.45/4328; PRO H.O.45/5632.
25 Charity Organisation Society Report on Italian Beggar Children 1877 (see Annual Report COS 1877); Arnold White.
26 Char. Organ. Soc. Reporter 28/2/1884.
27 Arnold White.
28 See ref. 27.
29 This is the date and composership given in the British Library Music Catalogue; however, original song sheets in my possession indicate publication 1879 or earlier, with words by A.W. French and music by G.W. Persley.

Chapter 6

1 See Dorothy Davis for early history of peddling. For licence law see Acts of 1810 (Chapt. 43) and 1831 (Chapt. 22). Hawkers required an extra £4 for each horse they used. The use of a conveyance or beasts of burden seems to have been the technical difference between a pedlar and a hawker. See also PP 1844, Vol. 32, p. 377.
2 James Dawson Burn.
3 RC on County Constabulary 1839.
4 Hansard 21/7/1870, Col. 701, debate on Pedlars Bill.
5 See Hansard 28/2/1871, Home Secretary Bruce; DC on Vag. 1906 Report para. 400, and Q7687 et seq.

6　See SC on Met. Police Officers 1837–8, ev. of Rowan and Mayne at Q912 and DC on Vag. 1906, ev. of E. Buchanan at Q11,091.
7　Mayhew, LL & LP, Vol. 4 (p. 439).
8　Frank Gray.
9　Crane.
10　Massie.
11　W.H. Davies (c).
12　Gape.
13　Walker.
14　Hill (a).
15　Guy.
16　Mayhew (Quennell).
17　Pierce Egan; Mayhew, LL & LP, Vol. 4 (p. 413).
18　Longmate.
19　Char. Organ. Society, Report on Italian Children 1877.
20　*Westminster Express* 24/11/1911.
21　Home Affairs Committee on Vagrancy Offences 1980–81 (HC 271), ev. of J. Wood, legal adviser to CHAR.
22　*Oxford English Dictionary*; see also Cohen and Greenwood for a general history of busking.
23　Jennings (a).
24　See W.H. Davies (a) and (b) for griddlers' tricks of the trade.
25　See W.H. Davies (b) and Jennings (b).
26　Jennings (a) and (b).
27　Lee.
28　See Cohen and Greenwood.
29　Guy.
30　*Westminster Express* 10/2/1911, advert. p. 2.

Chapter 7

1　For an eighteenth-century description (Henry Fielding) see Thomas Beames.
2　Hansard 6/6/1848; Ashley, Col. 428 et seq.
3　Mayhew, LL & LP, Vol. 1 (p. 408).
4　Hill (b).
5　PP 1857 (Sess.2), Vol. 41, Reports from various MO of H. on the Common Lodging House Acts. (Describing Macclesfield's just prior to the 1851 and 1853 Acts.)
6　Ashley: see ref. 2.
7　PP (Lords) 1842, Vols. 26–28. See also Reports on State of Large Towns and Populous Districts, PP 1844, Vol. 17 and PP 1845, Vol. 18.
8　For example, Ashley, see ref. 2 and the RC on County Constabulary 1839.
9　Mayhew, LL & LP, Vol. 1 (p. 410 et seq.). See also W.A. Miles, 'A Letter to Lord John Russell' (1837) for 'Kid Kens'.
10　For prices, London and provincial c. 1850, see e.g. Chadwick (ref. 7); Beames; the SC on Met. District Asylums 1846 at Q1760.
11　Mayhew, ref. 9 at p. 408–9.
12　See Mayhew, LL & LP, Vol. 4, Binny's contribution.
13　RC on County Constabulary 1839, ev. of Thomas Yates.
14　Smeeton; Low.
15　See Gape for Sullivan and Maria.
16　Codd. Important: Daniel King of Brighton.
17　SC on Met. District Asylums 1846, at Q3546.
18　Chadwick (ref. 7).
19　Charles Booth Vol.1; Chapter by R.A. Valpy on Comm. Lodg. Houses; Law.
20　Fredur.

21 Hotten; *Pall Mall Gazette* 24/4/1882: 'British Nomads: Uses of Tramp Houses'.
22 The RC on the County Constabulary 1839 contains statistics, but they are of dubious value.
23 This 1851 Act (14/15 Vict. Ch. 28) should not be confused with the Labouring Classes Lodging House Act of 1851 (14/15 Vict. Ch. 34) which empowered local authorities to build municipal dwellings for workers. 1853 Act (16/17 Vict. Ch. 41).
24 See Gauldie and Wohl for general background.
25 See DC on Vagrancy in Scotland, PP 1935–6; The Public Health (Scotland) Act 1897.
26 Goldsmid.
27 38/39 Vict. Ch. 55. London was excluded a propos c.l.h. regulation, and still remained under the 1851 and 1853 laws.
28 DC on Vag. 1906, p. 96–7 paras 361–2.
29 1936 Ch. 49 s.235. It defined a c.l.h as a house for accommodating poor persons by night, who not being members of the same family occupy one common room for sleeping or eating.
30 See PP 1852–3, Vol. 78, p. 525 et seq. (Capt. Hay's Report for London) and p. 555 et seq., reports from the provinces; see Gauldie; see PP 1870, Vol. 36, Report of Met. Police for 1869.
31 Gauldie.
32 See ref. 29.
33 See Gauldie; Met. Police Ann. Report, PP 1878/9, Vol. 33; PP 1854, Vol. 35, p. 117 (Capt. Hay's 2nd Report).
34 Hay's 2nd Report: see ref. 33.
35 Met. Ann. Reports: PP 1878–9, Vol. 33; PP 1875, Vol. 36.
36 Sims (c).
37 See Goldsmid; *New Survey* Vol. 3, Sir H. Llewellin-Smith; LCC Minutes 1927, Report of MO of H. on comm. lodg. hses. to Public Hlth. Comm. pp. 308–24.
38 Booth, Vol. 1. See ref 19; *New Survey*, Sir H. Llewellin-Smith; LCC Minutes 1927 (as in ref. 37). I must confess to some puzzlement over the statistics. The Met. Police transferred c.l.h. supervision to local sanitary authorities outside the Metrop. Bd. of Works area in 1872 (LCC area from 1888) – 'Greater London' here = Met. Police and City Police area. But do the figures I cite for the fall in c.l.h. nos. relate to the Met's remaining jurisdiction in the LCC area of 'Greater London'?
39 See LCC MO of H. Report 1927 in ref. 37 for state of affairs in 1894.
40 The Public Health Act of 1936, a consolidating and updating measure, did not extend licensing to other parts of England. The 1902 and 1907 Acts were re-enacted in the Public Health (London) Act 1936.
41 Wilkinson; chapter on Dosserland in George Sims (b) Vol. 2. See also MO of H. Report 1927 cited in ref. 37.

Chapter 8

1 Charles Booth, Vol. 3, Chapter by R.A. Valpy; LCC Minutes 1927, MO of H. Report (pp. 308–324); DC on Vag. 1906, p. 89.
2 See ref. 22 in Chapter 7.
3 Gauldie.
4 Higgs (c).
5 See the 1875 Public Health Act.
6 See LCC Minutes 1927 ref. 1.
7 LCC Minutes 1927 ref. 1; Mary Higgs (a).
8 Beams; Hole.
9 Hollingshead 1861.
10 DC on Vagrancy 1906, p. 91.

11 Collier; William Booth (a).
12 H. Llewellin-Smith in *New Survey*, Vol. 3.
13 See Jack London; Flynt; W.H. Davies (b).
14 Orwell.
15 Jennings (b).
16 Worby (a).
17 Crane.
18 Higgs (c) Chapt. 4, and Higgs (a).
19 W.H. Davies (b).
20 Higgs (c).
21 Higgs; see ref. 18.
22 See Edgar Rowan; PP 1893–4, Reports to the Board of Trade; DC on Vagrancy 1906, ev. of W. Carlile at Q8030 and Q1866 et seq.
23 Brandon (a); Arlington House file at CHAR HQ.
24 DC on Vag. 1906, Appendix 9, p. 56, Shirley Murphy's Report; and ev. at Q2781.
25 Sheridan.
26 W.H. Davies (b).
27 Sims (b) Vol. 3, p. 172 et seq.
28 Gray.
29 Gray; Orwell.
30 Sir H. Llewellin-Smith, *New Survey*, Vol. 3.

Chapter 9

1 Jerry White.
2 DC on Vag. 1906, Appendix 9, p. 52, Shirley Murphy's memorandum.
3 See Chapter 7 for Act of 1897.
4 DC on Vagrancy in Scotland, PP 1935–6.
5 Higgs (c).
6 Higgs (a) citing George Sims' investigations.
7 F. Jennings (b) p. 123.
8 See Fredur, and Goldsmid.
9 Paterson.
10 Charles Booth, Vol. 1, Chapter by R.A. Valpy on Comm. Lodg. Hses. 1892.
11 Mayhew, LL & LP, Vol. 1, p. 408–9.
12 W.H. Davies (c).
13 Fredur.
14 As in ref. 13.
15 W.H. Davies (c).
16 Frank Gray.
17 Higgs (c).
18 See ref. 10.
19 *People of the Abyss.*
20 Jennings (b).
21 See ref. 2 at p. 56; and Frank Gray (who reckoned 5%). But T.W. Wilkinson in George Sims (b) Vol. 2 ('Dosserland') says the majority are transients.
22 Frank Gray reckoned two-thirds.
23 Fried and Elman; Rowntree.
24 See ref. 2 at p. 55–6.
25 Report to Bd. of Trade PP 1893–4 (see bibliog.). For problem of ex-soldiers see also: Sir Baldwin Leighton MP in Hansard 12/5/1882 at Cols. 581–3; Howard Association Report . . . 1882 (see bibliog.); G. Stedman Jones; Charles Booth, Vol. 1, Chapter 4.
26 See Thomas Wright, and Eric Partridge, *Dictionary of Slang.*
27 W.H. Davies (c).

28 Hallifax; London.
29 W.H. Davies (c).
30 In George Sims (b) Vol. 2, Chapter on Dosserland.
31 George Sims (a).
32 See Smeeton; and *The Countryman*, April 1936, p. 132.
33 Brine; Smeeton.
34 Bentley; Gape; Hanmore; Edwards; Worby.
35 Hallifax.
36 Sims (b), Vol. 3, Chapter on Model Lodging Houses. Charles Booth, Vol. 1, Ch. 3.
37 Sims (a) Chapt. 4; C. Booth, Vol. 1, Ch. 3.
38 See also Gape for dossers' reaction; Orwell.
39 Barnardo, *Rescued for Life* (1888); A.E. Williams.
40 Mayhew, LL & LP, Vol. 1. See Geoffrey Pearson's *Hooligan*, however, for fears expressed in the Hungry Forties that to-day's Artful Dodgers would be tomorrow's radical agitators.
41 See also Peek (a).
42 Higgs (b).
43 Hanmore (1935) and Bentley (1933).
44 Kennedy.
45 Sims (b), by T.W. Wilkinson on Model Lodging Houses.
46 W.H. Davies (b) 1908.
47 DC on Vag. 1906, ev. of Sir Eric Buchanan at Q11,163.
48 Worby (b).
49 Wright.
50 See, for example, F.S. Stuart; and W.H. Davies (c) and (d).

Chapter 10

1 General source references as follows: S. & B. Webb; Vorspan; Annual Reports of P–L Commission, P–L Board and Local Govt. Board; Ann. Reports of Commiss. for Met. Police the Dept. Committee on Vagrancy 1906;
2 Everard Wyrall.
3 PRO HO45/19657/224947 Vagrancy Matters 1916–45. Letter from J. Theodore Dodd JP to the Home Office 1923.
4 Boase.
5 DC on Vag. 1906. Historical introduction; PP 1870, Vol. 36; Report of Ch. Commiss. for Met. Police; PRO HO45/10520/138276, Questions re Vagrancy Bill 1906–1912, file dated 3/1/1908.
6 PP 1850, Vol. 27, 2nd Ann. Report of Poor Law Board.
7 SC on Poor Relief, PP 1864, Vol. 9.
8 PP 1868–9, Vol. 28, Ann. Rept. of P–L. Board; and PP 1868–9, Vol. 53, Surrey justices' complaint about increase in vagrancy.
9 Amyatt; DC on Vag. 1906.
10 See *The Times*, 27/9/1910 (p. 3), 5/3/1912 (p. 17) and 9/2/1912 (p. 4); PRO MH 57/78 (Report on Vagrancy and Vagrancy Relief 1906–20).
11 For stats. of casual ward use from 1858–1905, see DC on Vag. 1906, Vol. 1 (Maj. Report, Cd.4499), Part 6, Chapter 1, p. 421.
12 PP 1897, Vol. 36, 20th Ann. Report of Loc. Govt. Bd., Appendix A; Frank Gray.
13 Dawson.
14 DC on Vag. 1906 (Part 3), Appendix 6 for stats.
15 DC on Relief of Casual Poor, PP 1929–30.
16 See PRO reference in ref. 5.
17 For labour and detention colonies see e.g. Report to the Board of Trade, PP 1893–4 (bibliog.); DC on Vag. 1906; William Booth (a) and (b); Wilson

and Victor Carlile; Dawson; Kelly (a) and (b); Report on Swiss Methods, PP 1904, Vol. 82 (see bibliog.).

18 See Report to Board of Trade . . . ref. 7 and DC on Vag. 1906 at p. 71
19 See Flynt; F.S. Stuart.
20 *Webster's Dictionary;* Jerome K. Jerome's *Three Men on the Bummel* is about a cycle tour through pre-1914 Germany.
21 The young Labour Party favoured them as did the RC on the Poor Laws (1909).
22 See Kelly (b); this attitude prevailed in the USA, too.
23 See RC on PL 1909 Maj. Report, Vol. 2 p. 337 et seq. Report to the Board of Trade 1893–4.

Chapter 11

1 See e.g. Peek (a); and his ev. before the Lords SC on Poor Relief 1888 at Q2618–20.
2 Howard Association's Report on Vagrancy and Mendicancy 1882.
3 Tallack (a); Peek (b) in 1888 gave a figure of four to five million pounds.
4 DC on Vag. 1906. Report Chapter 13; Sir Eric Buchanan's ev. at Q11,059.
5 *Confessions of an Old Almsgiver.*
6 Gape.
7 Colquhoun (c).
8 Mayhew, LL & LP, Vol. 4, p. xxvii et seq.; Mowat.
9 RCPL 1909, Min. Report, Part 2, p. 521; PP 1865, Vol. 48, p. 47, return re Certain Night Refuges in London.
10 RCPL 1834, Vol. 38, G. Henderson's Report; and ref. 17 (RCPL 1909).
11 Charity Organisation Society, Report on Soup Kitchens and Dinner Tables, 1871.
12 DC on Vag. 1906 at Q9605 et seq.
13 LL & LP, Vol. 3, p. 406 et seq.
14 See evidence of several witnesses before SC on Met. District Asylums 1846, e.g. William Jones and Thomas Lepard Knevitt.
15 Ref. 12 at Q1902.
16 Boase.
17 Ribton-Turner; RCPL Min. Report, Part 2, Chapter 2, p. 521–2.
18 See RCPL Min. Report, Part 2, p. 502–5; DC on Vag. 1906, Vol. 3, Appendix 32 and ev. at Q7758 et seq.
19 SC on Met. District Asylums 1846, ev. of John Sard.
20 RCPL 1909 Maj. Report, Vol. 1, Part 6, Chapt. 1.
21 Tallack (a).
22 Octavia Hill's ev. at Q243.
23 RCPL 1909 Maj. Report, as for ref. 9; C. Booth 1892, Vol. 1, Chapt. 4, 'Homeless Men'; Lords SC on Poor Relief 1888, ev. of Andrew Mearns Q68 et seq.
24 C. Booth, ref. 23.
25 Lords SC on Poor Relief 1888, ev. of Henry Hardcastle and Andrew Mearns.
26 For criticisms of relief work see e.g. Lords SC on Poor Relief 1888, ev. of Andrew Mearns at Q4349 et seq.; the RCPL 1909 – both Maj. and Min. Reports; Dawson; Peek (a); DC on Vag. 1906.
27 PP 1914, Vol. 44, p. 371, Report of Met. Inspectors Advisory Committee on Homeless Poor.
28 Gape.
29 For the SA and the Embankment, see Collier; William Booth (a). For the CA, see Rowman.
30 Wyrall.
31 See ref. 27 and PRO HO45/14571/202036 (File Dec. 1911). Eustace Miles and

Eustace Miles Barrow are given variously as his complete name.
32 Wyrall.
33 See PRO ref. 31. In files Feb. 1911 and Jan. 1912, Wilson Carlile to Home Office.
34 *New Survey*, Vol. 3. Sir H. Llewellin-Smith, 'Homeless Poor'.
35 Wyrall.
36 Smat (a).
37 Wyrall; W.H. Dawson.
38 See ref. 27 for the COS letter to *The Times*; ref. 31 (PRO); DC on Vag. 1906, Appendix 9 (Murphy's memorandum, p. 56).
39 See refs 31 (PRO); ref. 27; *The Times*, 1911: 21/1, 1/4, 24/10, 25/10, 3/11.
40 Those in need had first to obtain tickets of introduction to the N.O. from the police.
41 See ref. 31 (PRO), File 8.
42 LCC Annual Report 1933 (Vol. 1 Part 2) for stats.
43 *The Times*, 26/12/1912, p. 8.
44 See ref. 42.
45 See ref. 31 (PRO) and PRO MH 57/78.
46 See ref. (18).
47 *The Times* 26/12/05, 'The Legal Poor of London', cited in the MS Ann. Report for 1910.
48 See MS Ann. Reports for relevant years.
49 At Q11,067.
50 LCC Annual Report 1934, Vol. 1, Part 2, p. 23–4.
51 Amyatt.
52 See DC on Vag. 1906, Report, Chapter 5.
53 Orwell.
54 Michael Rose (a) for background; Mowat; Rooff.
55 COS Conference on Night Refuges, 1870; COS Report on Soup Kitchens and Dinner Tables, 1871.
56 DC on Vag. 1906, p. 91–8; and see Q9605 et seq.
57 W.H. Davies (b).

Chapter 12

1 Stats. in 'Alcohol-Reducing the Harm', pub. by Office of Health Economics, 1981.
2 G. Prys Williams and G.J. Brake, *Alcohol and the Nation* (1979).
3 *North British Daily Mail*, article 'The Dark Side of Glasgow', 1st Report 27/12/1870. This is the first reference I have found to the use of methylated spirits as a beverage, though it was evidently well-established by then.
4 See e.g.: Hallifax; George Zachary Edwards; Flynt; Charles Simmons' ev. before the DC on Vag. 1906; R.A. Valpy in C. Booth, Vol. 1, Chapt. 1 suggested that drink might not have been an original cause of vagrancy, but has since become an escape from misery.
5 C. Simmons in ref. 4.
6 DC on Vag. 1906, e.g. at Q227–8 and Q381–2.
7 Ibid., Appendix 9, Table D.
8 W.H. Dawson, citing the RC on PL 1909.
9 See Wilson Carlile's ev. before DC on Vag. 1906 at Q8225 et seq.
10 Home Office Working Party on Habitual Drunken Offenders, 1971.
11 Guy.
12 W.H. Davies (c).
13 Massie; see also Flynt.
14 Stamper; 'Housemaster'; Jennings (b).
15 DC on Vag. 1906, ev. of David C. Lamb of the SA.

16 DC on Relief of the Casual Poor 1929–30, Appendix 3.
17 Handley (a).
18 RCPL 1834, Vol. 28, Part 2, Capt. Chapman's Report.
19 As for ref. 16.
20 RCPL 1909, Min. Report, Part 2, p. 499 footnote, citing DC on Vag. 1906.
21 SC on District (Met.) Asylums 1846 at Q5815
22 Brine.
23 Act 11/12 Vict. Ch. 110, and P–L Board Bulletin 1848. The duties were reiterated and redefined in Circulars of 1868 and 1871.
24 London; see also Higgs (c) for another first-hand description.
25 Higgs (c); DC on Vag. 1906, ev. of R.J. Curtis at Q2627.
26 *On the Road* (a), Devizes, p. 33; and Frank Gray at Henley.
27 DC on Vag. 1906, Report, Chapter 11, p. 99 et seq., and ev. of Armstrong at Q3049 et seq.
28 Cited in Dawson.
29 See ref. 27.
30 DC on Vag. 1906, Appendix 9, p. 50–53, Shirley Murphy's Memorandum.
31 As for ref. 30.
32 See Flint; and ref. 30.
33 See ref. 30 and David Lamb's ev. before DC on Vag. 1906.
34 See ev. of Charles Simmons before 1906 DC on Vag.
35 See ref. 34 at Q3289 et seq.
36 W.H. Davies (b); Jennings (a).
37 Howard Association, Vagrancy and Mendicancy Report, 1882.
38 Cited in Dawson.
39 W.H. Davies (a); Jennings (a).
40 PRO HO/45/14571/202036, Treatment of London's Homeless Poor, 1909–32, file 2a, letter dated 6/3/1911.
41 Cited in José Harris.
42 At Q3134.
43 See e.g., ref. 15.
44 See RCPL 1909, Maj. Report, Vol. 1, Part 4, Ch. 5.
45 See British Library Music Catalogue under 'Tramp' and 'Vagabond' for the source of the ballads referred to here.
46 Words, Elphinstone Thorpe, music, H. Troters.
47 Words, G. Russell Jackson, music, Lloyd Wilson.
48 Words, Walter Travers, music, Charles M'Ace.
49 C.W. Murphy, writer and composer.
50 Bud Flanagan.
51 Massie.

Chapter 13

1 See DC on Habitual Offenders, PP 1895, Appendix LXXXII, p. 631, memo by C.S. Loch. A Gloucestershire tramp survey in 1893, if extrapolated nationwide, would give about 33,500 tramps. But this covered casual ward and c.l.h. inmates only, not those sleeping rough.
    The LCC conducted twice-yearly tramp censuses from 1904, which embraced those in shelters and institutions and those sleeping rough. Extrapolating London's figures in, say, January 1909, to the whole country, this would give an English tramp population estimate of around 41,000 (see Dawson).
2 Under the Scottish County and Borough Police Act 1857. Annual Reports (PP) of the Inspector of Constabulary for Scotland.
3 From December 1888 the statistics bear no relation to the series preceding that date. There was some radical change of definition. In 1887 103,662 vagrants were counted; but from December 1888 the figures fall below 10,000.

4 See Dawson for comparison; and the DC on Habitual Offenders 1895 at ref. 1.
5 Wal Hannington (b), and see RCPL 1909 Min. Report, Part 2.
6 Met. P–L Inspectors' Advisory Committee on the Homeless Poor, PP 1914–16, Vol. 32.
7 See also Frank Gray.
8 *The Countryman*, April 1936, 'My Queer Experiences as a Tramp'.
9 PRO MH 57/80, stats. on Vagrancy Matters for the DC of 1929: Boase's Reports on Vagrancy, PP 1847–8, Vol. 53 show no discernible common pattern for the places he lists.

Chapter 14

1 See Boase, PP 1847–8, Vol. 53.
2 See Doyle.
3 PP 1870, Vol. 36, Report of Commiss. for Met. Police for 1869.
4 PP 1844, Vol. 19, 10th Ann. Report of P–L Commissioners.
5 PP 1866, Vol. 35, see reports of W.H.T. Howley, and R. Weale.
6 Sir Richard Tangye, quoting from Local Govt. Ann. Report of 1894–5.
7 PRO MH 57/86, ev. of Salvation Army before DC on Relief of Cas. Poor 1929; see also Wyrall.
8 Neville
9 Frank Gray.
10 Jennings (a).
11 PRO MH 57/89.
12 See Wyrall.
13 Rachel Vorspan, p. 68.
14 Hobsbawm, chapter on the 'Tramping Artisan'; C.J. Ribton-Turner; RCPL 1909, Min. Report, Part 2, p. 584–5, footnote. PP 1893–4, Report to the Board of Trade.
15 Miles; Tobias (a).
16 Walker; DC on Vag. 1906, Appendix 9, p. 50, citing Mayhew.
17 Henry Fletcher MP, Hansard 12/5/1882, Col. 588.
18 Higgs (c); W.H. Davies (c).
19 Bentley; Gape; Jennings (a); *The Countryman*, April 1936, 'My Queer Experiences as a Tramp'.
20 See Fox for outline history of DPA Societies.
21 Salvation Army, 'In Darkest England Social Scheme' 1891, Edgar Rowan.
22 PP 1893–4, Report to the Board of Trade.
23 Quoted in Higgs (b).
24 DC on Vag. 1906, Carlile at Q8151–3.
25 See, e.g., Gape.
26 For hoppers, see, e.g., Tobias (a); Jones; Kennedy; RCPL 1909, Maj. Report, Part 8, Ch. 5, p. 162; DC on Vag. 1906, Report, para. 401.
27 For 'ins and outs' see RCPL 1909; DC on Vag. 1906; SC (Lords) on P–L Relief 1888.
28 See Mowat for Sir Charles Trevelyan's comment on them in 1870.
29 PRO MH 18/15, containing 10th Ann. Report of Loc. Govt. Board.
30 DC on Vag. 1906, Report at p. 32.
31 SC (Lords) on Poor Relief 1888, ev. of Robert Hadley at Q656 et seq.
32 RCPL 1909, Min. Report, Part 2, p. 505–7.
33 SC (Lords) on Relief 1888, Q4706 et seq. and Q4746, ev. of Robert Valpy.
34 RCPL 1909, Min. Report, Part 2, p. 507.
35 Vorspan.
36 RCPL 1909, Min. Report, Part 2, p. 578–9; DC on Vag. 1906, Report, para. 83.
37 Cited in Alden et al.

Chapter 15

1　PP 1844, Vol. 19, 10th Ann. Report of P–L Commissioners.
2　PP 1846, Vol. 36, p. 185 et seq.
3　PRO MH 18/5, Report on Unions not having vagrant wards; stats. from 10th Ann. Report of L.G. Bd.
4　Stats. from DC on Vag. 1906, Appendix 5, and Higgs (a).
5　See DC on Vag. 1906 at Q1466–7 and Q1040; Sir William Chance.
6　Cited in Ribton-Turner.
7　Cited in PRO HO45/14571/202036.
8　Stats. from PP 1914, Vol. 44, Metrop. Advisory Committee on Homeless Poor Report.
9　See ref. 7.
10　Higgs (a).
11　PP 1883, Vol. 28, Ann. Report of L.G. Bd. for 1882.
12　RCPL 1909, Min. Report, Part 2.
13　See Stallard.
14　Mary Kingsland Higgs.
15　Higgs (c).
16　Higgs (a) and (d).
17　As for ref. 16.
18　Report of LCC MO of H. to LCC, Public Health Comm. 1927.
19　LCC Minutes 1949 (Homelessness).
20　W.H. Davies (a), and Wilkinson's Chapter on 'Dosserland' in Sims *Living London*, Vol. 2.
21　Higgs (a).
22　See ref. 18 and Mrs Cecil Chesterton (a).
23　See ref. 18.
24　Mrs C. Chesterton (a).
25　As for ref. 24.
26　Mrs C. Chesterton (b).
27　Nigel Gray – Gladys Gibson's recollections.
28　PP 1927, Vol. 9, 8th Ann. Report of Min. of Health, Appendix 16, p. 228 et seq.
29　Frank Gray.
30　H. Llewellin-Smith. DC on Relief of Casual Poor 1929–30; PRO MH57/64, Survey of Casual Wards 1930–31; LCC, *London's Homeless* 1937.

Chapter 16

1　For admirers and promoters of Ragged Schools (e.g., Charles Dickens) see: Hodder, Philip et al; Carpenter (a) and (b); Watson (b), (c) and (d).
2　See Henry Mayhew's articles in the *Morning Chronicle* of 1850, viz. 25/3, 29/3, 22/4 and 25/4; also Mayhew and Binny.
3　Hansard 6/6/1848, Cols. 428–55.
4　Hodder; PP 1852–3, Vol. 3, p. 761, Juvenile Mendicancy and Vagrancy Bill; Hansard (Lords) 28/6/1853 and 5/7/1853, debates.
5　For Scotland, Industrial Schools were legally recognised in 1854, too.
6　1866. Acts, Chapter 117, Reformatories and Chapter 118, Industrial Schools. The laws were assimilated for England and Scotland.
7　Stats. from RC on Refs. and Indust. Schools 1884, Appendix A (1); PP 1899, Vol. 44, 42nd Annual Report of Inspector of Reformatories and Indust. Schools.
8　See DC on Vag. 1906, Report, p. 115, paras. 421–2.
9　Urwick, Chapter by J.G. Cloete, 'The Boy and his Work'.

10   DC on Vag. 1906, ev. of Robert Peacock at Q7927.
11   For history of the laws see Hermann Manheim, *Social Aspects of Crime between the Wars* (1940); and the contest of Edwardian concern about the baneful attractions of dead-end jobs for school-leavers see Geoffrey Pearson, *Hooligan* (1983).
12   DC on Vag. 1906, Report, p. 114–15, paras. 416 et seq.
13   A.E. Williams.
14   1908 Chapt. 67, sect. 118.
15   Though parents who withheld their children from elementary school as an antecedent in an Industrial School committal were liable.
16   PRO MH57/60, Adoption and Maintenance Powers of Vagrancy Committees (1924–30).
17   Wymer; A.E. Williams; Hitchman.
18   Annual Reports Dr Barnardo's Homes, 1890–1907.
19   Poor Law Acts 1889 (Chapt. 56) and 1899 (Chapt. 37).
20   The memorandum preceding the Vagrant Children's Protection Bill (PP 1900, Vol. 5, p. 561) indicates that the powers were the same. But the Spring Gardens Conference of MO of Health in 1904 called *inter alia* for the extension of adoption powers to vagrants' children, implying that the Bds. of Guardians were lacking in such powers (see DC on Vag. 1906, Appendix 33, page 165). In MH 57/60 (see ref. 16) it is stated that the guardians' right in relation to the children of casuals are dependent on the parents' consent.
21   DC on Vag. 1906 Report, p. 113–14. But Robert Parr of the NSPCC at Q11,008 believed that a 'good many' P–L guardians did avail themselves of adoption powers in relation to vagrants' children.
22   Source: see ref. 16.
23   *Child's Guardian*, Feb. 1899, p. 13.
24   Ibid., Feb. 1893.
25   Ibid., April 1897.
26   DC on Vag. 1906 at Q11,026.
27   DC on Vag. 1906 at Q11,016; and see Frank Gray.
28   *Child's Guardian*, Feb. 1899, pp. 14 and 18.
29   See *Child's Guardian*, Dec. 1899, May 1903, Feb. 1913.
30   Bills: PP 1899, Vol. 7; PP 1900, Vol. 5; PP 1901, Vol. 4; PP 1903, Vol. 4; PP 1904, Vol. 4; PP 1906, Vol. 5. The 1903 bill was sponsored by the State Children's Association and was different from the others in that it sought to exclude the Industrial Schools committal option to JPs in cases brought under other legislation. The SCA felt that the family-fostering possible under orphanage or workhouse committals was preferable to the comparative impersonality of Industrial Schools (see DC on Vag. 1906, ev. of Samuel Augustus Barnett at Q6066).
31   See DC on Vag. 1906 Report, p. 116–17, ev. of Robert Parr, and Home Office spokesman at Q1153 and 1161.
32   1908, Ch. 67, sect. 118
33   See ref. 16.
34   See ref. 16, Ministry memo 1927.
35   For 1840s examples: see PP 1847–8, Vol. 53. Reports on Vagrancy p. 43. Gloucestershire surveys 1878–83, see C.J. Ribton-Turner. London figures 1866, PP 1866, Vol. 61, p. 143, nos. admitted to Met. Cas. Wards; London figures 1871 and 1880, PRO MH18/5, stats. taken from 10th Ann. Report of Local Govt. Board.
36   The Gloucestershire figs. in ref. 35 show a higher percentage of children in the lodging houses; for Barnardo's statement see A.E. Williams.
37   DC on Vag. 1906, Appendix 5, p. 2, ev. of H. Preston-Thomas, and final Report; see ref. 16 for 1920s figures. Summer figures would be higher, with the addition of harvesters' children.
38   DC on Vag. 1906 Report, Chapters 13 and 18; a police census put it at 4.5%.

39   DC on Vag. 1906, ev. of Canon Barnett at Q5963–4; Q10931.
40   DC on Vag. 1906, Appendix 9; LCC Minutes 1927, Vol. 1, p. 425–6.
41   PP 1911, Vol. 38, Inspector of Police Annual Report.
42   DC on Vag. in Scotland, PP 1935–6.
43   See DC on Habitual Offenders, 1895.
44   See refs. 42 and 43 for descriptions and statistics.
45   Fergusson.

Chapter 17

1   See Judicial Stats. (Criminal) for relevant years; DC on Vag. 1906 Report, ch. 12, and Appendix 19.
2   See ref. 1 and figures cited in W.H. Dawson; and PRO HO45/15852/663451.
3   *Pickwick Papers*, 1837.
4   Judicial Stats. for relevant years; Ann. Reports of Chief Commissioner of Met. Police.
5   See SC on Met. (District) Asylums 1846, e.g. Q2769–71 et. Q3393–4; Q5507–14 for JPs' sympathy with vagrants.
6   SC on Met. Police Offices, PP 1837–8, ev. of J. Hawkins Elliott at Q1590–91, and Col. Rowan at Q1077.
7   See ev. of James Stewart Davy before the Lords SC on Poor Relief 1888.
8   At Q5825–8.
9   PP 1868–9, Vol. 53, Memorial of Surrey justices to the Home Office.
10   Ev. of J. Mulvaney at Q9551 et seq.
11   At paras. 186 and 187.
12   W.H. Dawson.
13   PRO HO45/5632 (OS) Dec. 1853, Met. Police Instructions re Beggars.
14   Ev. of Thomas Lepard Knevitt at Q958.
15   Cited in Dawson.
16   At Q481–2.
17   Robert Fabian, *Anatomy of Crime* (1970). He does not date the incident, but the 1920s seems likely.
18   At Q2618–20.
19   See Geoffrey Fletcher; Jack London; Mary Higgs (c) refers to 'Lousy Park'.
20   Mary Higgs (c), Ch. 8.
21   See PRO HO45/14571/202036; Bottomley in Hansard 30/4/1908 and 24/11/1910; Wedgwood in Hansard 20/11/1912.
22   Letter in PRO ref. 21.
23   Cited in William Chance: stats in Lloyd Wharton's letter in *The Times*, 10/3/1906.
24   Mary Higgs (c) citing DC on Vag. 1906.
25   Mayhew, LL & LP, Vol. 3 (p.377); Shaftesbury, Hansard (Lords) 5/3/1853, debate on Juv. Mendicancy Bill.
26   See Ann. Reports of Prison Comm., 1902–3 (PP 1904, Vol. 35), and 1905 (PP 1906, Vol. 50), and DC on Vag. 1906, Report p. 54–57; and H. Preston-Thomas's Memorandum (p. 76) and his evidence before the DC.
27   Ref. 26 H. Preston-Thomas at Q555.
28   DC on Vag. 1906 at Q3982.
29   PRO HO45/10520/138276; *The Times* 4/11/1910, p. 14.
30   *The Times*, ref. 29.
31   For Lincolnshire JPs see; Dawson (Lindsey Q. Sessions); ev. of H.J. Torr before DC on Vag. 1906; and *The Times* 6/1/1912, p. 8.
32   H.J. Torr (ref. 31) at Q10162.
33   *The Times* 6/1/1912, p. 8.
34   PRO HO45/10520/138276: Ostler's letters 16/2/07 and 11/3/08; Dawson also gives an instance of Lincolnshire JPs' harshness.

35 See ref. 42 for Podmore's details.
36 Jud. Stats. for 1886 (PP 1887, Vol. 90).
37 See ref. 34 (PRO, File 18).
38 Henry Mayhew, LL & LP, Vol. 1, p. 411–12.
39 See Hansard, e.g. 8/5/1889, Cols. 1437 et seq.
40 It was introduced as an amendment to the 1898 Vagrancy Bill (against pimping) but was disallowed as irrelevant to the specific purpose of the measure.
41 See Humanitarian League (Joseph Collinson).
42 Bills: PP 1909, Vol. 5, p. 567; Hansard 19/5/09: Macneill refers to the sentence of 12 lashes on a 65-year-old man for begging. This is scarcely likely to be anyone but Podmore. See Chapt. 2 for s. 4 of the Vagrancy Act.
43 PP 1938, Vol. 9, Dept. Comm. on Corporal Punishment (Cmd. 5684).

Chapter 18

1 PRO MH57/78, Vagrancy Relief 1906–20.
2 Ref. 1; Report of Met. Asylums Board Inspectors' Advisory Comm. on Homeless Poor, PP 1914–16, Vol. 32.
3 See ref. 1. I do not know if any War Office papers would shed further light on this.
4 See ref. 1; PRO HO45/14571/20236 (Homeless Poor in London 1908–32); Higgs (b); DC on Relief of Casual Poor 1929–30; PRO HO45/19657/224947, Vag. Matters 1916–45, File Feb. 1921.
5 Ref. 4; PRO MH57/80.
6 For unemployment figures inter-war; Hannington (a) and (c); Higgs (a).
7 See also the DC on Relief of Casual Poor 1929–30 for comments confirming this.
8 Nat. Assistance Board, Homeless Single Persons Survey 1966; and ref. 6.
9 Higgs (b) and (f).
10 *New Survey*, 1932, Vol. 3, p. 254, Ch. on Homeless Poor. These figures exclude Rowton's which were legally not comm. lodg. hses.
11 PRO MH57/72, Causes in Increase in Vagrancy 1927.
12 Ref. 11 and 9.
13 Ref. 9; John Burnett.
14 *New Survey*, 1932, Vol. 3, p. 254, Ch. on 'Homeless Poor' by H. Llewellin-Smith.
15 Frank Gray; ref. 11; *New Survey*, 1932, Vol. 3, p. 254, Chapter on 'Homeless Poor'.
16 See ref. 11.
17 See Chesterton (a).
18 Chesterton (b).
19 Ref. 11.
20 For the Night Office and Welfare Office, see *New Survey* (as in ref. 14); LCC, 'London's Homeless' (1937); LCC Annual Reports, 1934, Vol. 1, Part 2, p. 21–2, and 1936, Vol. 1, Pt. 2; Smart (a).
21 See Karl de Schweinitz and the writings of Wal Hannington for outline of inter-war unemployment relief system.
22 Higgs (b).
23 Hannington (a).
24 Hannington (c).
25 Stewart; Nigel Gray; Jennings (a).
26 Personal information supplied to the author.
27 See ref. 11 and PP 1927, Vol. 9, 8th Ann. Rept. Min. of Health, Appendix 16, p. 228 et seq.
28 S. & B. Webb; ref. 27, PP 1927; DC on Relief of Cas. Poor 1929–30.

29 Lorry and car lifts were remarked on elsewhere: see Frank Gray.
30 See ref. 11.
31 DC on Rel. of Casual Poor 1929–30; London casual ward superintendents were specialists, and probably knew their clientele better, so the London figures may be more accurate.
32 DC on Vag. in Scotland, PP 1935–6.
33 See PRO MH57/78, Report on Vagrancy. . . . Relief 1906–20; S. & B. Webb, Vols. 8–9; DC on Rel. of Cas. Poor 1929–30; Higgs (f).

Chapter 19

1   Higgs (b); PRO MH57/78 (Report on Vagrancy . . . Relief 1906–20).
2   Higgs (g); LCC Minutes 1927, p. 308–24; LCC Ann. Report 1937, Vol. 1, Part 2, Public Assistance; *New Survey*, 1932, Vol. 3, Chapt. by H. Llewellin-Smith; DC on Relief of Cas. Poor 1929–30.
3   Ref. 1 (PRO).
4   Smart.
5   DC on Relief of Cas. Poor 1929–30.
6   This doubtless reflected the hopes of the reforming Prison Commissioner, Alexander Paterson, who was a member of the DC of 1929–30. For his achievements see Lionel Fox.
7   Frank Gray.
8   *The Countryman*, April 1936: 'My Queer Experiences as a Tramp', p. 132 et seq.
9   See ref. 5 for limitation of JVC powers; Survey of Provincial Cas. Wards 1924, PP 1924, Vol. 19 (Cmd. 2267).
10 See ref. 9, PP 1924, Vol. 19.
11 Higgs (g).
12 Chesterton (a). But in 1931 Frank Gray said it survived in a very few places.
13 The first was a reprint of articles in the *Western Gazette*; I do not know about the latter.
14 Frank Gray had similar experiences when he went undercover as a tramp; W.A. Gape (1936) says that even if a casual did gain admittance to a workhouse infirmary, doctors and nurses gave him second-class attention; see also Higgs (g).
15 Frank Gray.
16 See also PRO MH57/64, p. 99, Survey of Casual Wards 1930–31 for same comment.
17 See RCPL 1909, Min. Rept., Part 2, p. 648–9.
18 Cited in 12th Ann. Report of Min. of Health, PP 1930–31, Vol. 14, p. 214.
19 *The Countryman*, October 1936: 'A Casual's Story'.
20 Callaghan.
21 Jennings (a).
22 See ref. 20.
23 LCC, 'London's Homeless' (1937); Smart (a); Battley.
24 *Manchester Evening Chronicle*, 20/11/1941, p. 5.
25 Stewart (1975); John Leach et al. (1980).

Chapter 20

1   Frank Gray 1931.
2   *New Survey*, 1932, Vol. 3, Ch. on 'Homeless Poor' by H. Llewellin-Smith.
3   Jennings (a) and (b); F. Gray.
4   F. Gray; Massie; Smart (a); ref. 2; *On the Road* (a), p. 40–41; Hanmore; PP 1927, Vol. 9, 8th Ann. Report of Min. of Hlth and C.F. Roundell's Report; LCC Ann. Report 1937, Vol. 1, Part 2 (Public Assistance).
5   PRO MH 57/89.

6 DC on Cas. Poor Relief 1929–30.
7 See ref. 4 (C.F. Roundell's Report).
8 Hanmore.
9 Worby (b).
10 Cited in Higgs (b).
11 Thomas Mason's statement, PRO MH 57/89.
12 PRO MH 57/78.
13 Callaghan.
14 Gape.
15 *On the Road* (a), p. 11–12.
16 Max Cohen.
17 W.J. Smart; DC on Vag. in Scotland 1935–6; LCC Ann. Report 1937, Vol. 1, Part 2 (Pub. Assistance).
18 PP 1929–30, Vol. 17, Appendix 3, Dr E.O. Lewis's Report.
19 DC on Vag. in Scotland, PP 1935–6; ref 2.
20 'Headmaster of Windlestone Hall'; for 'Knights of the Road' see also W.H. Davies; Lee; Jennings (a); Massie; Gape; Neville; Phelan.
21 Phelan (a).
22 Jennings (a).
23 See ref. 18.
24 *Justice of the Peace*, 19/9/1936, p. 618, 'Vagrancy in Scotland'.
25 Jennings (a).

Chapter 21

1 See Judicial Stats. for relevant years; PRO MH 57/80, stats. re Vagrancy Matters (1929).
2 *On the Road* (a) – at Poole casual ward.
3 Worby.
4 For inter-war beggars see, e.g.: Jennings; Worby; Orwell; F. Gray; Chesterton; Massie; Phelan.
5 Jennings (b); Orwell.
6 Orwell.
7 DC on Vagrancy in Scotland 1935–6.
8 Smart (a).
9 Bentley; Frank Gray calls her 'Silver Queen'. Was said to be run by a blonde society lady.
10 Bentley; Massie.
11 'The Headmaster. . . .'
12 See Orwell; Gape; Bentley.
13 Lee; Bentley.
14 PP 1927, Vol. 9, 8th Ann. Report of Min. of Health, Appendix 16, Duff's report.
15 PRO MH 57/60, powers of Vagrancy Committees (1924–30).
16 LCC; *London's Homeless* (1937); Rowan.
17 LCC Ann. Report 1933, Vol. 1 Part 2; and Ann. Report 1937, Vol. 1 Part 2.
18 John Edward Francis, 'Dick and Jef'.
19 Stewart; Smart; 'The Headmaster . . .'; Gape; F. Gray.
20 George Seaver et al.; Mary Kingsland Higgs; Mary Higgs (b); *Daily Chronicle* 26/6/1924 and 27/6/1924 – articles on Brother Douglas.

Chapter 22

1 Cited in Higgs (b).
2 As ref. 1.
3 PRO HO45/19657/224947, in letter from J. Theodore Dodd 3/10/1923.

4   PRO MH 57/89.
5   Massie.
6   Jud. Stats. for relevant years; and Stats. in PRO HO45/15852/663451, Inquiry into the death of John Thomas Parker.
7   *Justice of the Peace and Local Government Review*, 28/9/1931, p. 540, 'Visible Means of Subsistence'.
8   For coffee stalls and night life see Goldsmid; London; Gape.
9   See Orwell; Smart; Gape.
10 Orwell.
11 For the story of Parker and its aftermath see ref. 6 (PRO); Hansard 3/7/1933, 17/7/1933, 9/11/1933 (Gilmour); Hansard 26/3/1935, Col. 1743 (Spears); 'Howard Journal', Vol. 3 No. 4, 1933.
12 Hansard 9/11/1933, Gilmour and Mander.
13 Ref. 6 (PRO), File 32, Letter dated 30/11/1933.
14 Hansard 26/3/1935, Col. 1743.
15 Chapter 20, of 1935.
16 Jud. Stats. The percentage of convictions to prosecutions was very high after the Act, as just prior to it.

Chapter 23

1   For the background in its relationship to the homeless and vagrant, see Greve et al. (a); Stewart.
2   See Bailey (a) for the post-war phenomenon of squatting in response to the housing shortage.
3   LCC Minutes, 1949.
4   The NAB inherited 270 casual wards but immediately shut 136 of them; Stewart.
5   O'Connor.
6   Stewart.
7   NAB, Homeless Single Persons Report, 1966.
8   O'Connor.
9   Wilkinson (1981).
10 Wilkinson; Craig.
11 Greve (a); SHAC, 'Homelessness Prospects for the 1908s'.
12 Burke; Alderson; Brandon (b); Emlyn Jones of the Nat. Ass. of Voluntary Hostels in an interview with me.
13 For a challenge to the image of growing affluence in the 1950s and 1960s see writings of sociologists Peter Townsend and Royston Lambert; also Ken Coates and Richard Silburn: *Poverty: the Forgotten Englishmen* (1970); and the Milner Holland Report on London's Housing, 1965 (Cmnd. 2605).
    In the provinces homelessness was caused more by personal failings, e.g. rent arrears. In London it has been due to the housing shortage, and the astronomic levels of house prices and rents, as the private rented sector has shrivelled up.
14 Alderson.
15 The *Observer* 17/9/1961, cited in Alderson; and introd. in Sandford (a).
16 *New Statesman* 12/1/1962, 'In the Workhouse': reproduced in Burke.
17 Burke; Bailey (a); Sandford (b).
18 Sandford (b).
19 Brandon (b). See also Alan Murie.
20 Hansard 19/12/1975, Col. 2038, debate on Homeless Persons; British Youth Council, 'Young and Homeless' 1979.
21 Stewart.
22 See ref. 7.
23 OPCS, 'Hostels and Lodgings for Single People'; DHSS Survey 1972, pub. 1976.

24 For lodging house decline see also GLC/LBA 1981, 'Hostels for the Single Homeless in London'; Brandon (c).
25 Wallich-Clifford.
26 Simon Community, 'Non-Citizens of 1964'; J. Audrey Smith, *Casualties of the Welfare State* (Fabian Society); Breed; Trench; Brandon.
27 See ref. 7.
28 Page; see Burke for St Mungo's Survey of 1972, which revealed more.
29 Page citing Brandon; Burke (see ref. 28).
30 Brandon (b).
31 O'Connor; Page; Marshall; Stewart.
32 Leach et al. (1980)
33 Tony Wilkinson.
34 *Roof* May/June 1985, p. 26, article by Wilkinson.
35 See ref. 34 article on Fazakerly RC, Liverpool.

Chapter 24

1 For unemployment stats. from 1979 see e.g. Hansard 22/11/1982, Cols. 367–8 (written answers). For 1970s stats. see Hansard 2/8/1976, Cols. 551–2 (written answers).
2 Bailey (b); Hansard 14/12/1984, Debate on Homeless Persons Accom, Michael Meacher at col. 1354; SHAC, 'Homelessness: Prospects for the 1980s'.
3 I hesitate to give statistics comparing pre-1977 with post-1977 owing to the effect of the Housing (Homeless Persons) Act 1977. A Govt. Report 'Single and Homeless' in 1982 showed the unsurprising connection between unemployment and homelessness.
4 Central Statistical Office, *Social Trends*, 1973.
5 Burke; Bailey (b).
6 'Shelter' press release, April 1986.
7 Ref. 2, Hansard, Michael Meacher.
8 Hansard, debate ref. 2, Col. 1321 Roland Boyes; Hansard 21/11/85 Debate on Draft Board and Lodging Rules, Tony Newton; inform. from Chris Holmes of CHAR.
9 Chris Holmes of CHAR and Emlyn Jones of NAVH to the author.
10 The *Guardian* 25/11/85, p. 2, citing Greve (b).
11 Central Statist. Office, *Social Trends*, 1985.
12 Housing associations are 'charities' which offer accommodation for rent, not free shelter.
13 See Brandon (b) on this point.
14 Hansard 25/2/1983 (ref. 18), Col. 1192–4, statement by Sir George Young; *Roof*, May/June 1985, 'What will happen when the Spikes close?', p. 24; CHAR files, Report on Rowton Houses, and Arlington House – references to Camberwell therein; CHAR Occasional Papers, no. 4, 'The Future of the Resettlement Units' (Feb. 1985).
15 *Housing* magazine, Oct. 1985, Vol. 21, No. 10, Bob Hudson, 'Unsettling the Unsettled'.
16 Hansard 14/12/84, Debate on Homeless Persons Accommodation, Cols. 1321, et seq.
17 For Euston office controversy see Hansard 21/11/85, Michael Meacher, Col. 375–6; Shelter, B & L Campaign Broadsheet No. 5, Nov. 1985; *Guardian*, 27/2/86.
18 Hansard 14/12/84, ref. 2 – Ray Whitney; partly by Under-Sec. for DHSS; CHAR Bulletin, 7/12/1984; Hansard debate on Draft B & L Regs., 21/11/1985; Shelter, B & L Campaign Broadsheet No. 5, Nov. 1985; *Guardian* 27/2/86 – Camden Council Appeal.
19 Debate, Hansard ref. 2.

20   Debate, Hansard ref. 2.
21   Bailey (a) and (b); Burke; Richard Mills, *The Young Outsiders*, 1973, on the
     hippie sub-culture.

Chapter 25

1   Turner; Cook (b).
2   See: OPCS Survey, 'Hostels and Lodgings for Single People', 1972 (pub. 1976);
    GLC Central London Outreach Team, 1984, 'Sleeping Out in Central
    London'.
3   Cook (a), Chapter by Nick Beacock, 'Campaigning for Homeless and Roofless'.
4   See refs. 2 and 3; CHAR Occasional Paper No. 5, 'Replacing Night Shelter',
    1985; Stewart; Grafton.
5   Brandon (b).
6   *Sunday Times*, 23/9/1978, article on 'Highgate Hotel' Birmingham.
7   Ref. 6.
8   Sandford (b); for Bruce House as still being decent in the early 1950s, see
    O'Connor.
9   MIND/CHAR Campaign briefing, 1985.
10 Wilkinson, 1981.
11 Hansard (Lords), 16/4/73, Debate on Homeless Young, Lord Soper. CHAR
    news sheet, Nov. 1985.
12 CHAR, 'Arlington House' files, 1982 and 1983.
13 O'Connor.
14 Tower House (in Tower Hamlets); Arlington House (Camden); Rowton House
    (Southwark) plus Park View in Birmingham: see also Archards; *New Society*,
    10/3/83, John Laurance, 'A New Kind of Home'; *Observer* supplement,
    26/9/1982, Ian Walker, 'No Place Like Home'; CHAR, 'Tower House' file,
    based on Shelter report 1983; *Observer*, 10/4/83 on TB in East End of London.
    (Tony Wilkinson, however, speaks well of Arlington House.)
15 Craig 1984.
16 Wallich-Clifford; see also Sandford's postscript in *Edna the Inebriate Woman* 1971.
    I am grateful to Emlyn Jones of the NAVH for background information.
17 BBC 2 TV, *Forty Minutes*, 19/12/1985.
18 Page; writings of John Brandon; Sandford's article on vagrant women in
    Evening Standard 18/2/1970, and his play *Edna the Inebriate Woman*.
19 Breed; Marshall.
20 Chris Holmes of CHAR to the author, June 1986.
21 Emlyn Jones of NAVH to the author, Jan. 1986.
22 Page; Wilkinson; O'Connor; Brandon (b); Breed. Page and Breed do pay
    tribute to the SA's patience considering the human material it has to deal with.
23 GLC/LBA, 'Hostels for Single Homeless in London', 1981.
24 GLC Central London Outreach Team, see ref. 2; *Roof*, Nov/Dec 1984, p. 22 et
    seq.
25 Wilkinson; Craig; Marshall; Wallich-Clifford; Sandford in *Evening Standard*,
    16/2/1970, p. 21, 'Down and Out in London'.
26 Thomas Callaghan.
27 Shelter Report on Bed and Breakfast, 1974.
28 Craig.
29 Craig; Hansard Debate, ref. 2, Roland Boyes MP.
30 Hansard 1/12/1982, Debate on Houses in Multiple Occupation Bill, Cols.
    159–62, Tom Benyon MP quoting *New Statesman* article.
31 The Princes Lodge saga, newspaper cuttings etc., is contained in CHAR's
    'Tower House' file. I am grateful to CHAR for being allowed access to this file.
32 18/2/1981.
33 13/3/84.

34 Hansard ref. 2, e.g., Roger Gale, Gerrard Neale, Tony Speller MPs.
35 Hansard 25/2/83, Houses in Multiple Occupation Bill, see e.g., John Heddle, John Marshall, Tom Benyon MPs, Cols. 1142 et seq.
36 Cited in debate in ref. 18.
37 See ref. 18 John Wheeler MP at Cols. 1181–2.
38 *Roof*, Nov/Dec 1984; Hansard debate ref. 18, John Wheeler MP at Cols. 1181–2.
39 Hansard, ref. 2, Roland Boyes, citing the *Guardian* of 3/12/84.
40 *Roof*, Nov/Dec 1984, Vol. 9 No. 6.
41 Tony Wilkinson, 1981.
42 Ref. 23 and 22 (John Wheeler MP).
43 Bill 23 of the Sessions, introduced by Jim Marshall MP. Hansard 5/5/83, Col. 532; Sir George Young MP; Baroness Vickers Bill, Hse. of Lords, 1986.

Chapter 26

1 See Breed, Page, and O'Connor – for nostalgia for the 'gentlemen of the road'; largely illusory, I think.
2 Stats. supplied to the author by Alcohol Concern.
3 Home Office Working Party on Habitual Drunken Offenders, 1971.
4 GLC Outreach Team, 'Sleeping Out in Central London', 1984. However, a 1982 Govt. Report, 'Single and Homeless', says that only a small proportion of those interviewed were heavy drinkers. Perhaps this wider survey included many involuntarily homeless through unemployment, inability to pay London accom-modation prices, etc.
5 Geoffrey Fletcher; he says coal-gassed milk originated from Glasgow in the 1920s. I do not know if natural gas has the same effect.
6 Simon Community's 'Non-Citizens of 1964'; Fletcher; Breed; Trench. See also Wallich-Clifford; Cook (b); Marshall.
7 Emlyn Jones of the NAVH to the author.
8 Stewart.
9 Cook (b).
10 Information from Mr McKewan of 'Alcohol Concern'.
11 See ref. 10.
12 See Wallich-Clifford; Sandford (b) on Glasgow's down-and-out problem; GLC Outreach Team, 1984 see ref. 4; NAB Homeless Single Persons Report, 1966; OPCS Survey, 1972, 'Hostels and Lodgings for Single People' (pub. 1976).
13 Breed; Marshall; Emlyn Jones of NAVH for contemporary observation.
14 Sandford: article on vagrant women in *Evening Standard*, 18/2/1970.
15 See ref. 12.
16 Tony Wilkinson (1981).
17 MIND/CHAR Campaign Briefing 1985; see also Govt. Report 'Single and Homeless' 1982 for lowest estimate of 17 per cent (cited in CHAR Occasional Paper No. 3, 1983).
18 Henry Rollin, 'From Patients into Vagrants', *New Statesman* 15/1/1970. See also Stewart; Leach et al. (in bibliog) for critiques of community care in practice.
19 See ref. 17 (MIND/CHAR).
20 Trench; Wallich-Clifford.
21 Page.
22 Deakin and Willis.
23 Ron Bailey (b); Hansard (Lords) Debate on Young Homeless, 16/4/1973, Cols 991 et seq., Lord Soper.
24 Community Relations Commission, 'Unemployment and Homelessness' (1974).
25 Ref. 23 House of Lords debate.
26 Wallich-Clifford; Deakin and Willis.

27   Ref. 23 House of Lords; Grafton.
28   DHSS Working Group on Homeless Young People, 1976; ref. 4 GLC Outreach
     team.
29   Figs. cited in CHAR 'Arlington House' file (1982).
30   Hansard 13/3/1981, Debate on Govt's. policies regarding London, Cols. 1113
     et seq., A.W. Stallard MP.
31   Ref. 29.
32   *Daily Mirror*, 13/3/1984.
33   Programme on child runaways, Channel 4 TV, 17/2/1986.
34   See ref. 22 for the story of *Johnny Go Home*; DHSS, 'Working Group on
     Homeless Young People', 1976; Hansard 31/7/1975, Cols. 2359–80, Debate
     following *Johnny Go Home.*
35   Brandon (c).
36   Brian Masters, *Killing for Company*, 1985; *The Times*, 5/11/83, p. 8.

Chapter 27

1   Thomas Harman, 1573.
2   Home Office Working Party on Vagrancy and Street Offences, pub. 1974.
3   H. of C. Home Affairs Committee 2nd Report, Sess. 1979–80 (HC 559); Race
     Relations and the 'Sus' Law. Committee as above, 3rd Report, Sess 1980–1981
     (HC 271) – on Vagrancy Offences.
4   Trench; see Page for begging at Brighton; and see Chaps. 23 and 26.
5   *Star*, 23/4/1986, p. 9.
6   Author's own observation.
7   Judicial Stats. (Criminal) for relevant years. For most recent stats. (1980s) see
     Criminal Stats. Supplement (Vol. 1) – proceedings in Magistrates Courts; also
     stats. in Brennan (ref. 2) and the Home Affairs Committee 3rd Report (ref. 3).
8   As for ref. 7.
9   Judicial Stats. (Criminal) as for ref. 7.
10   See evidence of these groups before Committees in refs. 2 and 3.
11   In Feb. 1981 A.W. Stallard's Bill to repeal the Vagrancy Act re begging,
     sleeping rough and being found on enclosed premises, did not proceed
     (Vagrancy Offences Repeal Bill, No. 78, 1980–81 Session).
12   34/35 Vict., Ch. 112, section 15.
13   54/55 Vict., Ch. 69, sect. 7.
14   For technical legal discussion of sus. prior to 1980 see: *Solicitors Journal* 1964
     Vol. 108, p. 951 et seq., article by Florence O'Donoghue on 'Suspected
     Persons'; Dr Leonard Leigh: *Police Powers in England and Wales* (1975), and his
     chapter on Vag. and the Crim. Law in Tim Cook (ed. *Vagrancy, some new
     Prospectives* (1979); Glanville Williams: *Criminal Law: The General Part* (2nd ed.
     1961) at p. 657; cases of Rv. Frederick Dean 1924 18 Cr. App. R., p. 133 and
     Ledwith v. Roberts IKB (1937), p. 232; Gerald Gardiner and Andrew Martin,
     Law Reform Now (1963), Chapt. on Crim. Law Reform by C.H. Rolph.
15   Jud. Stats. (E. & W.).
16   The figures given by H. of C. Home Affairs Comm. (ref. 3, HC 559) differ from
     those I found in the Judicial Stats; for 1936 I found 2,989 pros. for frequenting
     under the Vag. Act. The Committee gives 3,549 pros. Does this include charges
     under the 1891 Act? Have I missed anything out?
17   'Sus' Comm. HC 559 (ref. 3), subject to my query in ref. 16.
18   For example, L.C. Justice Hewart in Rv. Frederick Dean (see ref. 14) and Lord
     Just. Scott in Ledwith v. Roberts (ref. 14).
19   See ref. 18.
20   Glanville Williams (ref. 14).
21   NCCL Ann. Report 1934; see also ref. 29, *Police Review*, article on police
     careerist exploitation of 'Sus'.

22 *News of the World* 1/12/1935, Cutting in file 56 in PRO HO45/19657/224947 (interpretation of S.4 of Vagrancy Act).
23 Home Affairs 'Sus' Committee (H.C. 559) (ref. 3), ev. of David McNee.
24 Hansard 6/2/1936, cited in *Justice of the Peace*, 15/2/1936, p. 107.
25 See ref. 14 for post-war commentators.
26 Brennan (ref. 1); I use the contemporary expression 'sus' exclusively in the 1970s and 80s context.
27 See ref. 23, McNee's ev.
28 Home Office Research Study no. 58, 'Race, Crime and Arrests' by P. Stevens and C.F. Willis; Clare Demuth – see bibliog.
29 For background to this paragraph see Home Affairs 'Sus' Committee, (ref. 3), ev. of witnesses, statistics final Report; Scarman Report on Brixton Disorders 1981 (Cmnd. 8427); *West Indian World* issue of 12-18/9/1980, article 'The Fight Continues against the Law for the Blacks'. Also, for unwitting admission how novice detectives exploit 'Sus' to boost their arrest record see *Police Review* 22/8/1980 article by Ian Will, 'The Case for Retaining "Sus"'.
30 Suspected Persons Abolition Bill (Bill 20, 1978), 1st reading 30/11/1978 (Lords); Hansard (Lords), debate on 2nd Reading 14/12/1978, Cols. 743 et seq.
31 Bill 45 1979/80 Session, Hansard 18/7/1979 debate.
32 See ref. 2.
33 Sect. 2, subsect. 5 of 1967 Act.
34 The H. of C. Home Affairs Committee's 4th Report 1980 (H.C. 744) warned the government that if it took no action, it would introduce a bill of its own. For the Law Commission's Report on Crim. Attempt see H.C. 646 (25/6/1980).
35 See Scarman Report (ref. 29).
36 Crim. Stats for 1980, Supplement Vol. 1, Proceedings in Magistrates Courts.
37 'Stop and Search' and the Crim. Law Act s.2(5) remained, but I understand that Home Office guidelines to the police have eroded 'Stop and Search' to virtual inoperability.
38 Vagrancy Offences Repeal Bill 1981 (Bill 78 1980–81 Session).
39 See ref. 3 (H.C. 271).

Index